# The UN-Santa Book

**LEGACY PRESS®**

Andy Smith

# Kathy Widenhouse

To Brett, Britta and Kurt
Together we celebrate Christ in Christmas

THE UN-SANTA BOOK
Copyright ©2005 by Legacy Press
ISBN 1-58411-062-7
Legacy reorder# LP48032
church and ministry/ministry resources/children's ministry

Legacy Press
P.O. Box 261129
San Diego, CA 92196

Interior Illustrator: Chuck Galey
Cover Illustrator: Tom Voss

Scriptures are from the *Holy Bible: New International Version* (North American Edition),
©1973, 1978, 1984 by the International Bible Society. Used by permission of Zondervan
Bible Publishers.

*Printed in the United States of America*

# Contents

What is The Un-Santa Book? ........7
   Ways to Use This Book ...............8

Getting Started ..........................9
   Prayer.........................................9
   Setting a Date ............................9
   What Type of Event? ................10
   Volunteers ................................11
   Budget ......................................13
   Publicity....................................13
   Stocking Surprises ....................15
   The King's Having a Birthday!.....15
   Registration ..............................16

Planning...................................17
   Selecting Activities....................17
   Games and Prizes......................17
   Decorations, Crafts and Gifts ......18
   Snacks .....................................20
   More Activities!.........................20
   Santa Claus ..............................22
   Your Pastors .............................23
   Parents and Family Members ......23
   Weather ...................................24
   Enlarging Patterns ....................24
   Creating Pattern Templates.........25
   Party and Lesson Themes ...........25
   Planning Timetable.....................28

Set-up Time! ............................30
   Stations ...................................31
   Registration Table.....................32
   Take-home Bags .......................33
   Posted Schedule .......................33
   Traffic Flow ..............................33
   Decorations ..............................34
   Christmas Kindness Tree............35
   "Happy Birthday, Jesus!" Banner .....36
   Sing, Sing, Sing!........................37
   Sparkling Snowflakes..................38

Star of Wonder .............................39
Welcome Wreath............................39
Crepe Paper Cascades ...................40
Crepe Paper Arches .......................41
Balloons .......................................41
Balloon Arches and Pillars .............42

After the Celebration.................43
   As Guests Leave .......................43
   Clean-up ...................................43
   Program Evaluation ...................43
   Follow-up ..................................45

Decorations..............................49
   Candy Tree................................50
   Cardboard Tube Caroler .............51
   Chrismon ..................................52
   Cinnamon Ornament ..................53
   Frosty Icicle Wreath...................54
   Grocery Sack Reindeer ...............55
   Luminaries for the Light of the World .........56
   Paper Clip Heavenly Host ............57
   Plastic Basket Snowflake ............58
   Ribbon Teardrop Swag ...............59
   Silver Bells Door Hanger.............60
   Tabletop Crèche ........................61
   Tree Garland of Trust.................62

Crafts ......................................63
   Advent Treat Calendar ...............64
   Bethlehem Sky Star Caper ..........65
   Christmas Card Magnets .............66
   Gabriel Macaroni Pin ..................67
   Gingerbread Magi Men.................68
   Happy Birthday Pin ....................69
   King's Crown .............................70
   Magi Gift Bag.............................71
   Miniature Poinsettia ...................72
   Pocket Crèche Puppets ...............73
   Reindeer Candy Cane...................75
   Santa Take-home Sack.................76

Sheep Lollipop ................................78
Shepherd Treat Holder ........................79
Star of Bethlehem Pencil Topper ...............81
Walnut Mouse ................................82

## Gifts ..........................................83

Bouncy Balls ................................84
Celebration Soap Bar ........................85
Christmas Card Roundabout ....................86
Confetti Treat Tin ..........................87
Cookie Mix in a Jar .........................89
Cozy Cocoa Kit ..............................90
Cranberry Grapevine Wreath ..................91
Hand Towel for a King .......................92
Holiday Heart Gift Tag ......................93
Holly Door Stopper ..........................94
Im-pastable Canister ........................95
Jingle Bell Gloves ..........................96
Night of Wonder Headband ....................97
Noel Coffee Mug .............................98
Rock Trivet .................................99
Santa Stamps ...............................100
Shining Light Votive Holder .................101
Shoelace Elves .............................102
Silver and Gold Sachet .....................104
Snowflake Fleece Scarf .....................105
Spicy Scented Coasters .....................106

## Games .........................................109

Build a Stable Relay .......................110
The Call from King Herod ....................111
Camels and Donkeys .........................112
The Census in Bethlehem ....................113
Christmas Story Match-up ....................114
Escape to Egypt ............................115
Fields of Snow .............................116
Grow a Beard ...............................117
The Land Where Jesus Was Born ...............118
Race Down the Chimney ......................120
Santa's Belly ..............................121
Sheep on the Hillside ......................122
Snow Shoveling in the Dark ..................123
Stocking Stuffers ..........................124

## Snacks ........................................127

Angel Clouds ...............................128
Animals in the Stable ......................129
Bright Morning Stars .......................130
Cheesy Popcorn .............................131
Cornflake Wreaths ..........................132

Cozy Christmas Cocoa .......................133
Crunchy Shepherd's Staffs ...................134
Donkey Biscuits ............................135
John the Baptist's Snack Mix ................136
The King's Cupcakes ........................137
Mangers with Straw .........................138
Shepherd's Dip .............................139
Snowman Sticks .............................140
Spicy Hot Cider ............................141
Sprinkle Spoons ............................142
Stained Glass Candies ......................143
Sugarplums .................................144
Swaddled Dates .............................145

## More Activities ...............................147

Caroling Fun ...............................148
The Christmas Story ........................152
Gingerbread Houses .........................156
Hanging the Greens .........................158
Live Nativity ..............................161
The Mitten Tree ............................163

## Lessons .......................................165

Ask for Good Gifts .........................166
Don't Miss the Party! ......................167
Getting Ready for Christmas .................169
God's Messengers ...........................170
Immanuel ...................................171
J.O.Y. .....................................172
Jesus Came for Everybody ...................174
The Light of the World .....................175
No Room at the Inn .........................177
Spread the News ............................178
Which King Will You Follow? ................179
Why a Baby? ................................181
Worship the King ...........................183
Wrapping Gifts with Jesus ..................184

## Reproducibles & Patterns ...............185

## Christmas Symbols and Their Meanings ............254

## Scripture Reference Index ............255

# ❄ What is The Un-Santa Book? ❄

**Christmas is Jesus' birthday.**
For Christians, it is a time of great joy as we remember and celebrate the birth of our Savior. But while Christians rejoice at the coming of Immanuel, the rest of the world blindly makes merry. They enthusiastically embrace the season, but still don't know the Good News: "God so loved the world that he gave his one and only Son" (John 3:16). This real message of Christmas is difficult to hear amidst the commotion of parties, baking, gifts and meals!

**You and your congregation can seize this opportunity by** sponsoring a one-of-a-kind holiday event in your community – one that capitalizes on all the outward trimmings of Christmas to underscore the birth of Christ. The holiday's high profile provides an open door for us to share and demonstrate the story of God's love wrapped in a baby.

**A Christmas event is a natural inroad.** Members of your congregation may be intimidated about sharing their faith with others, but it is easy to invite a neighbor to a Christmas party! Fun, treats and excitement resonate with families. By using the trappings of the season to explain Jesus Christ, we can give others a precious gift: an introduction to the King of Kings.

**The focus on Christ can touch every participant.** As congregation members work together to honor Jesus, their bonds of fellowship will strengthen. Families will build memories. Children will feel the joy of belonging. Unchurched friends will see God's love in action and join in. In fact, an invitation to a birthday party for Jesus can be the invitation to a miracle. **That is the purpose of *The Un-Santa Book*: To allow Jesus and His birthday to take center stage during the Christmas season.**

# ❄ There is no better way to celebrate Christmas! ❄

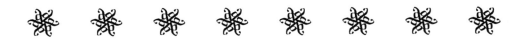

# Ways to Use This Book

You will find a variety of ways to use this book during the Christmas season.

### ❄ Direct an outreach event at your church

Whether you are a novice volunteer or an experienced Christian Education professional, this book will take you step-by-step through what you need to do to plan a special Christmas outreach event for the children and families in your community.

### ❄ Create smaller, specialized events at your church

Arrange an afternoon of gift making. Coordinate an evening of caroling. On pages 10-11, you will find a list of the types of events your church can plan that will have an impact for Christ. Afterward, invite new faces to join you for worship during Advent, on Christmas Eve, and in the New Year. The **Follow Up** section on page 45 explains how.

### ❄ Enhance your children's ministries

All the activities in **The Un-Santa Book** are based on Scripture. Use them to reinforce a Sunday school lesson with a game or snack. Supplement a children's church lesson with crafts. Let the members of your mid-week Bible club make decorations for your fellowship hall. The **Scripture Reference Index** on page 255 shows you where to turn in the book for a hands-on Bible activity related to your pre-selected Scripture. **Party and Lesson Themes** on page 25 provide you with activities grouped by Christmas season themes.

### ❄ Present children's sermons

Find ready-made children's **Lessons** beginning on page 165 as you prepare to communicate the message of Christmas. The other activities in this book can be converted to lessons for children's church, too.

### ❄ Plan activities for home

Let this book be your Christmas toolkit in your home and neighborhood. Select and launch a new family holiday tradition. Invite the kids from next door to create gingerbread houses. Prepare a plate of treats for a shut-in friend. Decorate your home with chrismons. Help your children craft gifts for their teachers. Make and display a tabletop crèche!

*The angel said to them... "I bring you good news of great joy that will be for all the people."*
*Luke 2:10*

#  ❄ Getting Started ❄

## Prayer

Begin planning your celebration for Jesus with prayer. Commit to regular, personal time with the Lord from now until the last tree ornament is stowed away. Invite a close friend to pray for you as you plan and organize the event.

Seek out prayer partners in your congregation and ask them to intercede for you. Reproduce the **Prayer Checklist** on page 187 for them to use. Meet with your pastors and pray with them. Put your request for prayer on your church's prayer chain.

Satan has "blinded the minds of non-believers, so that they cannot see the light of the gospel of the glory of Christ" (2 Corinthians 4:4). An event that honors Jesus Christ is not part of Satan's plan, so don't be surprised if roadblocks are thrown in your way. Prayer paves the way around those obstacles. Don't underestimate its importance!

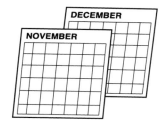

## Setting a Date

Check your church calendar to see what is scheduled for the Christmas season (Advent begins four Sundays before Christmas). Make sure that your event does not overlap or replicate other activities planned for children. A conflict will not only limit the number of people who can attend; it will also drain your volunteer pool.

Because the Christmas season extends for several weeks, your event does not need to take place in mid-December. In fact, late November can be an ideal time for a party because the year-end holidays have just begun and people are not overwhelmed with activities yet. An early-season event also allows for plenty of follow-up time to invite new families to worship during Advent (see pages 45-47 for **Follow-up** ideas).

Another way to avoid the holiday rush is to hold your celebration in the days following Christmas. Most kids and many adults have time off school and work during that time, so they would be able to participate. Also, your church's college students will be home to join in the fun (and perhaps offer their help!).

Choose the day of the week and time of day that is best for your situation. A weekday evening accommodates working parents. Saturday morning and evening also are good times for family events.

A two-hour time frame for small to mid-size celebrations lets participants enjoy most activities. If you plan on hosting more than 150 guests, schedule your party for at least 2½ hours so participants aren't rushed.

When you reserve your church's facilities, allow time for set-up and clean-up. For an evening party, reserve the building for the entire day. If your event is scheduled for a Saturday morning, plan to use the space on the preceding Friday as well.

# What Type of Event?

Seek input from your children's ministries team, church board and pastors as you determine what kind of Christmas celebration your church should sponsor.

Consider gearing the event toward families rather than youngsters only. Adults want to experience the wonder of Christmas and share that awe with their children and grandchildren. Your party can be an important opportunity for families to spend time together, strengthen and grow.

If your church is large and you have adequate staff, you might want to put on a full-scale gala that includes several or all of the following elements. However, a smaller church can do an equally meaningful event with careful planning and focused activities. Choose the celebration that will best allow your church to share the joy of Christmas.

※ **A Birthday Party for Jesus:** Organize a carnival-type festival complete with games, crafts, balloons, prizes and snacks. Stage a presentation of the **Christmas story** at the conclusion of your event (see pages 152-155). Invite parents and grandparents to join in the fun.

※ **Hanging the Greens:** Plan for members and guests to decorate your church building and fill your sanctuary with fresh greenery, swags and tree trimmings just before Advent. You will build excitement in your congregation for the coming of Christ, and also grab the attention of passers-by, who will note that your church is prepared for Christmas. See pages 158-160 for ideas.

※ **Santa's Gift Shop:** Gift giving is central to Christmas. Choose several gift projects, assemble supplies, make samples, set up a gift-wrapping station and let children and adults fashion quality presents for those on their gift lists. Instructions for **Gifts** begin on page 83.

※ **Santa's Gift Shop Giveaway:** Have members of your church's Bible club or teens' groups make gifts for shut-ins and missionaries. Afterward, the young people can deliver the gifts to the shut-ins while caroling, or wrap and send Christmas packages to missionary families.

※ **Santa's Secret Shop for Kids:** Give parents the gift of time: a free evening or Saturday morning to do their Christmas shopping. While the parents are away, help children make and wrap their own gifts. Have parents return to your church at a designated time for snacks and a presentation of the Christmas story.

❄ **Christmas Caroling Party:** Singing gives praise to God and creates camaraderie and goodwill among neighbors. Organize a caroling party, and invite the community to participate. Have families in your church bring along their friends. Provide **Caroling Songbooks** (page 148) for each participant. Leave an invitation to your church's holiday services at every stop. If your numbers get too large as you go door to door, split into smaller groups. Meet back at your church at a pre-determined time to play games, make crafts and enjoy refreshments. Ideas for **Caroling Fun** begin on page 148.

❄ **An Epiphany Party:** Traditionally celebrated on January 6, Epiphany ("The Twelfth Day") is a festival that recalls the arrival of the Magi to honor baby Jesus. Plan an Epiphany Party during the days after December 25, using a "We Three Kings" theme. Parents of schoolkids on Christmas break will welcome the activities. (And a party after Christmas allows extra time to prepare!)

# Volunteers

Recruiting volunteers for a Christmas celebration is easy because it is a short, one-time commitment. People are more apt to help when asked to contribute only a few hours. In addition, your event gives volunteers the chance to "get into the Christmas spirit" while serving Christ at the same time.

To estimate how many helpers you need, make a list of the kinds of activities you want to include in your program (for help deciding, see **Selecting Activities** on page 17). Each game, craft, snack, gift and activity will require at least one volunteer on the day of the event – and possibly two. Don't forget to count the helpers you will need at the registration table and for the Christmas story presentation.

❄ **Recruiting:** As soon as you know the date of your event – even if it is months ahead of time – begin recruiting volunteers. Here are a few tips for enticing helpers:

**Work in advance.** If you wait until only a couple of weeks before your party to ask for help, people may be too busy. But when you ask volunteers to save the date early on, you have a better chance of getting firm commitments. Planning early also heightens the importance of the event in your congregation.

**Ask personally.** One or two volunteers may offer their services without your asking them. But by far the most effective means for getting people on board is approaching them individually. Get a directory from your church office. Ask your pastors, Sunday school superintendent, youth group coordinator, church secretary and other church leaders for lists of potential volunteers. Set aside a few hours on a weekend or evening to call or e-mail the people on your list. Enthusiastically explain the program and invite them to be a part of it. If some people have conflicts with the date of your event, find out if they are willing to help with publicity, preparation or follow-up instead.

## Let them choose their tasks.
Have a list of the jobs you need filled. As volunteers agree to help, ask them what they would like to do. Some helpers love crafts, while others are more comfortable working in the kitchen. Try to put people where they serve the best. Also, ask for names of other potential recruits. Volunteers (especially teens) enjoy working alongside their friends.

## Get people's attention.
Submit a "Help Wanted: Elves" ad to your church bulletin and newsletter. Make creative announcements during worship services. Post fun flyers. (See an **Announcement Sample** on page 188.)

## Talk to adult and teen
Sunday school classes, Bible study groups, choirs and other groups that meet weekly so you can share the plans for your event.

## Post a sign-up sheet to create momentum.
People who see that others have already agreed to help are more likely to commit. Reproduce the **Volunteer Sign-up Sheet** on page 189 and post it in your church lobby. Contact those who sign up, confirm that you have received their information and thank them for volunteering.

## ❄ Training.
It is important that volunteers catch the vision for making Christ the focus of your celebration. They also need to understand how to carry out their particular roles. There are several different ways you can provide orientation for your team (see below). You might need to use a combination of these training methods to prepare your workers for your Christmas event.

## One large training session.
With this format, you can explain the program thoroughly to the entire group. Your staff can pray, sing and celebrate together prior to instruction about individual responsibilities. To be effective, this kind of training requires extra organization ahead of time, but it has these advantages:

> ❄ **All training is completed at once.**

> ❄ **Volunteers see how their jobs fit into the entire program.**

> ❄ **Workers experience unity of purpose and excitement about their participation in the event.**

## Individual or small group training.
When it is not possible to assemble all of your workers in one place at the same time, you can meet with them individually or in small groups. To be effective, this kind of training also requires extra time, but it has these important advantages:

❉ **Volunteers receive individualized instruction.**

❉ **You can instill the purpose of the program in each helper.**

❉ **You can get to know each worker personally.**

❉ **Volunteers can be trained at their convenience.**

**Telephone Training.** When it is not possible to meet in person with volunteers, contact them by telephone to review the program and their individual responsibilities.

A **Volunteer Training Checklist** is provided on page 190 for help in planning your training sessions.

# Budget

Use your projected activity list to create an inventory of necessary supplies – use the **Supply Checklist** on page 191 to help you organize the details. Then estimate how many guests you expect, and project the total cost of your program.

Avoid charging admission for your event. You are throwing a party to honor Jesus' birth – not to raise money. Instead, consider other financing methods:

❉ **Find out if your church's evangelism or outreach budgets have resources you can use.**

❉ **Request financial assistance from your education or Sunday school departments.**

❉ **Seek permission to solicit financial donations from the congregation.**

❉ **Ask the church office for help with copying and postage to reduce expenses.**

❉ **Make a list of needed supplies, distribute the** Supply Donations Form **(on page 188) to your congregation and invite them to contribute those items. Designate a collection point at a central location in your church, and label it clearly.**

# Publicity

Begin publicizing your event at least six weeks in advance. Start within your own congregation, then branch out your efforts into your community. Turn the page for ideas on getting the word out.

## In your congregation:

❈ **Ask for permission to explain your event from the pulpit and to invite members to participate.**

❈ **Put announcements in your church newsletter.**

❈ **Create a** Bulletin Insert **using the sample on page 192, and include it in worship bulletins during the weeks leading up to your event.**

❈ **Reproduce the** Publicity Flyer **on page 193. Fill in the appropriate information, make copies on colorful paper and hang the flyers on bulletin boards, walls and in your church's windows.**

❈ **Make** Publicity Postcard Invitations **(see page 192) and mail them to every child and family on your church's mailing list.**

## In your community:

❈ **Give church members copies of the publicity flyer. Have them share the flyers with neighbors and friends.**

❈ **Ask local businesses, libraries and community centers for permission to hang your publicity flyers in their windows. Some may also allow you to leave stacks of flyers in their checkout or display areas.**

❈ **Find out if schools in your area will allow you to distribute flyers to their students.**

❈ **Let children in Sunday school classes and mid-week Bible clubs make invitations to your event. Suggest that everyone give or send an invitation to a friend.**

❈ **Hang a waterproof banner in front of your church that announces "Happy Birthday, Jesus!" and the details of your celebration. Specify to the printer (or whoever makes the banner) that the event's dates and times should be made from replaceable lettering so you can re-use the banner every year.**

❈ **Submit information about your event to the local newspaper for its free "Community Events" calendar.**

Word of mouth is always the best publicity. If you put on a quality event the first time around, more people will attend the next year because they know your celebration is organized, meaningful and worthwhile.

Ask various organizations in your church (women, kids, teens, seniors) to make posters for your party. Some ideas to get started are on the next page.

# Stocking Surprises

## What You Need

* stocking pattern on page 194
* poster board or construction paper
* markers or crayons

## What to Do

1. Enlarge the stocking pattern on poster board or construction paper. (See page 24 for how to enlarge patterns.)
2. Across the top of the poster, write, "There's a stocking full of surprises at…"
3. Fill in specific information on the stocking.
4. Use markers or crayons to decorate it.

There's a stocking full of surprises at…

**Santa's Gift Shop**

Crafts Games Stories

Saturday, December 5
10-Noon

Faith Community Church
215 Oak Street

Kids 4-12

# The King's Having a Birthday!

## What You Need

* crown pattern on page 195
* poster board or construction paper
* markers or crayons

## What to Do

The King's Having a Birthday
And You're Invited!

Crafts Games Snacks Stories

Elmwood Bible Church
6405 Oregon Blvd.
Tuesday, December 12
7-9 p.m.

Kids 4-12

1. Enlarge the crown pattern on poster board or construction paper. (See page 24 for how to enlarge patterns).
2. Across the top of the poster, write, "The King's Having a Birthday and You're Invited!"
3. Fill in specific information on the crown.
4. Use markers or crayons to decorate the crown.

# Registration

Encourage pre-registration for your event. If you know an approximate number of guests to expect, you can plan accordingly.

Reproduce the **Registration Form** on page 196. Give copies to your church secretary. Ask the secretary to record guest information when parents call to register their children. Tell congregation members to sign up their youngsters and friends as early as possible.

Keep accurate registration information records. The names and addresses you collect can be used as a mailing list when you promote other family events at your church, such as vacation Bible school, Sunday school kick-off day and next year's Christmas celebration.

Make sure your registration form includes these key questions:

❄ **"May we contact you by e-mail?" By law, you must have permission to place individuals on an electronic mailing list.**

❄ **"Do you have a home church?" Your church's visitation committee can follow up with families who have no regular place to worship.**

❄ **"How did you hear about us?" When you plan future events, you will know which methods of publicity were the most effective.**

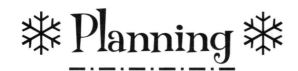

# ❄ Planning ❄

## Selecting Activities

All of the decorations, games, crafts, gifts, snacks and activities in this book are based on Scripture. Each one reinforces a specific biblical principle or story. They can be used in any combination. They can also stand alone as individual activities for class, club or home.

Take advantage of this flexibility as you plan your Christmas celebration. Pick and choose the elements that appeal to you and your team.

It is important to strike a balance with the right number of options for the kind of program you are offering. For example, just a few games and snacks make a caroling party complete. But a gala festival requires a wide range of activities to achieve a "midway" atmosphere.

Each guest will participate at his or her own pace. Some will choose to spend 30 minutes making a gift for Grandma. Others will want to repeat the same game three or four times. On average, calculate that each participant will take 3-5 minutes to play a game, 7-10 minutes to make a craft and 8-15 minutes to make a gift.

Consult other Sunday school teachers and children's workers as you select activities for your program. Ask them what has worked well at your church in the past. Solicit their opinions about how many activities to include, where to stage them and which new ideas to try.

To streamline preparation, recruit station leaders for the various components of your event. Each station leader can be responsible for one particular area of the program: for example, a crafts station leader, a gifts station leader and a snacks station leader. You can work directly with station leaders as they select activities, collect supplies and train volunteers in their respective areas. By distributing some responsibility to others, you will not shoulder the burden for the entire event. In addition, your celebration will benefit from the creative input of several organizers. Station leaders will gain crucial leadership experience in the process.

You and your team may opt to focus your celebration on a particular Christmas theme. If so, you will find the **Party and Lesson Themes** on pages 25-28 particularly helpful.

## Games and Prizes

As you choose games for your celebration, make sure to include some for younger children (ages 3-6) as well as those that will challenge older children (ages 7-12). Complete instructions for **Games** begin on page 109.

Some games, such as **Build a Stable Relay** (page 110) and **Escape to Egypt** (page 115), require at least two helpers because of the need to re-set pieces and time the players. However, simple games – particularly those that are appropriate for preschoolers – can be grouped together and managed by a single volunteer.

Each volunteer should play his or her game several times before the event and understand its biblical message. That way volunteers will know how long each game takes to play, how to re-set the games and how to reinforce the games' spiritual meanings as the kids play.

The volunteers should explain the rules to the children before play begins. Allow the kids to play the games as many times as they want. Helpers can point out that if others are waiting to play, repeat players should go to the end of the line.

Provide baskets of prizes at each game station. Each child who plays should receive a prize, regardless of "success." Choose prizes that are fun, colorful and inexpensive, such as stickers, pencils, erasers, penny candy and small toys with non-commercial Christmas themes.

# Decorations, Crafts and Gifts

**Party Decorations.** Add a touch of sparkle to your celebration by decorating your facility. An ideal time to do this is during Set-up. Recruit volunteers specifically to help with decorating. Instructions for simple party decorations begin on page 34.

## Christmas Decorations. **Christmas Decorations** (pages 49-62) are additional projects specifically designed to decorate doors, walls, windows and tabletops in your church or home. Christmas tree ornaments are included (**Chrismons**, page 52, **Cinnamon Ornaments**, page 53, **Paper Clip Heavenly Host**, page 57 and **Plastic Basket Snowflakes**, page 58).

Use these Christmas decorations to supplement your party décor. With your team, decide which ones add to the spirit of your celebration. Have volunteers prepare these decorations during Set-up. Tell your workers that even though the directions were created for teachers to use with children, they can adapt the instructions for themselves.

Christmas Decorations also can be included as craft items for your party guests to make and take home. Choose some that fit your theme. Set up extra tables for decorations in your craft area.

## Crafts. The **Crafts** in this book (pages 63-82) are items that children can use for Christmas games and activities, in day-to-day activities during Advent and as preparation for Christmas. All activities are suitable for elementary-aged children. Preschoolers will need adult assistance.

Have your helpers make a sample of each craft and decoration prior to your event. That way they will be able to share with the guests what to do, what pitfalls to avoid and how long  each item takes to complete. Also, the children can follow the examples while working. Most important, helpers who are familiar with the crafts and decorations will be able to share the biblical significance of each one with the children.

Allow one craft or decoration per table. Participants can stand around the tables as they work. Have extra supplies on hand. Some guests will make more than one of their favorite items.

Cover an extra table or shelf with newspaper and designate it as a drying area. The crafters can leave their completed projects there to dry while they participate in other activities (make sure your volunteers label each guest's craft with his or her name). Afterward, remove the newspaper for easy cleanup.

Gifts. Each project in the **Gifts** section of this book (pages 83-107) is a simple, high-quality item. However, these gifts will take longer to make than the craft and decoration items, and the materials are slightly more expensive, so plan accordingly.

Set up the Gift station as for crafts and decorations. Offer a range of gift options. Prepare and display samples so the guests can choose what to make. Volunteers will need to be familiar with the available gift choices so they can help participants select appropriate gifts for their relatives, teachers or friends.

Each item can stand alone as an individual gift. However, related projects can be grouped together as gift sets. For example, the **Celebration Soap Bar** (page 85), **Hand Towel for a King** (page 92) and **Silver and Gold Sachet** (page 104) combine appropriately. Likewise, the **Noel Coffee Mug** (page 98) and **Spicy Scented Coasters** (page 106) fit together well. Mix and match gift items as you like.

Each gift project has a biblical objective. The helpers should reinforce the points to participants making gifts. The biblical points can also be reproduced on gift tags and tied to the gifts so that crafters can share the message of God's love with the recipients. Instructions for **Holiday Heart Gift Tags** are on page 93.

Set apart one section of the gift area as a wrapping station so participants can wrap their gifts and take them home without fear of prying eyes. Supply gift wrap, ribbons, bows, tape and scissors. Have pens or markers on hand to write on the Holiday Heart Gift Tags. You might choose to let participants prepare specialty **Magi Gift Bags** (page 71) for their gifts. If so, provide tissue paper to fill the bags.

Consider having extra volunteers at the gift station. The children might want to work privately without their parents' help in order to prepare their gifts, yet they still could require adult assistance.

# Snacks

Decide whether you want to serve snacks to all your guests at the same time or allow participants to visit the snack station when they are ready. Each method has its plusses.

If you are using a Jesus' birthday party theme, a group snack time will reinforce that atmosphere. Serve **The King's Cupcakes** (page 137), sing "Happy Birthday" to Jesus and blow out the candles together. A group snack is also convenient because once it's over, workers at that station can begin clean-up.

At larger parties, it might be easier to keep the snack station open the whole time so kids can come and go as they please. To guarantee that each child gets an opportunity to have a snack (and to fend off kids who might try to gobble all the goodies early!), require tickets for the snack station. Reproduce the **Snack Tickets** on page 197 and distribute one to each guest at registration. Then have the kids hand in their snack tickets at the station when ready to eat.

Determine whether you want helpers to prepare snacks in advance or if you want the children to make their own snacks as an activity. Either way, assemble sufficient ingredients to provide enough snacks for not only the kids but also their parents and your helpers. Have extra plates, napkins and cups on hand, just in case.

Have the children wash their hands prior to food preparation and eating. Use tape or chairs to designate a specific eating area. Have plenty of trash cans nearby for easy clean-up. Watch that kids do not take the food into other parts of your facility!

# More Activities!

Caroling. "Sing to the Lord a new song, his praise in the assembly of the saints" (Psalm 149:1). Music is synonymous with Christmas celebrations. But you don't need to be a professional musician to include Christmas music as part of your program. Ideas for **Caroling Fun** (pages 148-151) can show you what to do.

A warm, old-fashioned Christmas caroling party gets participants into the "holiday spirit" and creates treasured memories. It is also a worship experience. Over the course of the party, carolers repeatedly sing praise to God and narrate the Christmas story through song. A well-run caroling party can have significant spiritual influence on the lives of your participants, so plan your time carefully.

Greet guests at your facility, distribute **Caroling Songbooks** (page 148) and rehearse the carols before venturing out into the neighborhood. Have participants make **Caroling Candleholders** (page 149) to use as they go door to door, or provide flashlights. After caroling, return to the church for refreshments and games.

If you are caroling at night with children, have extra adults to help corral the group. Ask small children to hold hands. To help recruit adult participants, specify in your publicity that parents must accompany their children.

# Gingerbread Houses. Volunteers who help with gingerbread
houses don't need to be culinary experts. They simply need to know a few easy techniques, be tolerant of sticky fingers and enjoy helping children be creative!

To generate decorating ideas, cut out photographs of gingerbread houses from magazines. Cover the photos with clear, self-stick plastic. Collect a variety of candies and snack foods with which to decorate the houses.

Helpers can follow the **Gingerbread Houses** instructions on pages 156-157 and assemble one or more houses ahead of time. That way they will have samples to follow while they help the children. Use royal icing "glue" to fasten house parts together and attach the candies. Because the prepared icing is made from meringue powder and does not include raw egg whites, it will not present a health risk.

Making gingerbread houses is a favorite Christmas activity. Guests may spend up to an hour at this station, creating their "masterpieces." Have extra helpers to accommodate a crowd.

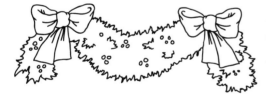

# Hanging the Greens. Let families work
together to make their own evergreen swags or wreaths to take home. Be sure to have an assortment of pine, cedar, fir and spruce branches on hand. Have participants work outside if the weather is mild, or in a large open area indoors. Lay down a tarp to collect excess needles. **Hanging the Greens** instructions begin on page 158.

# Live Nativity. Erect a simple lean-to, line it with hay, ask a local
farmer to bring his or her sheep, goats or cows and have volunteers from your congregation portray the Christmas story characters in a live setting. The scene's sounds, textures and smells bring the first Christmas to life. Find complete **Live Nativity** instructions on pages 161-162.

# The Christmas Story. There will be visitors to your event
who will hear the Christmas story for the first time. Others will experience it in a whole new light. Don't underestimate the importance of this element in your program. Pages 152-155 describe different ways to present the story of Jesus' birth. Choose the option that best uses your resources.

Decide if you want to feature the Christmas story as an individual station with repeat presentations, or as a one-time, group presentation. The advantage of repeat presentations is flexibility. Participants can enjoy the story when they are ready. If you choose this option, put the story station in a noticeable area of your facility.

On the other hand, a group presentation at a designated time will guarantee that all your guests hear the story. A good time to do this is in combination with a group snack time.

Remember that there will be young children in your audience. To keep their attention, streamline your presentation to 10 minutes or less. Or, choose an interactive version that will involve the audience and be a memorable experience for every guest.

A favorite way to conclude a Christmas party is to combine a carol sing and the Christmas story in a pageant with narration and carols. Pages 153-155 show how to bring these two elements together.

## The Mitten Tree.
Contact a local shelter or family crisis agency and offer to provide warm winter accessories for disadvantaged children and adults. Set up an extra Christmas tree in a prominent location of your facility. Designate it as the collection point for mittens, hats, scarves and socks. Keep the **Mitten Tree** up for one day, one week or one month. You can even suggest that guests to your party offer a mitten or cash donation to the **Mitten Tree** in lieu of an entrance fee. Page 163 outlines the **Mitten Tree** activity in detail.

# Santa Claus

Should you have Santa Claus participate in an event centered on Christ's birth? Discuss this question with your pastors, team and church board.

Today's image of Santa Claus traces its roots to Saint Nicolas, a godly bishop in fourth century Turkey who distributed all his wealth to poor people, especially children. Likewise, a beloved Christian image of Santa Claus is the jolly, red-suited gentleman kneeling beside Jesus' manger in worship. Including Santa in this way – emphasizing St. Nicolas' generosity and compassion, always in deference to Christ – can enhance the message of Jesus as the focal point of Christmas.

If you decide to include a live Santa Claus at your party, determine the extent of his involvement. You could have him simply circulate among your guests. He can encourage the children in the games, compliment them on their handiwork, help wrap gifts, serve snacks to the families or carry a sack of candy canes to share.

Or, you could have Santa Claus take children onto his lap so they can share their Christmas wishes. This is a wonderful opportunity to give individual attention to each child and talk about God's wonderful gift of His Son.

Either way, enlist an outgoing older man to portray him (this is a great way to involve seniors!). Rent or borrow a suit for the occasion. Or, ask a seamstress in your congregation to sew one. You might even discover that a member already owns a Santa suit that can be used.

Use photos with Santa as an outreach tool. Have a congregation member snap candid shots of Santa interacting with the children. (Make sure your photographer records the names of the children in each photo.) After your party, mail the developed photos to visiting children and include a note: "Thank you for celebrating Jesus' birth with us! We hope you will join us again for Christmas Eve [or Sunday school, or another appropriate event]." See pages 45-47 for more **Follow-up** ideas.

# Your Pastors

Your event is an excellent opportunity for your pastors to meet community residents who are not members of your church, and to build relationships with people who are. Tell your pastors the date and time of the party as soon as it is on the calendar.

Ask your pastors to attend in whatever capacities they choose. Your pastors might feel comfortable as greeters. They can welcome participants as they arrive and help them get involved with the activities. Or, your pastors might want to be involved "hands-on" at the stations in order to interact with guests and helpers.

Your pastors should invite people to other events at your church. In particular, they can share a listing of Christmas worship services with guests who do not have a church home. They might also want to offer information on pastoral care, such as hospital visitation or counseling. Make sure your pastors wear name tags.

# Parents and Family Members

While your Christmas celebration is programmed to be kid-friendly, it is very much a family event. Invite parents, grandparents, older siblings, aunts and uncles to attend. Do everything you can to make them feel comfortable and welcome.

Encourage parents and family members to circulate through your party with their children. Offer them the opportunity to participate in games. Adults may want to assist their children with the crafts, or even make a few gifts themselves. Invite families to work together to create personal decorations for their homes.

Provide coffee at the snack station. Have plenty of chairs at all points so parents and family members can take breaks if they need. Remind your helpers to introduce themselves to visiting adults and get to know them.

Make sure your publicity is inviting to adults: "A celebration for children and their families. Kids – bring your parents! Youngsters ages six and under require adult supervision." That way adults will know that the fun has been planned with them in mind, too. It will also prevent your party from becoming too much of a "drop-off" event.

# Weather

As you plan, consider the typical winter climate in your area, and your available space. If you live in a temperate zone, you may be able to set up some of your activities outside. For those in central and northern regions, remember that your party likely will be all indoors because of wintry conditions.

Plan what you will do if there is rain, sleet or snow. Enlist helpers to clear the sidewalks and parking lot. Set aside an area in your building's vestibule for coats, hats and boots. Make sure the heat is working!

If you are planning an evening program, you may want to decorate outside walkways with **Luminaries for the Light of the World** (page 56). Recruit an adult volunteer to light the luminaries just before your guests arrive, periodically check that the candles are safely burning and extinguish them at the conclusion of the evening.

# Enlarging Patterns

Some of the activities in this book require oversize parts that are easy to enlarge from patterns. Here's how.

 ## What You Need

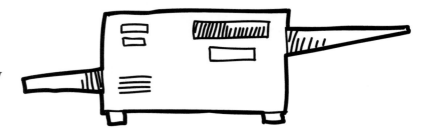

✳ pattern to be enlarged
✳ overhead projector
✳ reusable overhead transparency
✳ transparency marker
✳ poster board or poster paper
✳ clear tape
✳ pencil
✳ permanent marker

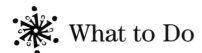 ## What to Do

1. Use a transparency marker to trace the pattern onto an overhead transparency.
2. Tape poster board or paper on a wall.
3. Place the transparency on the reflecting surface of the overhead projector.
4. Position the projector so the pattern image projects onto the poster board or paper.
5. Trace the image onto the poster board or paper with a pencil.
6. Go over the lines with a permanent marker.

# Creating Pattern Templates

Many activities use patterns, which are included in the **Reproducibles and Patterns** section at the back of the book, starting on page 185. It is easy to make your own templates from patterns.

 ## What You Need

❄ pattern to be copied
❄ lightweight paper
❄ poster board
❄ pencil
❄ scissors
❄ clear, self-stick plastic

 ## What to Do

1. Photocopy the pattern onto lightweight paper.
2. Cut out the pattern.
3. Trace the pattern onto poster board and cut it out.
4. Cover the pattern with clear, self-stick plastic for durability.
5. Trim the edges.

# Party and Lesson Themes

You might decide to organize your event around a single theme. Or, for a small party, you might need to streamline activities. Perhaps you would like to emphasize specific components of the Christmas story during a Sunday school class, teen meeting or children's program.

Pages 26-28 show how to group this book's activities thematically. Each theme is labeled with an icon, both here and throughout the book. Use these groupings to help you coordinate your program, or simply to make planning easier.

## Getting Ready for Christmas (Advent)

**Decorations:** Christmas Card Roundabout, page 86
Cinnamon Ornament, page 53
**Craft:** Advent Treat Calendar, page 64
**Gifts:** Bouncy Balls, page 84
Im-pastable Canister, page 95
**Games:** Christmas Story Match-up, page 114
Grow a Beard, page 117
Stocking Stuffers, page 124
**Snack:** John the Baptist's Snack Mix, page 136
**More Activities:** Hanging the Greens, page 158
**Lessons:** Don't Miss the Party!, page 167
Getting Ready for Christmas, page 169

## A Stable in Bethlehem (Mary and Joseph)

**Decorations:** Tabletop Crèche, page 61
**Crafts:** Christmas Card Magnets, page 66
Gabriel Macaroni Pin, page 67
Pocket Crèche Puppets, page 73
**Gifts:** Confetti Treat Tin, page 87
Hand Towel for a King, page 92
**Games:** Build a Stable Relay, page 110
Camels and Donkeys, page 112
The Census in Bethlehem, page 113
**Snacks:** Animals in the Stable, page 129
Donkey Biscuits, page 135
Mangers with Straw, page 138
Stained Glass Candies, page 143
Sugarplums, page 144
Swaddled Dates, page 145
**More Activities:** The Christmas Story, page 152
Live Nativity, page 161
**Lessons:** No Room at the Inn, page 177
Why a Baby? page 181

## Angels and Shepherds (Celebrating the Savior's Birth)

**Decorations:** Cardboard Tube Carolers, page 51
Paper Clip Heavenly Host, page 57
**Crafts:** Miniature Poinsettia, page 72
Sheep Lollipop, page 78
Shepherd Treat Holder, page 79

**Gifts:**  Jingle Bell Gloves, page 96

   Night of Wonder Headband, page 97

   Noel Coffee Mug, page 98

**Game:** Sheep on the Hillside, page 122

**Snacks:**  Angel Clouds, page 128

   Crunchy Shepherd's Staffs, page 134

   Shepherd's Dip, page 139

**More Activities:** Caroling Fun, page 148

**Lessons:**  God's Messengers, page 170

   Spread the News, page 178

# A Visit from the Magi (Epiphany)

**Crafts:** Bethlehem Sky Star Caper, page 65

   Gingerbread Magi Men, page 68

   King's Crown, page 70

   Magi Gift Bag, page 71

   Star of Bethlehem Pencil Topper page 81

**Gift:** Spicy Scented Coasters, page 106

**Games:** The Call from King Herod, page 111

   Escape to Egypt, page 115

   The Land Where Jesus Was Born, page 118

**Lessons:**  Which King Will You Follow? page 179

   Worship the King, page 183

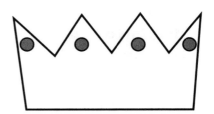

# The Light of the World (The Names of Christ)

**Decorations:** Chrismon, page 52

   Luminaries for the Light of the World, page 56

   Silver Bells Door Hanger, page 60

**Gifts:** Rock Trivet, page 99

   Shining Light Votive Holder, page 101

**Snacks:** Bright Morning Stars, page 130

   The King's Cupcakes, page 137

**Lessons:**  Immanuel, page 171

   The Light of the World, page 175

# Winter Wonderland (Walking with Jesus)

**Decorations:** Candy Tree, page 49

   Frosty Icicle Wreath, page 54

   Plastic Basket Snowflake, page 58

   Ribbon Teardrop Swag, page 59

**Craft:** Happy Birthday Pin, page 69

**Gifts:**  Celebration Soap Bar, page 85

   Silver and Gold Sachet, page 104

   Snowflake Fleece Scarf, page 105

**Games:** Fields of Snow, page 116
Snow Shoveling in the Dark, page 123
**Snacks:** Cheesy Popcorn, page 131
Spicy Hot Cider, page 141
Sprinkle Spoons, page 142
**Lesson:** J.O.Y., page 172

## Santa and His Reindeer (The Joy of Giving)
**Decorations:** Grocery Sack Reindeer, page 55
**Crafts:** Reindeer Candy Cane, page 75
Santa Take-home Sack, page 76
**Gifts:** Holiday Heart Gift Tag, page 93
Shoelace Elves, page 102
**Game:** Santa's Belly, page 121
**More Activities:** The Mitten Tree, page 163
**Lessons:** Ask for Good Gifts, page 166
Wrapping Gifts with Jesus, page 184

## A Cozy Christmas (The Love of God)
**Decorations:** Tree Garland of Trust, page 62
**Craft:** Walnut Mouse, page 82
**Gifts:** Cookie Mix in a Jar, page 89
Cozy Cocoa Kit, page 90
Cranberry Grapevine Wreath, page 91
Holly Door Stopper, page 94
Santa Stamps, page 100
**Game:** Race Down the Chimney, page 120
**Snacks:** Cornflake Wreaths, page 132
Cozy Christmas Cocoa, page 133
Snowman Sticks, page 140
**More Activities:** Gingerbread Houses, page 156
**Lesson:** Jesus Came for Everybody, page 174

# Planning Timetable

Use this checklist to plan your Christmas celebration from start to finish!

## 4 months ahead
❑ Begin praying for your event
❑ Recruit prayer partners; give each one a **Prayer Checklist** (page 187)
❑ Set a date
❑ Choose a type of celebration
❑ Schedule set-up time
❑ Reserve your facility

## 2 months ahead

- ❏ Begin publicity in your congregation
- ❏ Place announcements in church newsletter
- ❏ Order outside banner
- ❏ Prepare publicity flyers, posters, bulletin inserts, publicity postcards and registration forms
- ❏ Recruit station leaders and volunteers
- ❏ Select activities
- ❏ Establish a budget
- ❏ Organize a supply list

## 1 month ahead

- ❏ Post publicity flyers in your church
- ❏ Post banner outside your building
- ❏ Post publicity flyers in community businesses
- ❏ Include a bulletin insert and announcements in worship bulletin each week until event
- ❏ Begin accepting pre-registrations
- ❏ Distribute supply list to congregation
- ❏ Designate a supply collection point
- ❏ Begin collecting supplies and prizes
- ❏ Finish recruiting volunteers

## 3 weeks ahead

- ❏ Mail publicity postcards
- ❏ Continue pre-registration
- ❏ Schedule volunteer training sessions
- ❏ Organize game parts, Christmas story materials and caroling booklets
- ❏ Reproduce craft and gift patterns
- ❏ Prepare necessary craft parts
- ❏ Make decorations
- ❏ Assign volunteers to their tasks

## 2 weeks ahead

- ❏ Plan set-up
- ❏ Finish collecting supplies
- ❏ Make sample crafts, gifts, decorations, gingerbread houses
- ❏ Conduct volunteer training sessions (see **Volunteer Training Checklist**, page 190)

## 1 day ahead

- ❏ Set up for your party (see **Set-up Checklist**, page 198)

## Celebration Day

- ❏ Light luminaries
- ❏ Celebrate the birth of our Savior and King!

# ❄ Set-up Time! ❄

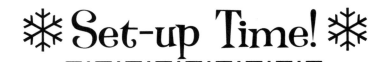

While a Christmas celebration is an opportunity to share the message of Christmas with the families in your community, it also builds unity within your congregation. Camaraderie is evidence of God's work among you. Do everything you can to foster this kind of teamwork.

One way to do this is to have a well-planned set-up time. As your volunteers make preparations together, excitement will grow. You might hear them saying, "This is getting me into the Christmas spirit." In addition, setting up ahead of time lets your entire team take a break before the party starts, so they will feel rested and ready to go.

An organized set-up time is one of the building blocks of a successful event. Use the **Set-up Checklist** on page 198 to help you plan this important segment of your program. Be sure to take these steps before set-up:

❅ **Publicize the set-up date and time in the church bulletin and newsletter several weeks in advance. Invite your congregation to participate. Some people who aren't able to help at the actual party might be available the day before to help you prepare.**

❅ **Create a festive atmosphere. Start celebrating while you set up! Supply snacks for your workers. Play Christmas music on the sound system. Provide childcare so parents of young children are free to fulfill their responsibilities.**

❅ **Organize your time. Make a list of tasks that need to be done.**

> ✔ Set up stations
> ✔ Arrange tables and chairs
> ✔ Make and put up decorations
> ✔ Prepare sample crafts and gifts
> ✔ Set up game parts
> ✔ Post signs
> ✔ Rehearse the presentation of the Christmas story
> ✔ Set up and decorate Christmas trees
> ✔ Fill luminaries
> ✔ Prepare snacks

❄ Complete volunteer training for those who missed the earlier sessions.

❄ Have a clipboard handy so you can jot down any last-minute supplies you need or details you want to remember.

❄ Use your volunteers wisely. As volunteers arrive, assign them a task. Follow up later to see if they need help, instructions, supplies or an additional job to do. Well-directed volunteers ease your work burden, build enthusiasm for the program and are more likely to help again next time.

❄ Match experienced volunteers with newcomers.

❄ Make and give a Happy Birthday Pin **(page 69)** to each volunteer as a thank-you gift for his or her contribution to the event. Distribute the pins during your set-up time or immediately before the party. Invite the volunteers to wear their pins during the celebration so guests can easily identify them, and then keep the pins as an expression of appreciation from your church.

## Stations

Each set of activities (decorations, crafts, gifts, games and snacks) needs its own special area, or station. Spend some time thinking about where to locate each one by assessing the available space in your facility. Here are some tips for savvy stations:

❄ **A fellowship hall works well as a central location for your party. You can designate different sections for specific stations. Arrange tables in a U-shape, T-shape or square to encourage participants to work through the set-up in an orderly fashion.**

❄ **A series of classrooms in your education area is another easy way to designate stations. Separate rooms keep noise levels manageable. A hallway lends itself well to foot traffic.**

❄ **Allow one table for each individual craft, gift or decoration activity. Let participants stand around the tables while working.**

❄ **If you live in a temperate area or expect mild weather, consider setting up some of the games outside. Otherwise, find an open area for relays and tossing games.**

❄ **Snacks should be located near the kitchen so the refrigerator, microwave and stove are accessible for preparations and a sink is nearby for quick clean-up.**

❄ **If you plan to present the Christmas story several times throughout the** course of your party, select a quiet location and label it clearly. That way guests can enjoy the presentation without distractions. If you decide to give one group presentation, use your sanctuary, auditorium or large multi-purpose room to ensure adequate seating.**

- **Try to cluster activities for very young children in one place. This will allow the little ones to move freely around their area while parents keep a close eye on them.**
- **Designate each activity with a sign that includes its title and Bible reference.**
- **Draw a simple map showing where each activity is located. Distribute copies of the map to your volunteers. You can also include a copy of this map in guests' registration packets (see** Registration Table **below).**
- **After the stations are set and stocked, take photos of each one to put in your** Christmas Celebration File **(see page 43) for next year.**

# Registration Table

Set up a large table near the entrance to your facility. Pre-registered guests will check in here. Walk-in visitors can fill out registration forms. If you keep careful records of participants, you will have a substantial list of families to invite to your next outreach event.

Registration table volunteers should be familiar with the set-up so they can give guests directions. They should also be able to answer questions about your church and its ministries. Have plenty of markers, pens and pencils at the registration table.

Prepare registration packets to give guests when they arrive. Each packet should contain a **Schedule of Events** (page 196), a name tag, a copy of your set-up map and a snack ticket for each child. You might also want to include your church's brochure with a list of Advent activities and Christmas services.

Volunteers at this station should welcome visitors and have them add personalized "branches" to the **Welcome Wreath** (page 39). If the **Christmas Kindness Tree** (page 35) or **The Mitten Tree** (page 163) is part of your program, then volunteers can point out these activities to your guests, too.

Make sure that registration table helpers distribute the **Visitor Evaluation Form** (page 199) with registration packets. Have them explain that visitors' feedback will help your church provide quality programs to meet the needs of the families in your community. Place a gift-wrapped box, with an opening in it for completed forms, near the exit.

# Take-home Bags

During the celebration, families will accumulate prizes, crafts, decorations and gifts. To prevent chaos, provide take-home bags.

If you opt to have participants make **Santa Take-home Sacks** (page 76), have helpers at the registration table direct them to that station first.

Pre-printed small plastic sacks are an inexpensive option for take-home bags. A local printer can print your church's address, phone number, e-mail address and web site address on the bags. Printed bags are not only practical carryalls, but also publicity tools.

Another option is ready-made Christmas gift bags. Check discount stores or look on-line for gift bags in bulk quantities that are more affordable.

The simplest take-home bag is a brown grocery bag. Provide markers and let families draw Christmas trees, stars or other Christmas symbols on the outsides.

Make sure all participants write their names on their take-home bags.

# Posted Schedule

Make several copies of your **Schedule of Events** (page 196) on poster board. Post them at the registration table and at several locations throughout your facility. When participants ask, "When does the carol sing begin?" or "How long until snacks are served?" volunteers can refer to the posted schedule. They can also remind visitors to check the schedules in the registration packets.

Be sure that clocks in your building are synchronized. Remind helpers to wear watches!

# Traffic Flow

As guests arrive, they might be uncertain about what to expect and what to do. By giving good directions, you will make things easy for them and keep confusion to a minimum.

❄ **Post maps. Make poster copies of your set-up map, similar to the smaller copies in the registration packets. Post the big maps near the registration table and in other key areas. Volunteers can use these maps to help guests get started or to help guests decide where to go next.**

❄ **Use directional signs. Label stations with large signs or banners, such as "Crafts," "Gifts" and "Games." Use arrows with signs to show where activities are located. For example, an arrow with a sign, at the foot of a staircase, might read "Gingerbread Houses upstairs."**

❅ **Make sure to label rest rooms.**

❅ **Encourage movement. When lines get too long, offer guests the option to try something else first. Say, "We need a few more people to play Camels and Donkeys. Would you like to join us, and then come back to make a gift for your mom when it's less crowded here?"**

# Decorations

If your church usually decorates for Christmas, some of your decoration work for this party will be done for you! If you're not sure what kinds of decorations your church will provide, ask your pastor or church secretary so you don't duplicate efforts.

Secure permission to add special accents for your celebration. Choose decorations that reinforce the season: Christmas trees, greenery (fresh or artificial), wreaths and swags. Borrow winter props from congregation members, such as sleds, ice skates, snowsuits, boots, scarves and hats. Hang a series of Christmas stockings along a hallway. Twinkling lights can sparkle on trees and outline doorways and windows. Ideas for **Decorations** you can make are on pages 34-42. Decorations that adults or kids can make for your celebration or to take home are on pages 49-62.

Complement theme parties with these special touches:

❅ **A Birthday Party for Jesus.** Balloons and crepe paper streamers will highlight the fact that Christmas is Jesus' birthday. Inflate and knot balloons, tie on curling ribbon tails, assemble the balloons in bunches and attach to railings, chair backs and table legs. Twist, hang and tape crepe paper streamers in doorways. Loop streamers across ceilings. Distribute party noisemakers with registration packets. Make and post a **"Happy Birthday Jesus!" Banner** (page 36).

❅ **Hanging the Greens.** Because decorating will be the main activity at this party, preparation is easy. Simply assemble what you will need: decoration supplies (from the activities you choose on pages 158-160), Christmas lights, fresh greenery, garden shears, gardening gloves, sturdy wire and ladders. Set up Christmas trees ahead of time. Figure out where decorations are to be placed.

❅ **Santa's Gift Shop.** Collect assorted empty boxes. Wrap them in Christmas gift wrap, add ribbons and bows, and pile the packages beneath Christmas trees. Have your workers wear red stocking "elf" hats with white trim. Hang **Sparkling Snowflakes** (page 38) from ceilings.

❋ **Christmas Caroling Party.** String mittens, gloves and hats along hallways and in doorways. Hang **Sing, Sing, Sing!** notes (page 37) from ceilings. Spray artificial snow around windowpanes and place electric candles on windowsills. Set out **Luminaries for the Light of the World** (page 56) along outdoor walkways.

❋ **An Epiphany Party.** Decorate with a "royalty" theme. Purchase a long length of inexpensive red fabric and lay it near your entrance or registration table so guests can "walk the red carpet." Gather containers of different shapes and cover them with aluminum foil or gold gift wrap. Group these "gifts" in different areas around your set-up. String small white lights across ceilings to resemble starry skies. Cut out stars from metallic or holographic paper and hang them from the ceilings and in doorways. Construct a **Star of Wonder** (page 39). Let guests make and wear **King's Crowns** (page 70).

Overwhelmed with making decorations? Ask women's groups, Sunday school classes, Bible clubs or teens to make some for you. Provide small goody bags of treats or candy canes as a thank-you. They will enjoy the satisfaction of contributing to one of your church's ministries – and you will have decorations for your party!

# Christmas Kindness Tree

If possible, leave the Christmas Kindness Tree hanging up all season long. Members of your congregation will enjoy reading how the Holy Spirit is working in the lives of those in your community. They can also add their own anecdotes to the tree.

## ❋ What You Need

- ❋ tree pattern, page 208
- ❋ star pattern, page 209
- ❋ ornament pattern, page 209
- ❋ green poster board
- ❋ construction paper, assorted colors
- ❋ pencil
- ❋ markers
- ❋ clear tape
- ❋ basket
- ❋ step stool or ladder

## ❋ What to Do

1. Enlarge the tree pattern on green poster board to about 22" x 28" (see page 24 for how to

enlarge patterns). Note: Each tree will hold 20-25 bulbs. If you are having a large party with many volunteers, prepare several trees.

2. Cut out the tree.

3. Make a template of the star pattern using poster board (see **page 25** for how to make pattern templates).

4. Trace and cut out a star from yellow construction paper.

5. Tape the star to the top of the tree.

6. Use markers to draw garlands as shown on the tree. Decorate the **garlands** with the words from Galatians 5:22-23: "The fruit of the Spirit is love, joy, peace, patience, kindness, goodness, faithfulness, gentleness and self-control."

7. Use markers to write "Gifts from God" on the tree trunk and stand.

8. Tape the Christmas Kindness Tree to a wall in a prominent location.

9. Make a template of the ornament pattern using poster board.

10. Trace and cut out ornaments from various colors of construction paper.

11. As volunteers and guests arrive for your party, give each one an ornament. Say, **Think of a situation where you saw someone demonstrate one of the Fruits of the Spirit.** Review the list that is printed on the tree: love, joy, peace, patience, kindness, goodness, faithfulness, gentleness and self-control. Have volunteers and guests use markers to record one observation per ornament. Let them **attach** ornaments to the tree with clear tape. Let them complete as many ornaments as they wish.

12. Leave a basket of extra ornaments, markers and tape next to the tree so people can add to it throughout the party.

# "Happy Birthday, Jesus!" Banner

## ❄What You Need

- ❀ poster paper
- ❀ construction paper, assorted colors
- ❀ pencil
- ❀ markers
- ❀ ruler or yardstick
- ❀ scissors
- ❀ craft glue
- ❀ clear tape
- ❀ step stool or ladder

## ❄ What to Do

1. Measure the wall where you want to place your banner. Cut a piece of newsprint or shelf paper that length.

2. With a pencil, sketch "Happy Birthday, Jesus!" onto the banner.

3. Trace over the lettering with markers.

4. Cut construction paper into 1" squares.

5. Randomly position the squares on the banner to resemble "confetti." Glue the confetti into place. Allow the glue to dry.

6. Hang the banner on the wall with clear tape.

# Sing, Sing, Sing!

## ❄ What You Need

- ❄ music note patterns, pages 210-211
- ❄ poster board, assorted colors
- ❄ pencil
- ❄ markers
- ❄ glitter
- ❄ craft glue
- ❄ hole punch
- ❄ fishing line or heavy thread
- ❄ clear tape
- ❄ step stool or ladder

## ❄ What to Do

1. Enlarge the music note patterns on poster board (see page 24 for how to enlarge patterns). Make them at least 12" high so they are noticeable. Metallic-colored poster board works especially well for this decoration.

2. Cut out the music notes.

3. Use a pencil to write "Sing!" "Sing to the Lord!" or "Sing praises!" on the bodies of the music notes.

4. Outline the letters with markers.

5. Decorate the notes with glitter and glue.

6. Punch holes in the stems of the music notes.

7. Cut fishing line or thread to desired lengths. Thread the line through the note holes. Knot to secure.

8. Use clear tape to hang the notes from the ceiling.

# Sparkling Snowflakes

## ❄ What You Need

❄ snowflake pattern, page 212

❄ white poster board or heavy paper

❄ scissors

❄ glitter

❄ craft glue

❄ hole punch

❄ fishing line or heavy thread

❄ clear tape

❄ step stool or ladder

## ❄ What to Do

1. Enlarge the snowflake patterns on poster board or heavy paper. (See page 24 for how to enlarge patterns.) About 16" x 16" makes a nice size.

2. Cut out the snowflakes.

3. Decorate the snowflakes with glue and glitter. Allow to dry.

4. With a hole punch, make a hole in the top of each snowflake.

5. Cut fishing line or thread to the desired lengths (be sure they are not so low that adults will bump into them!).

6. Thread a strand through the hole in one of the snowflakes. Knot to secure. Repeat for the other snowflakes.

7. Use clear tape to hang the snowflakes from the ceiling. Make and hang as many as you want to create your own "winter wonderland." Sparkling Snowflakes are particularly beautiful when intermingled with strings of miniature white lights.

# Star of Wonder

## ❄ What You Need

- ❄ star pattern, page 209
- ❄ poster board or large piece of cardboard
- ❄ aluminum foil
- ❄ ruler
- ❄ scissors
- ❄ craft glue
- ❄ clear tape
- ❄ step stool or ladder

## ❄ What to Do

1. Enlarge the star pattern on poster board or a large piece of cardboard to about 22" x 28" (see page 24 for how to enlarge patterns).

2. Cut out the star.

3. Cut aluminum foil into 6" squares.

4. Crumple each square into a cluster.

5. Glue the clusters onto the star, covering it completely. Allow to dry.

6. Use clear tape to hang your Star of Wonder on the wall. Hang the larger stars throughout your facility. Or, make one larger star and several smaller ones, positioning the smaller stars as a "tail."

# Welcome Wreath

## ❄ What You Need

- ❄ wreath pattern, page 213
- ❄ bow pattern, page 214
- ❄ green and red poster board
- ❄ green construction paper
- ❄ pencil
- ❄ markers
- ❄ craft glue
- ❄ clear tape
- ❄ step stool or ladder

## ❄ What to Do

1. Enlarge the wreath pattern on green poster board to about 22" x 28" (see page 24 for how to enlarge patterns). Note: Each wreath will hold 25-30 hands. If you are having a large party with many volunteers, prepare several wreaths.

2. Cut out the wreath.

3. Enlarge the bow pattern on red poster board.

4. Cut out the bow.

5. Write "Welcome" on the bow with a marker.

6. Glue the bow to the wreath.

7. Hang the wreath at shoulder height on a wall near your registration area.

8. Have the volunteers trace their hands on green construction paper, write their names on the hands and cut them out.

9. Show how to position the hands on the wreath and tape in place.

10. As guests arrive at the registration table, let them make their own hands to hang on the wreath. (Occasionally check the wreath to make sure names aren't covered up as new ones are added.)

# Crepe Paper Cascades

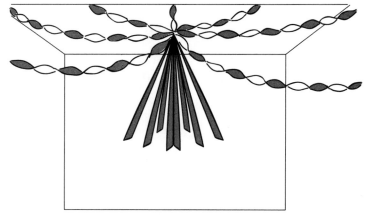

## ❄ What You Need

- ❄ rolls of crepe paper streamers in assorted colors
- ❄ clear tape
- ❄ scissors
- ❄ step stool or ladder

## ❄ What to Do

1. With clear tape, secure the end of one streamer to the ceiling where it meets the corner and the wall.

2. Unravel the streamer to the center of the room.

3. Twist the streamer for a ripple effect.

4. Tape the streamer to the ceiling at the center of the room. Cut the streamer about two or three feet below this taped position.

5. Repeat these steps for the other streamers, stringing them in each corner of the room and at periodic intervals along the walls.

**Note:** Take extra care with your balance as you tape streamers to the walls and ceiling.

# Crepe Paper Arches

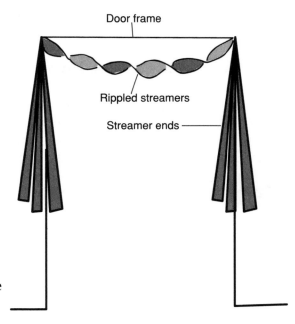

Door frame

Rippled streamers

Streamer ends

## ❉ What You Need

- ❉ rolls of crepe paper streamers in assorted colors
- ❉ yardstick or tape measure
- ❉ clear tape
- ❉ scissors
- ❉ step stool or ladder

## ❉ What to Do

1. With the tape measure or yardstick, measure the width of the doorway you want to decorate.

2. Double that figure. Measure and cut two or more contrasting crepe paper streamers to that length.

3. Layer the cut streamers and treat the stack as one.

4. Find the center of the streamers and position this point at the middle of the doorway's top frame.

5. Let the streamers loop down slightly below the top of the door frame, creating an arch. Twist the streamers for a ripple effect and tape them to the corners of the door frame.

6. Allow the remaining ends to hang down along the door frame.

**Note:** Take extra care with your balance as you tape streamers to the walls and ceiling.

# Balloons

Because balloons lose their buoyancy in a few hours, you must inflate them just before your event. They will be one of the final touches you add to your celebration.

Helium balloons stay aloft, are versatile in decorating and are easier to inflate than regular balloons. Regular balloons are less expensive and free to inflate.

If renting a helium tank fits in your budget, select good-quality balloons (usually labeled "helium quality") to avoid breakage during inflation. Because string tends to tangle, use curling ribbon to anchor the balloons instead. Five- to six-foot lengths of ribbon can be cut in advance.

Whether you select helium or regular balloons, have an assembly-line team of volunteers ready to inflate and tie them. Secure bunches of balloons at the entrance, the corners of all rooms and all large stations. Add single balloons or pairs on the backs of chairs and around table legs or poles.

If your budget allows, consider ordering bunches of pre-inflated helium balloons from a gift store or florist. Many businesses will deliver these just in time for your event.

Ask a few volunteers to gather all the balloons before the conclusion of the party. Have them distribute the balloons to children as the guests leave.

# Balloon Arches and Pillars

One way to create a dramatic effect at an entrance or station is with balloon arches and pillars.

## ❋ What You Need

❋ inflated balloons

❋ curling ribbon

❋ measuring tape

❋ scissors

❋ clear tape

Arch

Pillar

## ❋ What to Do

1. Measure the desired length of your arch or pillar. Add two feet (24") to that figure to allow you to secure the completed arch or pillar. Cut a piece of curling ribbon to the total length to make the "backbone" of the arch or pillar.

2. Tie a 6-8" piece of curling ribbon onto each inflated balloon.

3. Tie inflated balloons to the backbone as close together as possible. Trim excess ribbon close to the backbone.

4. If you are using helium balloons, create an arch by securing each end of the backbone to the floor, a piece of furniture or a handrail. The helium will cause the balloons to "arch" upward.

5. If you are using regular balloons, create a hanging pillar by securing one end of the backbone to the wall or ceiling. Balloons will then cascade down.

**Note:** If you plan a long arch or pillar, or you are contending with windy weather, use a double backbone.

# ❄ After the Celebration ❄

## As Guests Leave

Have volunteers posted at exits to say good-bye to departing families. The volunteers can remind guests to turn in their completed **Visitor Evaluation Forms** (page 199). Have forms, pens and pencils available at your exit. Make sure guests take home all the items they made.

Volunteers can assist guests with coats and boots. If the weather is inclement or sidewalks are icy, they can escort visitors to cars.

Have your volunteers thank families for coming by saying things like "It was wonderful to have you here," "Glad you had a good time" or "Merry Christmas."

## Clean-up

Have your crew save craft and gift samples, reusable game parts, decorations and extra supplies. Neatly store these items in plastic storage bins. Label each bin with a packing list for easy reference.

Make a copy of the packing list for your **Christmas Celebration File** (see the next page).

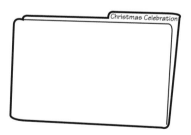

Christmas Celebration

## Program Evaluation

Assess the strengths and weaknesses of your program so you know what to do the same or differently next year. Here are some ways to effectively evaluate your event.

❄ **Ask your volunteers. Your team will be your most valuable source of feedback. They were on the front lines assisting with preparations, participating in activities and interacting with visitors. Talk to volunteers individually and ask for their observations. Distribute** Volunteer Evaluation Forms **(page 199) and ask workers to complete them before they leave the party. Set a form collection box near your exit.**

❄ **Review the submitted Visitor Evaluation Forms. Make notes for your Christmas Celebration File (see the next page). Pass along specific words of encouragement to your volunteers.**

❄ Gather the information you have accumulated and start a Christmas Celebration File. In your file, be sure to include:

- *Notes on how you chose type of celebration, theme and date*
- *Your planning timetable*
- *Names and jobs of volunteers, and the training you scheduled*
- *Samples of publicity flyers, bulletin inserts, publicity postcards and registration forms*
- *Activity list*
- *Photos of stations*
- *A copy of your set-up map*
- *Schedule of events*
- *Samples of the additional paperwork in the registration packets*
- *A copy of your budget*
- *Supply list*
- *Donor list*
- *Record of supplies obtained*
- *Copies of the packing lists in the storage bins*

❄ Make notes about which activities worked best. Were some games, crafts and gifts more popular than others? Refer to the Visitor Evaluation Forms and Volunteer Evaluation Forms as you record your impressions.

❄ Decide if your planning was adequate. Did you have enough time to prepare? Were there enough volunteers? What kind of training did you use? Was it effective?

❄ Record how many visitors attended. From the information on the registration forms, tally how guests heard about your program and determine which forms of publicity were most effective. Log your results.

❄ Evaluate the day and time of your program. Did you receive comments such as "I wish you had done this on a Saturday instead" or "I'm glad we had our party in November"?

❄ Write a brief weather report. Were you able to adjust to conditions on the day of your event?

❄ Assemble your file while ideas are still fresh in your mind. What you document will help you and your church host an even more effective party next year.

# Follow-up

The gift wrap, candy canes and bows have been put away. The lights have been taken off the trees and the ornaments put in boxes. Your Christmas celebration is over.

But an introduction to the Savior in the manger can be the beginning of a whole new life for any of the families who participated in your event. Take advantage of the enthusiasm and momentum initiated by your party. Make a plan to follow up with visitors both immediately and over the long term.

The first step is to sort through registration forms and your volunteer registry. From this information, assemble these lists.

❅ **Children.** Include the names, addresses and birthdays of the children who attended your celebration.

❅ **Non-member families.** Include the names and addresses of families who attended your celebration but are not members of your congregation.

❅ **Member families.** Include the names and addresses of families who attended your celebration and are members of your congregation.

❅ **Volunteers.** Include the names and addresses of volunteers who helped with your event in any way.

## Immediate follow-up. Take these steps to follow up with participants, volunteers and your congregation right away, preferably during the week after your party.

❅ **Photos with notes.** Send copies of candid shots or photos with Santa to the children who attended your party. Include a note that says "We're so glad you could join us for our day of fun! We hope you can come to our Children's Christmas Eve Service [or any children's event]."

❅ **Follow-up letters.** Let non-member families know that your church appreciated their participation by sending them follow-up letters. In this letter, thank them for attending, tell them about your church's ministries and list other Christmas events they can attend. You might want to include a copy of your church's brochure. Be sure both you and your pastor sign the letter. Use the **Follow-up Letter** on page 200 as a model, or compose your own.

❅ **Letters of appreciation.** Express your gratitude for the support of member families who attended your party by sending them letters of appreciation.

Encourage them to invite their friends and families to other events at your church during the Christmas season. You might want to craft your own letter, or simply personalize the **Letter of Appreciation** on page 200. This small gesture not only strengthens bonds within your church, but can also cultivate future volunteers.

❋ **Thank-you notes.** Write a personal thank-you note to each volunteer, including those who helped with preparation, set-up, publicity, registration, stations, clean-up and prayer.

❋ **Feedback to your congregation.** Share the successes of your event with your congregation. Thank them for hosting it. Publicly acknowledge your volunteers. Write a short article for your church newsletter that lists positive comments from guests. Provide anecdotal details about how the celebration affected lives.

❋ **Telephone and home visits.** Invite friendly, outgoing members of your congregation to follow up with visitors who don't have church homes. Explain that the purpose of these calls and visits is to demonstrate love and support to those who came to your party, and to thank them for coming. Encourage your team to make home visits as soon as possible. Have them place courtesy telephone calls ahead of time so that they can arrange convenient days and times.

When they visit, they might want to give each family a small gift, such as a **Frosty Icicle Wreath** (page 54) or a **Shining Light Votive Holder** (page 101). They can also give out copies of your church brochure and listings of your church's Christmas events.

During visits, your team should thank guests for coming to your party, and should ask for feedback. Good ways to initiate conversations are "Did your children have fun?" "What was your favorite part?" "How long have you lived in the community?" or "How did your learn about our celebration?" Your team can invite families to Advent and Christmas worship services. They may also ask if your church can serve the families in any way.

Have your visitation team share with you what they learned. Add these new comments to your **Christmas Celebration File**. Share details with your pastors and church's evangelism committee.

If time constraints prevent your volunteers from making home visits immediately after your event, have them follow up with phone calls instead. They can arrange for a home visit a few weeks later.

A personal visit takes time and initiative – valuable commodities in today's fast-paced world. Yet people are touched when others go out of their way to demonstrate compassion. Let your visitors see this tangible expression of Christ's love in action.

## Long Term Follow-up

✳ **Add visitors' names and addresses** to your church's existing mailing list. If your church doesn't have an outreach mailing list, start one! People who have already attended an event at your church and enjoyed it are likely to come to another one. Keeping families informed about programs at your church is an excellent way to continue to offer them the message of salvation in Jesus Christ.

✳ **Send invitations to children's events**, vacation Bible school and Sunday school celebrations to the kids on the children's list. (Note: Periodically update the children's list by checking birthdays. Names of children over age 12 can be transferred to a teen list and shared with your teen group leaders).

✳ Send both member and non-member families **invitations to family events**.

✳ Begin or add to **your church's electronic mailing list** with data from registration forms. Make sure you have permission from individuals to use their e-mail addresses. E-mail is quick and inexpensive. However, don't rely exclusively on e-mail as a publicity tool. Many computer users receive dozens of messages in their in-boxes, and they may hit the "delete" button if they see that too many are sent too often from your church. But when combined with other types of promotion, e-mail is a convenient way to reinforce your message.

# Decorations

# Candy Tree

 AGES 3-12

**Bible Reference:** A healthy tree / *Psalm 1:1-3*

 ## Overview

A healthy tree, like a joyous Christian, yields good fruit and then continues to grow and prosper. The children will make trees from foam cones and wrapped candies as examples of healthy trees bearing good "fruit."

 ## Helpers: 1

one for every 3-4 children

 ## What You Need

❊ foam cones, various sizes
❊ lollipops
❊ wrapped candies (bring extra for snacking!)
❊ double-sided foam tape
❊ scissors
❊ masking tape

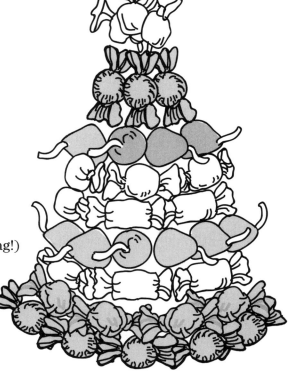

## What to Do

1. Give each child a foam cone.

2. Show the children how to attach double-sided foam tape in angled, parallel rows to the "trees" until they are completely covered.

3. Help the children remove the tape backings to expose the adhesive.

4. Say, **Let's add fruit and leaves to our trees.** Let the children cover their trees with wrapped candies.

5. Have them insert lollipop sticks in the tops of the trees.

6. Say, **The Bible says that a healthy tree is like a joyful person. A healthy tree bears good fruit, and then continues to grow and flourish. What kinds of fruit does a joyful person produce?** Allow the children to respond. Say, **When you take these trees home, eat one piece of candy a day from now until Christmas. Each time you do, name one fruit you see God growing in your life.**

7. Have the children write their names on masking tape and stick the names to the bases of their trees.

8. Have the children arrange their Candy Trees in a display area.

# Cardboard Tube Caroler

❄ ❄ ❄ ❄ ❄ ❄ ❄ AGES 3-12

**Bible Reference:** Shepherds tell about Jesus / *Luke 2:17-18*

 Overview

Like the shepherds who spread the word about baby Jesus, carolers spread the Good News in song. The children will make carolers out of cardboard tubes, gift wrap and socks.

 Helpers: 1

one for every 3-4 children

 What You Need

❄ Cardboard Tube Carolers patterns, page 215
❄ poster board
❄ toilet tissue, paper towel or gift wrap rolls
❄ Christmas gift wrap
❄ children's socks
❄ pink and white construction paper
❄ yarn          ❄ glue sticks
❄ scissors       ❄ craft glue
❄ ruler          ❄ black and red markers

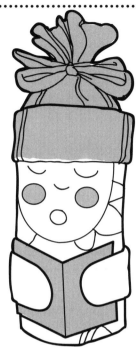

 Preparation

Make templates of the patterns using poster board. Trace and cut the faces and hands from pink construction paper. Trace and cut the caroling books from white construction paper. Measure and cut 10" lengths of yarn. Lay the socks flat. Cut off the tops just above the ankle. Reserve the tops. Cut the cardboard tubes into sections that are at least 4.5" tall. (Toilet tissue tubes do not need to be cut.) You will need one cardboard tube, one face, one hand assembly, one caroling book, one yarn length and one sock cuff for each caroler.

 What to Do

1. Ask, **Have you ever gone caroling?** Allow the children to respond. Say, **Christmas carolers share the joy of Christmas by going door-to-door and singing about Jesus' birth.**

2. Let each child select a cardboard tube. Older children can roll tubes on Christmas gift wrap to measure for coverage, and then cut. Younger children will need help measuring paper to cover the tubes. Have the children use glue sticks to attach the paper to the tubes, turning the top edges into the tubes' insides.

3. Distribute pre-cut carolers' faces. Tell the children to use markers to add eyes, noses, rosy cheeks and mouths to the carolers. The children can use glue sticks to attach the carolers' faces and hand assemblies to the tubes. Have the children use dabs of craft glue to place the caroling books in the carolers' hands.

4. Give each child a pre-cut sock. Show how to turn up the cuffed edge of a sock, creating the rim of the caroler's hat. Have the children use craft glue to attach the "hat rims" to the tops of the cardboard tubes, adjusting the hats to fit over the carolers' foreheads.

5. Older children can use pre-cut yarn lengths to tie tassels on the tops of the hats. Younger children will need help with the yarn and hats. Let the children trim the yarn ends.

6. Have the children write their names on their carolers.

7. As the children are working, reaffirm the theme by saying, **After the shepherds found baby Jesus, they spread the Good News to everyone they knew. Carolers spread the Good News by singing Christmas carols.**

# Chrismon

 **Ages 7-12**

**Bible Reference:** The Name above all names / *Philippians 2:9-11*

 ## Overview

The term "chrismon" is a combination of "Christ" and "monogram." Tradition holds that Chrismons – symbols of Jesus – are white and gold, the liturgical colors for Christmas Day. White symbolizes Christ's purity, and gold symbolizes His majesty.

 ## Helpers: 1

one for every 3-4 children

 ## What You Need

❋ Chrismon patterns, pages 216-218
❋ poster board
❋ white craft foam
❋ gold metallic spray paint
❋ gold glitter glue    ❋ pencil
❋ white paint pens    ❋ scissors
❋ gold sequins    ❋ hole punch
❋ gold and white beads    ❋ ruler
❋ gold glitter    ❋ gold metallic thread
❋ craft glue    ❋ newspapers

 ## Preparation

Make templates of the patterns using poster board. Trace and cut out the Chrismons from poster board and white craft foam. Use a hole punch to make a hole at the top of each one. Spread newspapers on your work surface. Lay out the Chrismons and spray both sides of the poster board with gold metallic paint. Foam pieces do not need to be sprayed. Allow to dry. Measure and cut 12" lengths of gold metallic thread. You will need one length for every Chrismon. Set out glitter glue, paint pens, sequins, beads, glitter and craft glue. Note: For safety purposes, do not use beads, sequins or glitter around very young children.

## What to Do

1. Say, **We are going to make special ornaments called "Chrismons." The word "chrismon" is a combination of "Christ" and "monogram." Each Chrismon is a symbol of Jesus Christ.**

2. Let the children select Chrismons to decorate with glue, paints and craft supplies. Say, **We use only two colors for Chrismons: white and gold. White represents Christ's purity. Gold represents His majesty.**

3. While the Chrismons are drying, point to each one and ask, **Why does this symbolize Jesus Christ?** If the children struggle to answer, help them with the appropriate information (see page 218 for the Chrismons' symbolic meanings).

4. Help the children loop gold metallic thread through the Chrismons' holes and tie the ends in knots. Say, **God gave His Son the Name above all names: Jesus.**

5. Have the children write their names on the backs of the Chrismons. They can use the Chrismons to decorate a Jesus Tree (see page 160), or they can take them home to hang in windows, on mirrors or from gift bows.

# Cinnamon Ornament

❄ ❄ ❄ ❄ ❄ ❄ ❄ ❄ ❄ **AGES 3-12**

**Bible Reference:** Spices were used in temple worship / *Luke 1:8-13*

 ## Overview

The children will make ornaments from ground cinnamon and applesauce to show how nice-smelling spices are a reminder of God.

 ## Helpers: 1

one for every 3-4 children.

 ## What You Need

❄ ½" satin ribbon
❄ scissors
❄ ruler or tape measure
❄ ground cinnamon
❄ unsweetened applesauce
❄ wire rack
❄ bowl ❄ cookie cutters
❄ measuring cup ❄ plastic drinking straws
❄ wooden spoon ❄ spatula
❄ wax paper ❄ puff paints (optional)
❄ rolling pin

 ## Preparation

In a bowl, measure and combine one cup ground cinnamon and ½ cup applesauce. If the dough is overly dry and crumbly, add applesauce one tablespoon at a time until the mixture holds together. Cut ribbon into 10" lengths. You will need one length for each ornament.

 ## What to Do

1. Have the children use rolling pins to roll the dough into ½" thickness between sheets of wax paper.
2. Let the children use cookie cutters to cut out ornaments. Show how to use the end of a drinking straw to make a hole in each ornament for its hanger.
3. Help the children transfer the ornaments to a wire rack with a spatula. Allow the ornaments to dry completely, which will take at least 24-36 hours.
4. The children can decorate the ornaments with puffy paints, if desired. Allow the paint to dry.
5. Have older children thread satin ribbons through the straw holes and tie the ribbon ends together to make hangers. Younger children will need help threading and tying ribbons.
6. Say, **Cinnamon Ornaments have a delightful aroma. In Bible times, priests used incense, which contained spices like cinnamon, in God's temple when the people worshiped. The scent was pleasing to God.**
7. Be sure the children write their names on their crafts. Suggest that they hang their Cinnamon Ornaments on trees, in windows or on gifts.

# Frosty Icicle Wreath

❄ ❄ ❄ ❄ ❄ ❄ ❄ ❄ ❄ **AGES 7-12**

**Bible Reference:** Jesus cleanses us from sin / *Isaiah 1:18*

  ☞ **Overview**

The children will make wreaths that highlight the contrast between sin and forgiveness.

 **Helpers: 1**

one for every 3-4 children.

 **What You Need**

❄ 12" wire wreath frame (available at craft stores)
❄ masking tape
❄ pencil, pens or markers
❄ plastic sandwich bags, fold-top (not zipper – style)
❄ red curling ribbon
❄ wrapped hard candies
❄ ruler
❄ scissors

**Preparation**

Cut ribbon into 8" lengths. You'll need 12 lengths of ribbon for each wreath. You also will need 50-100 plastic sandwich bags per wreath depending on the desired thickness of the "icicles" and the attention spans of the children tying them.

**What to Do**

1. Give each child a wreath frame.
2. Have each child fold a 4" piece of masking tape around a wire frame so it forms a tail. The children should write their names on the tapes.
3. Show how to tie a sandwich bag onto a frame with a single knot, making an "icicle" (see diagram at right). Have the children cover their frames with icicles.
4. Give each child 12 hard candies and 12 ribbon lengths. Help the children tie ribbons onto hard candies, and then onto their wreaths at regular intervals between icicles.
5. Help the children use scissors to curl the ends of the ribbons.
6. As the children are working, say, **This wreath shows what happens when God forgives our sins. Even though sin stains us on the inside, God can take that sin away, cleanse us and make us clean like frosty snow.** As you speak, pull one of the hard candies and ribbon off of a wreath to demonstrate God taking away our sins.
7. Suggest that the children hang their wreaths on doors, in windows or on walls.

# Grocery Sack Reindeer

 **AGES 3-12**

**Bible Reference:** Flocks of sheep / *Micah 2:12-13*

 ## Overview

As they make reindeer from grocery sacks, the children will compare Santa's reindeer with Jesus' care for His flock.

 ## Helpers: 1

one for every 3-4 children.

 ## What You Need

* Grocery Sack Reindeer pattern, page 219
* poster board
* brown paper grocery-size sacks
* newspaper
* brown poster board
* red, white and black tissue paper
* 25 mm movable plastic eyes
* old newspapers
* 20 mm jingle bells
* red curling ribbon
* spring-type clothespins
* hole punch
* scissors
* ruler or tape measure
* clear tape
* craft glue
* pencil

 ## Preparation

Make templates of the pattern using poster board. Use the template to trace and cut antlers from brown poster board. Trace and cut 6" squares from red tissue paper and 2" squares from white and black tissue paper. Cut 1-yard lengths of curling ribbon. You will need two antlers, two red tissue squares, eight white tissue squares, eight black tissue squares and one ribbon length for each reindeer.

## What to Do

1. Give each child a grocery sack. Tell the children to crush newspapers and put them in the sacks, packing loosely until almost filled, then fold the top to the back and tape.
2. Distribute antlers and show where to glue them on the backs of the reindeers' "heads." Let the children use clothespins to hold the glued antlers in place until the glue dries.
3. Let the children attach plastic eyes to their reindeers' faces.
4. Give each child two red tissue squares. Have each child lay one square flat on the work surface. Show how to crumple a second square and place it in the center of the first, then gather the edges and glue them together. Show where to attach the nose to the face.
5. Let the children crumple white and black tissue squares and glue them onto the bags, alternating the two colors in a line, to form the reindeers' mouths.
6. Show how to use the hole punch to make two holes, one on each side of each reindeer's face. Make sure the children punch through all the bag layers. Let the children thread ribbon from the holes in the backs of the bags to the fronts, pausing in between folds to string bells on each side of the bags. Once the children have threaded ribbon through the front holes, help them tie the ends in bows.
7. Allow each child to make several reindeer and leash them together, through side holes, with extra ribbon. Have them write their names on the backs of their reindeer.
8. Say, **Reindeer travel together in teams or herds, like sheep. During Bible times, it was the shepherd's responsibility to keep the flock of sheep together. Jesus is our Shepherd. We are the flock. He takes care of us!**

# Luminaries for the Light of the World

 AGES 7-12

**Bible Reference:** Simeon praises God for Jesus / *Luke 2:25-32*

 ## Overview

The children will make luminaries to light a sidewalk, pathway or entrance as a reminder that Jesus is the Light of the world.

 ## Helpers: 2

one person to help children put together luminaries
one person to light luminaries and check them regularly

 ## What You Need

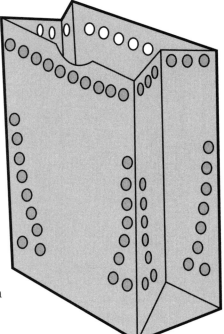

❄ Luminaries for the Light of the World pattern, page 220
❄ poster board
❄ brown or white paper lunch sacks
❄ pencils
❄ hole punch       ❄ votive or tealight candles
❄ sand             ❄ fireplace matches or propane torch
❄ scoop or spoon   ❄ Caroling Songbooks, page 148

 ## Preparation

Make a template of the Luminaries for the Light of the World pattern using poster board. If you plan to have a group of children make luminaries simultaneously, you will need to prepare several templates so the children can use them at the same time.

## What to Do

1. Distribute paper lunch sacks. Have the children use the pattern templates and pencils to mark where to punch holes in their luminaries.
2. Let the children punch out the patterns with the hole punch. They should also write their names on the bottoms of their bags.
3. Show how to unfold the bags to see the completed candle patterns. Say, **A candle gives light. Jesus is the Light of the World.**
4. Let the children use the scoop or large spoon to fill the bottoms of the bags with 2" of sand.
5. Let each child place a votive or tealight candle in his or her luminary.
6. Help the children position their luminaries on outside sidewalks, pathways and entrances. Let them watch while an adult lights the luminaries using fireplace matches or a propane torch. As the adult lights the candles, lead the children in songs from the Caroling Songbooks.
7. Say, **After Jesus was born, His parents dedicated Him to God. Simeon, the priest at the temple, said that Jesus is our Light and our Salvation.**
8. Make sure an adult regularly checks the luminaries. An adult should extinguish the luminaries when the candles begin to burn low.
9. After the candles are extinguished and the bags are cool, allow the children to find their bags to take home.

# Paper Clip Heavenly Host

❄❄❄❄❄❄❄❄ AGES 3-12

**Bible Reference:** Angels praise God / *Luke 2:13-14*

 **Overview**

The children will make angels out of butterfly-style paper clips.

 **Helpers: 1**

one for every 5-6 children.

 **What You Need**

❄ butterfly-style paper clips
❄ ½" wide satin ribbon
❄ silver pony beads
❄ ruler
❄ scissors

 **Preparation**

Measure and cut satin ribbon in lengths of 9", 11" and 13". You will need one length of ribbon for each angel.

 **What to Do**

1. Give each child a butterfly-style paper clip and a length of satin ribbon. Show how to hold the paper clip so its tips (the angel's "wings") are pointing up. Demonstrate how to thread satin ribbon through the center of the clip in between the "wings."

2. Each child should match the ribbon ends together and string them through a silver pony bead. Have the children push the pony beads all the way down the ribbons to the clips. They will see how the bead becomes the angel's "head."

3. Help the children tie the ribbon ends together in knots to secure, and to trim the ribbon ends, if needed.

4. Let each child make three angels, if desired, using a different length of ribbon for each one. Say, **An angel announced Jesus' birth to shepherds on a hillside. Then a large group of angels appeared and praised God. They are called the "heavenly host."**

5. Show how to hang the Paper Clip Heavenly Host in a window or on a Christmas tree. The different ribbon lengths will ensure that the angels will not overshadow each other.

# Plastic Basket Snowflake

❄ ❄ ❄ ❄ ❄ ❄ ❄ ❄ ❄ **AGES 7-12**

**Bible Reference:** God is sovereign / *Job 37:5-6*

 ## Overview

The children will make snowflake ornaments out of plastic produce baskets and facial tissue as reminders of God, the Creator.

 ## Helpers: 1

one for every 3-4 children.

 ## What You Need

❄ plastic produce baskets (as for berries or cherry tomatoes)
❄ facial tissue
❄ foam plates
❄ glitter     ❄ 3-ounce paper cups
❄ fishing line     ❄ scissors
❄ small paint brushes     ❄ blunt needle
❄ craft glue     ❄ ruler
❄ water     ❄ masking tape

 ## Preparation

Cut the sides and bottoms of the plastic baskets to create branches for snowflake arms. Cut fishing line into 18" lengths. You will need one length of fishing line for each snowflake. Just before craft time, make the glue mixture in paper cups by combining glue and water in a 3-1 ratio. Note: For safety purposes, keep glitter away from very young children.

 ## What to Do

1. Give each child a foam plate and a facial tissue. Have the children lay the tissues flat on the plates. Let them use paintbrushes to spread a thin layer of the glue mixture over the tissues.

2. Show how to arrange plastic branches in a snowflake pattern on top of a moistened tissue. After they place their branches, the children should place a second tissue on top of the patterns and tap gently with their fingertips. Tell them to apply a thin layer of glue to their second tissues. Remind the children not to soak the tissues with excess glue.

3. Allow the children to sprinkle the wet snowflakes with glitter.

4. Say, **God makes every snowflake! How many snowflakes fall during a snowstorm?** Allow the children to respond.

5. Let the Plastic Basket Snowflakes dry for at least 8 hours or overnight. When the snowflakes are dry, help the children carefully peel the edges away from the foam plates. They can trim away excess tissue.

6. Demonstrate how to use a scissors point or a blunt needle to poke a hole in the tip of one of each snowflake's branches. Help the children thread the pre-cut fishing line through the holes and knot to secure.

7. Say, **Snowflakes remind us that God is the Creator. He is in charge of everything – even the weather.**

8. Have the children write their names on masking tape to stick on the backs of their snowflakes. They can hang their Plastic Basket Snowflakes on their Christmas trees or in windows.

# Ribbon Teardrop Swag

❊ ❊ ❊ ❊ ❊ ❊ ❊ ❊ ❊ AGES 3-12

**Bible Reference:** God wipes our tears / ***Revelation 21:3-4***

 Overview

The children will make swags of hanging teardrops to decorate doorways as a reminder that Jesus wipes every tear from our eyes.

 Helpers: 3

one to help every 3-4 children to make swags
two to hang swags

 What You Need

❊ tinsel garlands
❊ ¾"-wide gift ribbon in seasonal colors
❊ 2 mm wide metallic lamé chord
❊ scissors
❊ ruler or tape measure    ❊ clear tape
❊ stapler                  ❊ step stool or ladder
❊ hole punch               ❊ masking tape

 Preparation

Measure and cut strips of ribbon for the teardrops. You will need two 11" strips, two 9½" strips and one 8" strip for each teardrop. Measure and cut various lengths of metallic lamé cord. You will use the cord to attach the ribbon teardrops to the tinsel garlands. Measure and cut tinsel garlands into 8' lengths.

 What to Do

1.  To make the teardrops, show how to stack ribbons in this order, keeping one set of ends even: 11", 9½", 8", 9½", 11".
2.  Have the children staple the even sets of ends together, about 1" from the end.
3.  Show how to create a teardrop by adjusting the opposite set of the ribbon ends so they are even, bending outside strips as necessary. Help the children staple these sets together, about 3" from the ends.
4.  Let the children fringe the 3" tails with scissors.
5.  Have each child attach tape to one teardrop so they can write their names on them.
6.  Say, **God sent His Son, Jesus, to the earth to be our Savior. The Bible tells us that Jesus will be with us forever and wipe every tear from our eyes. These teardrops are tears of beauty and happiness, because of the joy we can know in Jesus!**
7.  Have the children use a hole punch to make holes in the 1" ends of the teardrops. They can loop metallic lamé cords through the holes and tie them to secure them.
8.  Instruct the children to lay their tinsel garlands on a work surface, adjusting the corners to bend as they would in a doorway.
9.  Let the children position the ribbon teardrops in the center sections of the garlands, tie on the teardrops and trim the excess cord ends. Suggest that the children hang their swags in doorways, securing with clear tape.

# Silver Bells Door Hanger

❊ ❊ ❊ ❊ ❊ ❊ ❊ ❊ ❊ AGES 3-12

**Bible Reference:** Jesus is the Door / *Revelation 3:20*

 ## Overview
A door hanger made of foil and bells is a reminder that Jesus knocks on the doors to our hearts.

 ## Helpers: 1
one for every 3-4 children

 ## What You Need
❊ egg cartons
❊ aluminum foil
❊ 20 mm jingle bells
❊ silver tinsel chenille wire
❊ 3½"-4"-wide plastic container lids,
   as for frosting or yogurt
❊ tinsel garlands        ❊ craft glue
❊ ½" wrapping ribbon      ❊ scissors
❊ ruler or tape measure   ❊ masking tape

 ## Preparation
Cut apart the egg carton sections. Cut foil into 6" squares. Cut out the middle sections of the lids, leaving a ½" outer edge on each. Cut the tinsel garlands into 30" lengths. Cut the ribbon into 10" lengths. You will need three egg carton sections, three foil squares, one pre-cut lid, one pre-cut tinsel garland and one wrapping ribbon length for each door hanger.

 ## What to Do
1. Give each child a pre-cut plastic lid and tinsel garland to make the door hanger assemblies.
2. Have the children apply glue to their lids. They can attach the garlands to the lids by weaving the tinsel in and out until the plastic is completely covered. Allow to dry.
3. To make the bells, let each child wrap three egg carton compartments in aluminum foil squares. Give each child three jingle bells and three tinsel wire stems. Show how to thread ½" end of each tinsel wire stem through a bell, bend it back, and twist it together to secure.
4. Demonstrate how to use a scissors blade point to poke holes in the tops of the egg carton bells. Help younger children in poking holes.
5. Each child should thread one tinsel wire/jingle bell assembly up through the bottom of an egg carton bell. The jingle bell will remain inside the bell. Have each child thread a total of three bells. Help the children twist the tinsel wire ends onto their prepared door hangers. Explain that each of the three bells can hang at different lengths.
6. Let the children trim the excess tinsel wire after attaching the bells to the door hangers.
7. Have the children tie ribbons into bows, trim the ends and glue onto the door hangers.
8. Have the children write their names on tape and stick inside one bell each.
9. As the children are working, say, **Once you put the hanger on the doorknob, the bells will ring every time you open or close the door. They will remind you of Jesus. He knocks at the door of your heart, and He wants to come in.**

# Tabletop Crèche

AGES 7-12

**Bible Reference:** The Christmas Story / *Luke 2:1-20*

 **Overview**

Craft foam is used to make this contemporary version of a traditional crèche scene.

 **Helpers: 1**

one for every 3-4 children

 **What You Need**

❄ Tabletop Crèche patterns, pages 221-223
❄ poster board
❄ dark brown, light brown, black, blue, yellow, white, pink and purple craft foam
❄ scissors   ❄ hole punch
❄ craft glue  ❄ fishing line or metallic thread
❄ pencils    ❄ markers

 **Preparation**

Make templates of the Tabletop Crèche patterns with poster board.

 **What to Do**

1. Say, **A crèche scene is a traditional Christmas decoration. It shows a stable where Mary and Joseph are next to the baby Jesus in a manger with shepherds and wise men worshipping nearby.**

2. Distribute the templates. Let the children trace and cut out crèche figures from craft foam using these colors:

   Black: shepherd's crook, sheep feet and ears       Blue: Mary
   White: sheep body, angel, blanket                  Pink: baby Jesus' face
   Light brown: manger, shepherd, camel and feet      Purple: wise men
   Dark brown: Joseph, stable, shepherd's headpiece
   Yellow: halos for Mary, Joseph and manger; wise men's crowns and gifts; angel's halo; star

3. Demonstrate how to hold the two pieces of each figure at right angles and slide them together at the notches, creating a three dimensional object.

4. Show how to attach baby Jesus' face to the manger halo with glue. Let each child set a manger blanket on the top edge of a manger and glue to secure.

5. Let the children add halos, headpieces, crooks, crowns, gifts and feet to the crèche figures where appropriate. Have the children use craft glue to secure the parts together.

6. Let each child use the hole punch to make a hole at the top of one star part. Show how to loop fishing line or metallic thread through the top of the stars, knot and hang above the stables.

7. Have the children write their names on their figures. Suggest that they display the Tabletop Crèche on shelves, mantles, bookcases or tables.

# Tree Garland of Trust

❄❅❆❅❆❅❆❅❆❅ AGES 3-12

**Bible Reference:** God surrounds the faithful / *Psalm 32:10*

 ## Overview

These tinsel garlands wrap around a tree the same way God's unfailing love surrounds those who trust in Him.

 ## Helpers: 1

one for every 3-4 children

 ## What You Need

❉ tinsel garland
❉ ½" wrapping ribbon
❉ wrapped hard candies with twisted paper ends
❉ stapler
❉ clear tape
❉ scissors
❉ ruler

 ## Preparation

Cut tinsel garlands to desired lengths. Measure and cut one ribbon length to match each garland. Cut 6" strips of ribbon to tie onto the garlands.

 ## What to Do

1. Lay out the pre-cut garland-length ribbons on a work surface. Have the children select wrapped candies and arrange them 2" apart along the ribbons, with twisted paper ends lying on the ribbons.

2. Show how to staple one end of each piece of candy onto the ribbons.

3. Demonstrate how to lay the tinsel garlands on top of the candy-decorated ribbons. The children can then attach the garlands to the ribbons by stapling the two together about every 6 inches.

4. Let the children conceal the tinsel staples by tying 6" ribbons around the garland/ribbon/candy assemblies at each stapled interval. The children can trim the decorative ribbons as desired.

5. Help the children flip over the garlands. Show how to use pieces of clear tape to cover the staples to avoid injury.

6. Have the children write their names on their garlands.

7. Say, **When you wrap this garland around your Christmas tree, remember that we trust God to wrap us in His love, just like this garland wraps around tree branches.**

# Crafts

# Advent Treat Calendar

❋ ❋ ❋ ❋ ❋ ❋ AGES 3-12

**Bible Reference:** Prepare the Way of the Lord / *Mark 1:1-3*

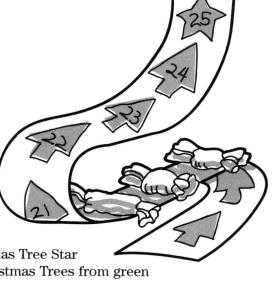

☞ ## Overview

Each child will make a calendar that has one treat for each day in December leading up to Christmas.

## Helpers: 1

one for every 3-4 children

## What You Need

❋ poster board
❋ Advent Treat Calendar patterns, page 224
❋ Christmas gift wrap, 36" wide
❋ green and yellow construction paper
❋ ½"-wide gift ribbon
❋ 2"-wide clear packaging tape
❋ wrapped candies      ❋ markers
❋ craft glue              ❋ stapler
❋ pencil                  ❋ ruler
❋ scissors                ❋ clear tape

## Preparation

Make a template of the Christmas Tree and Christmas Tree Star patterns using poster board. Trace and cut out Christmas Trees from green construction paper and Christmas Tree Stars from yellow construction paper. You will need 24 trees and one star for each child. Measure and cut one 2" x 36" strip of gift wrap for each child. Measure and cut one 36" length of ribbon and one 8" length of ribbon for each child.

## What to Do

1. Give each child a 2" strip of gift wrap. Say, **We're going to make a calendar that will help us think about Jesus as we prepare for Christmas.**

2. Distribute the 8" ribbon. Show how to loop a strip and staple it onto one end of the gift wrap. Cover staples with tape to avoid injury. Explain that this is a hook for hanging.

3. Have the children lay their calendars on a work surface. They should glue 36" ribbon down the centers of their calendars. Have them trim any excess at the ends.

4. Give each child 24 Christmas trees and one star. Let the children number the trees 1-24 and arrange them in ascending numerical order, beginning at the bottoms of their calendars.

5. Each child should write the number 25 on a star, and place it at the top of a calendar. Say, **The days and weeks leading up to Christmas are called "Advent."**

6. Let the children glue the trees and stars on their calendars.

7. Help the children cover both sides of their calendars with packaging tape, for durability.

8. Give each child 25 candies. Have the children position the candies on the backsides of the calendars so each treat is behind a tree or star, and tape the candies into position.

9. Say, **Advent is a time when we prepare for Christmas. Use this calendar in December to remind you that Jesus is coming. When you eat your treat each day, thank God for sending Jesus to save us and love us.**

# Bethlehem Sky Star Caper

❄ ❄ ❄ ❄ ❄ ❄ ❄ ❄ ❄ AGES 3-12

**Bible Reference:** The star leads the wise men to Jesus / *Matthew 2:9*

 ## Overview

The children will create a poster board landscape with a movable star to remind them that stars filled the sky when Jesus was born.

 ## Helpers: 1

one for every 3-4 children

 ## What You Need

❄ Bethlehem Sky Star Caper patterns, page 225
❄ dark blue and white poster board
❄ green and brown construction paper    ❄ ruler
❄ foil star stickers    ❄ craft glue
❄ glitter glue    ❄ pencil

 ## Preparation

Make pattern templates using poster board. Trace and cut hills from green paper and stables from brown paper. You will need one hill and one stable for each child. Cut 6" x 11" pieces of blue poster board for the backs and the fronts. On each landscape front, cut a center window ½" from the top, measuring 9" x 1½". Cut 2" x 12" pieces of blue poster board for the movable strips. Cut 3½" x 11" pieces of poster board (any color) for the landscape liners. You will need a back and front, one movable strip and one landscape liner for each child.

## What to Do

1. Give each child a sky front, hill and stable. Say, **We are going to make a picture of the stable in Bethlehem.** Show where to glue the hill and stable on the right side.

2. Distribute the sky backgrounds and landscape liners. Have the children attach the liners to the lower sections of the backs. Explain that the liners will be hidden beneath the fronts. The liners will help the movable strips stay in place.

3. Help the children attach the sky fronts to the backs by dropping glue in the top right corners of the backs and continuing counterclockwise around the boards. Each child should stop the glue at the top of the liner on the right side to leave an opening for the movable strip.

4. Say, **The Bethlehem sky was filled with stars.** Let the children use foil star stickers and glitter glue to decorate the sky backgrounds that appear in the windows.

5. Hand out strips. Say, **God put a special star in the sky when Jesus was born.** Have the children use glitter glue to create stars on the left ends of the strips.

6. Allow the landscapes and movable strips to dry. Then have the children insert their strips into the openings on the right sides, moving toward the left.

7. Say, **The wise men asked for help to find baby Jesus.** Show how to gently pull the movable strip so the star moves to the right, closer and closer to the stable. Say, **God moved the star until it was right over the stable where Jesus lay. The wise men followed the star. God will always lead us to Jesus when we ask for help.**

8. Help the children to reposition their movable strips to move the stars again. They should write their names on their crafts.

# Christmas Card Magnets

AGES 3-12

**Bible Reference:** The Christmas Story / *Luke 2:4-20*

 **Overview**

The children will make magnets out of used Christmas cards to help them remember the Christmas story.

 **Helpers: 1**

one for every 3-4 children

 **What You Need**

* ❄ used Christmas cards
* ❄ clear, adhesive-backed plastic
* ❄ self-stick magnet strips
* ❄ scissors
* ❄ craft glue
* ❄ resealable plastic sandwich bags
* ❄ masking tape
* ❄ pens or markers

 **Preparation**

Select Christmas cards that illustrate the Christmas story: Mary, Joseph, baby Jesus, donkeys, the stable in Bethlehem, sheep, shepherds, angels, wise men, camels and the star. Include those that depict Christian symbols, such as candles, wreaths, crowns, shepherd's staffs, trees, holly, mistletoe and gifts. Cut self-stick magnet strips into ½" pieces.

 **What to Do**

1. Set out the assortment of cards. Let the children select their favorites.

2. Tell the children to cut out the pictures that illustrate the Christmas story or Christian symbols.

3. Help the children cover the pictures with clear, adhesive-backed plastic.

4. The children can attach magnet strip pieces to the backs of their card magnets. Small cards will need only one magnet. Larger cards could need two or three magnets. (Craft glue will hold the magnets to the cards more securely.)

5. As the children are working, ask, **How does the picture on your magnet tell part of the Christmas story?** Let the children respond. If they struggle to answer, help them with a brief review (see page 254).

6. Give each child a piece of masking tape and a plastic sandwich bag. Have the children write their names on the tapes and stick the tapes on their bags, then place their magnets inside the bags for carrying home.

# Gabriel Macaroni Pin

AGES 7-12

**Bible Reference:** Gabriel announces Jesus' birth to Mary / *Luke 1:26-38*

 ## Overview

The children will make a clever pin from dry pasta that represents the angel Gabriel.

 ## Helpers: 1

one for every 3-4 children

 ## What You Need

* dry bow tie pasta
* dry elbow pasta
* 14 mm wooden craft balls
* 8 mm brass craft rings
* satin craft rosettes
* white spray paint
* craft glue
* pin backs
* paper plates
* old newspapers

 ## Preparation

Spread newspapers over your work surface. Lay out the bow tie pasta, elbow pasta and wooden craft balls. Use white spray paint to cover the pasta and balls. After they dry, turn over the pieces and repeat for the other sides. Allow the pieces to dry thoroughly. You will need two bow ties, two elbows and one wooden ball for each angel.

 ## What to Do

1. Give each child a paper plate on which to work. Show how to place one bow tie perpendicular to the other to create Gabriel's body and wings. Have the children glue the bow ties into place.
2. Help each child use glue to affix the elbows (arms) to Gabriel's body, and the wooden ball (head) to the top of his body. Allow the glue to dry.
3. Each child should use glue to attach the brass ring halo to Gabriel's head, and to place the satin rosette in the angel's hands. Allow the glue to dry.
4. Have each child turn Gabriel over. Show where to place a pin back. Help them attach the pin backs with glue.
5. As the children are working, say, **The angel Gabriel came to Mary and told her that she would have a baby boy. He said she should name the baby "Jesus." He told her that Jesus would be the Savior of the world!**

# Gingerbread Magi Men
❈❈❈❈❈❈❈❈❈❈ AGES 3-12

**Bible Reference:** Magi come from the East / *Matthew 2:1-2*

 ## Overview
The children will make beanbags to represent the wise men in the Christmas story.

 ## Helpers: 1
one for every 3-4 children

 ## What You Need
❈ Gingerbread Magi Men patterns, page 226
❈ poster board
❈ brown and gold felt
❈ gold braid or rickrack
❈ sequins
❈ white fabric paint
❈ fabric glue
❈ scissors
❈ popcorn kernels
❈ funnel with ½"-wide spout
❈ masking tape

 ## Preparation
Make a template of the Gingerbread Magi Men patterns using poster board. Trace and cut out two gingerbread men from brown felt and one crown from yellow felt for each beanbag.

 ## What to Do
1. Give each child two gingerbread men and one crown. Have each child lay one of the felt gingerbread men on the work surface. Show where to attach the crown to the gingerbread man's head with fabric glue.
2. Demonstrate how to pipe a bead of fabric glue around the entire outer edge of a gingerbread man, leaving an opening along the crown at the top of the head. Each child should place the second gingerbread man on top of the first and gently seal the edges. Allow the gingerbread men to dry.
3. Help each child insert the funnel into the opening at the crown and fill the gingerbread man with popcorn kernels.
4. Show how to secure the top edges of the beanbags with fabric glue.
5. Let the children decorate their Gingerbread Magi Men. They can cut and attach gold braid or rickrack belts and sequin buttons with fabric glue. Show how to outline the edges and add facial features with white fabric paint.
6. As the children are working, say, **After baby Jesus was born, He had visitors. The wise men, also called "Magi," saw a special star in the sky. They followed it for many miles until they reached the stable in Bethlehem.**
7. Have the children write their names on masking tape and stick the tapes on the backs of their Gingerbread Magi Men.
8. Allow the Gingerbread Magi Men to dry. The children can use their beanbags to play The Call From King Herod (page 111).

# Happy Birthday Pin

 AGES 3-12

**Bible Reference:** Jesus is born / *Luke 2:11*

 Overview

This pin made from paper, craft foam and gift wrap announces Jesus' birthday.

 Helpers: 1

one for every 3-4 children

 What You Need

❄ Happy Birthday Pin patterns, page 224
❄ poster board
❄ brightly colored paper
❄ clear, adhesive-backed plastic
❄ craft foam
❄ foil or metallic gift wrap
❄ 1" metal pin backs
❄ markers
❄ craft glue
❄ scissors
❄ ruler
❄ craft paint pens

 Preparation

Use the Happy Birthday Pin patterns to reproduce the pin fronts on brightly-colored paper. Make templates of the Happy Birthday Pin patterns. Use the templates to trace and cut out pin backings from craft foam. On foil or metallic gift wrap, trace and cut out pin fringe borders. Cut 3" squares of adhesive-backed plastic. You will need one pin front, one pin backing, one pin fringe border and one square of adhesive-backed plastic for each pin.

## What to Do

1. Distribute the pin fronts and markers. Tell the children to color the pin fronts as they like.
2. Help the children cover the pin fronts with adhesive-backed plastic for durability. Have them trim the edges.
3. Give each child a pin fringe border. Show how to fringe the borders by making ½" cuts around the circle's perimeter.
4. Each child should glue a pin together like a sandwich, layering the fringe border on top of the foam pin backing, and the pin front on top of the fringe border.
5. Have the children position metal pin backs on the foam backings and attach them with glue.
6. Let the children use paint pens to decorate the circular edges of the pin fronts.
7. Be sure the children write their names on the backs of their pins.
8. Say, **Christmas is Jesus' birthday. Wear your pin to celebrate!**
9. Allow the pins to dry before the children attach them to their clothing.

# King's Crown

**Bible Reference:** Jesus is King / *1 Timothy 6:14-16*

 **Overview**

The children will make and wear crowns that honor Christ the King.

 **Helpers: 1**

one for every 3-4 children

 **What You Need**

* King's Crown pattern, page 227
* gold poster board
* glitter glue
* paint pens
* rhinestones, sequins and buttons
* pencil
* scissors
* craft glue
* stapler
* clear tape
* old newspapers

 **Preparation**

Make a template of the King's Crown pattern using poster board, making sure to trace the pattern end to end 2½ times so that the template is 25" long. Trace and cut the crowns from gold poster board. You will need one pre-cut crown for each child.

 **What to Do**

1. Give each child a pre-cut crown. Say, **Jesus is King. Kings wear crowns!**

2. Have the children decorate their crowns with glitter glue, paint pens, rhinestones, sequins and buttons. Allow the crowns to dry.

3. Fit a headband around each child's head and staple the ends together to secure. Cover the staples with clear tape to avoid injury.

4. Be sure the children write their names on the backs of their crowns.

5. Say, **Wear your crown in honor of Christ the King!**

# Magi Gift Bag

❄ ❄ ❄ ❄ ❄ ❄ **AGES 3-12**

**Bible Reference:** Magi present the Infant Jesus with gifts / *Matthew 2:11*

 ## Overview

The wise men brought gifts to baby Jesus. The children can use these gift bags when they give their own Christmas gifts.

 ## Helpers: 1

one for every 3-4 children

 ## What You Need

❋ Magi Gift Bag patterns, page 228
❋ poster board
❋ purple paper bags
❋ yellow, pink and brown card stock or construction paper
❋ sequins
❋ 15 mm moveable plastic eyes
❋ craft glue
❋ scissors
❋ black and red markers
❋ clear tape
❋ paper plates

 ## Preparation

Make templates of the Magi Gift Bag patterns using poster board. Trace and cut crowns and gift boxes from yellow card stock or construction paper, Magi faces and hands from pink, and Magi beards from brown. You will need one crown, one gift box, one face, two hands and one beard for each gift bag. Set out sequins on paper plates.

 ## What to Do

1. Say, **When Jesus was born, men from a faraway land traveled to bring Him gifts. Some people called these men "kings." Other people called them "wise men" or "magi."**
2. Distribute pre-cut beards, faces and crowns. Show how to use glue to layer the faces on top of the beards, and then the crowns on top of the faces.
3. Have the children position eyes on the faces and attach them with glue. They can use black markers to draw noses and red markers to draw mouths.
4. Hand out pre-cut gift boxes, which will become gift tags. Have the children use markers to write "To" and "From" on the tags, leaving spaces to fill in later. Let the children use sequins and glue to decorate the crowns and gift box tags.
5. Give each child a bag. Say, **In Bible times, purple was a color of royalty. Only kings and leaders, like the Magi, wore purple.** Instruct the children to lay the bags flat, with the folds on the bottom, then fold over 1½" of the bag tops toward the fronts.
6. Each child should glue the face assembly to the folded flap. Have the children position the hands along the lower fronts of the bags. Tell them to apply glue to the hand palms only, leaving the thumbs free to hold the gift box tags.
7. Show how to apply glue to the tags' backs, tuck the tags under the thumbs and attach.
8. Be sure the children write their names on the backs of their bags. Say, **The Magi brought gifts to Jesus. We honor Jesus by giving gifts to others at Christmas.**

# Miniature Poinsettia

✳ ✳ ✳ ✳ ✳ ✳ ✳ ✳ ✳ AGES 7-12

**Bible Reference:** The desert rejoices in the Savior / *Isaiah 35:1-2*

 **Overview**

The bright colors of poinsettia leaves during the darkest weeks of the year are a reminder of the joy Christ brings to sinners everywhere.

 **Helpers: 1**

one for every 3-4 children

 **What You Need**

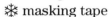

※ Miniature Poinsettia patterns, pages 229-230
※ plastic lids from detergent or spray cans (optional)
※ red, green and yellow tissue paper　※ pencils
※ poster board　　　　　　　　　　　　※ craft glue
※ scissors　　　　　　　　　　　　　　※ masking tape

 **Preparation**

Make templates of the Miniature Poinsettia patterns using poster board. Use the templates to cut poinsettia leaves from red tissue paper, stems from green tissue paper and seeds from yellow tissue paper. You will need one red square, one green square and three yellow squares for each poinsettia. See diagrams on page 230 for the steps below.

 **What to Do**

1. Say, **A poinsettia is a special plant that grows in the dry desert areas of Mexico. Its leaves change color in December, right around Christmas time. Let's make our own Miniature Poinsettias.** Give each child a square of red tissue paper. Show how to fold the square in half to make a rectangle, in half again to make a square and a third time to make a rectangle once more.

2. Have the children position leaf patterns on top of their red tissues so the leaf points are on the unfolded edges of the rectangles (see Diagram 1). Let them outline the leaf points with pencils and trim away the excess tissue with scissors. Help the children unfold the red tissues and lay them flat (see Diagram 2).

3. Show how to gather the centers of the red tissues from the ends working in, pinching together the extra tissue below the petals (see Diagram 3). The leaves will swirl outward.

4. Distribute green tissue squares. Have the children coil the green "stalks" onto the poinsettia bases beneath the flowers, twist the remaining green tissue into stems and glue.

5. Let each child crunch three yellow tissue squares into poinsettia "seeds" and attach them to the centers of the flowers with glue.

6. A child can use a single Miniature Poinsettia to decorate gifts, bulletin boards or walls. Or children can assemble three or more poinsettias to make an arrangement in a laundry detergent or aerosol lid "flowerpot." Make sure they anchor the poinsettias in their pots with craft glue.

7. Have the children stick tape on the flowers or holders and write their names on the tape.

8. Say, **Even in the dark days of winter, the poinsettia plant celebrates the birth of Christ with color and joy.**

# Pocket Crèche Puppets

❄ ❄ ❄ ❄ ❄ ❄ ❄ ❄ AGES 7-12

**Bible Reference:** The Christmas Story / *Matthew 2:1-12, Luke 2:1-20*

## Overview

The children will make Christmas story puppets from glove fingertips, fabric and yarn.

## Helpers: 1

one for every 3-4 children

## What You Need

❄ knit gloves in brown, blue, white and purple
❄ fabric scraps
❄ pink, brown, yellow and blue yarn
❄ brown and gold chenille wire
❄ 7 mm moveable plastic eyes
❄ 1" wide white lace
❄ clear nail polish
❄ ruler or tape measure
❄ scissors
❄ pinking shears
❄ fabric glue
❄ small-mouthed bottles (as for water, condiments or soda)

## Preparation

Cut the fingers off the gloves: brown for the manger, Joseph and shepherds; blue for Mary; white for angels and purple for wise men. To prevent fabric from raveling, spread clear nail polish on the cut fingertip edges. Use pinking shears to cut 2" x 2½" headpieces from fabric scraps for Joseph, Mary, the shepherds and the wise men. Cut 6" lengths of yarn for headbands: brown or yellow for Joseph and the shepherds, and blue for Mary. Cut 3" lengths of brown chenille wire for the shepherds' staffs. Cut 3" lengths of gold chenille wire for the angel's and manger's halos and the wise men's crowns. Cut 1" lengths of lace for angels' wings. Cut ½" lengths of pink yarn for mouths.

## What to Do

1. Let the children choose which Nativity figure to make. (If time allows, each child can make more than one figure or even an entire set.) Distribute pre-cut glove fingertips.
2. Show how to station a glove fingertip on the top of a bottle so your hands are free to work.
3. For Joseph, Mary, shepherd and wise men puppets, give the children pre-cut fabric headpieces. Have the children spread fabric glue on the backs of the fabric. Help them

*continued on next page...*

apply the headpieces to the puppet figures, placing the fabric on the backs of the puppets, wrapping the side edges around to the fronts, and folding down the tops. Let the children tie pre-cut yarn headbands around the figures' foreheads, trim the ends and glue to secure.

4. For shepherd puppets, let the children bend brown chenille wire into staffs and glue one onto the back of each shepherd's body.

5. For wise men puppets, let the children twist gold chenille wire into crown circles and glue one on each wise man's head.

6. For angel puppets, have the children glue two pre-cut lace lengths to the back of each angel to make wings, then twist gold chenille wire into halo circles and glue one onto each angel's head.

7. For manger puppets, let the children bend gold chenille wire into semi-circle halos and glue one onto each puppet. The manger puppet should be held horizontally with the halo its only feature.

8. For all figures other than the manger, have the children make faces by gluing on moveable plastic eyes and yarn mouths.

9. Allow the figures to dry completely.

10. Say, **Use these figures to tell the story of Jesus' birth.** Have the children place their puppets on their fingers. Help them pantomime Joseph and Mary traveling to Bethlehem, the arrival of baby Jesus, the angel's announcement to the shepherds, the shepherds at the stable and the wise men's trip from the East.

# Reindeer Candy Cane

❉❉❉❉❉❉❉❉❉ AGES 3-12

**Bible Reference:** God strengthens us / *Psalm 18:32-33*

## Overview

The children will decorate candy canes to resemble reindeer, and learn that God gives us strength to get through difficult times.

## Helpers: 1

one for every 5-6 children

## What You Need

❉ 6" wrapped candy canes
❉ brown chenille wire
❉ 7 mm moveable plastic eyes
❉ 10 mm red pompons
❉ ½"-wide red satin ribbon
❉ scissors
❉ craft glue
❉ ruler or tape measure
❉ masking tape

## Preparation

Cut chenille wire into 6" and 3" lengths. Cut red satin ribbon into 10" lengths. You will need one 6" length of brown chenille wire, two 3" lengths of brown chenille wire and one 10" red satin ribbon for each reindeer.

## What to Do

1. Give each child a candy cane and a set of pre-cut chenille wire. Show how to lay the candy cane on the work surface, slip the 6" chenille wire length underneath the curve of the cane, bend it in half and twist the center of the wire around the cane to make the reindeer's antler shafts.

2. The children should twist 3" chenille wire lengths around each of the shafts to add limbs to the antlers. Let them use craft glue to secure the antler assemblies to the candy canes.

3. Show where to attach moveable plastic eyes and red pompons to the candy canes to make eyes and noses.

4. Let older children tie red satin ribbon bows around the reindeer's "necks" and trim the ends, if desired. Younger children will need help tying bows.

5. As the children are working, ask, **Where do reindeer live?** Allow the children to respond. Say, **Reindeer move around on mountains, in snow and ice. God made reindeer strong so that they can survive in difficult conditions. We are like reindeer – God gives us strength when life gets difficult.**

6. Allow the Reindeer Candy Canes to dry. Have the children write their names on masking tape and stick the tape on their candy canes.

# Santa Take-home Sack

**Bible Reference:** Jesus prepares a place for us / *John 14:2-3*

 ## Overview

The children will convert brown paper sacks into decorative bags that resemble Santa Claus, and be reminded that Jesus wants to take us home with Him to heaven some day.

 ## Helpers: 1

one for every 3-4 children

 ## What You Need

- ❊ poster board
- ❊ Santa Take-home Sack patterns, pages 231-232
- ❊ brown grocery-size paper sacks
- ❊ red, pink and black construction paper
- ❊ cotton balls
- ❊ 20 mm movable plastic eyes
- ❊ 20 mm pink pompons
- ❊ glitter glue
- ❊ curling ribbon
- ❊ 20 mm jingle bells
- ❊ 2" packing tape (clear or brown)
- ❊ craft glue
- ❊ scissors
- ❊ hole punch
- ❊ ruler

 ## Preparation

Make templates of Santa Take-home Sack patterns. Trace and cut out Santa's face from pink construction paper, Santa's hat and mouth from red construction paper, and Santa's belt and buttons from black construction paper. Score the fold line on Santa's hat. You will need one face, one hat, one mouth, one belt and three buttons for each sack. Measure and cut ribbon into 36" lengths. You will need two lengths of ribbon for each sack.

 ## What to Do

1. Give each child a grocery sack. Say, **We're going to decorate these bags to look like Santa. Then you'll have somewhere to put all the things you want to take home with you from our party today.**
2. Help the children attach 2" wide packaging tape around the top edges of their bags for durability.

*continued on next page...*

3. Give each child an 8½" x 11" piece of red construction paper. Show how to center the paper vertically on one side of the bag so that it becomes Santa's torso. The children can position Santa's face and hat on their bags. Let them glue all three pieces into place on each bag.

4. The children should arrange movable plastic eyes, pink pompon noses, and red construction paper mouths on their Santa's faces and attach them with glue.

5. Show how to fold down the scored line on Santa's hat and glue it into place.

6. Let each child glue on cotton balls to make Santa's beard, the top rim of his hat and the pompon for the hat tip.

7. Show how to position a black construction paper belt and buttons onto Santa's torso and glue them into place. The children can use glitter glue to outline the buttons and draw square buckles in the centers of the belts.

8. Have the children lay their Santa Take-Home Sacks flat on the work surface. Use the hole punch to show how to make two holes, one on each side of Santa's face. Make sure the children punch through all the folded layers of the bags when they make the holes.

9. Help each child string a jingle bell onto each of two pre-cut lengths of curling ribbon. Each child should thread one ribbon through each hole on the side of the bag and tie it in a bow to secure. The tied ribbons become the sack's handles.

10. Be sure the children write their names on their sacks.

11. Say, **We are special to Jesus. He wants to take us home to heaven with Him some day. He's preparing a place for us there right now – just like you prepared this wonderful Santa Take-home Sack to take home your special things.**

# Sheep Lollipop

❋ ❋ ❋ ❋ ❋ ❋ ❋ AGES 3-12

**Bible Reference:** We are His sheep / *John 10:14-16*

 Overview

The children will decorate lollipops to look like sheep as reminders that we are Jesus' sheep and He is the Good Shepherd.

 Helpers: 1

one for every 3-4 children

 What You Need

- ❋ poster board
- ❋ Sheep Lollipop patterns, page 233
- ❋ round lollipops
- ❋ white muslin or sheeting
- ❋ white and pink felt
- ❋ rubber bands
- ❋ ½"-wide black satin ribbon
- ❋ 6-7 mm movable plastic eyes
- ❋ cotton balls       ❋ ruler
- ❋ scissors            ❋ craft glue
- ❋ pinking shears    ❋ masking tape

 Preparation

Make templates of the Sheep Lollipop patterns. Trace and cut out sheep's ears from white felt. Trace and cut out sheep's ear linings and nose from pink felt. Measure 6" squares of white muslin or sheeting. Cut out squares with pinking shears. Measure and cut 8" lengths of black satin ribbon for sheep's neck collars. You will need one square of white muslin or sheeting, one set of ears and ear linings, one nose and one neck collar for each sheep.

 What to Do

1. Give each child a lollipop and a square of white fabric. Each child should position a lollipop "head" in the center of a square, then draw up the corners to a point. Show how to wrap a rubber band around the base of the lollipop to secure the fabric.
2. Show how to position and glue the sheep ear linings to the center of the ears. Point out where to glue the ear assemblies onto the backs of the sheep heads.
3. Have the children pinch off pea-sized pieces of cotton from the cotton balls. Show how to roll the cotton pieces in between index fingers and thumbs to make the sheep "wool." The children should use glue to cover the sheep's heads with wool.
4. Let the children attach movable plastic eyes and felt noses to their sheep faces with glue.
5. Help the children tie black satin ribbons into bows around the sheep's necks, covering the rubber bands, trimming the ribbon ends if desired.
6. Say, **Jesus says that we are His sheep. He is our Good Shepherd.**
7. Allow the Sheep Lollipops to dry. Have the children write their names on masking tape and stick the tape on their lollipops.

# Shepherd Treat Holder

❄ ❄ ❄ ❄ ❄ ❄ AGES 7-12

**Bible Reference:** Jesus is the Good Shepherd / *John 10:11*

 ## Overview

The children will make a treat holder that represents a shepherd.

 ## Helpers: 1

one for every 3-4 children

 ## What You Need

- ❄ poster board
- ❄ Shepherd Treat Holder patterns, page 234
- ❄ toilet tissue tubes
- ❄ fabric scraps
- ❄ light brown craft foam
- ❄ light brown felt
- ❄ pink felt scraps
- ❄ natural-colored raffia
- ❄ jumbo craft sticks
- ❄ 15-16 mm movable plastic eyes
- ❄ ½"-wide black satin ribbon
- ❄ red yarn
- ❄ craft glue
- ❄ scissors
- ❄ pinking shears
- ❄ pencil
- ❄ candy canes

 ## Preparation

Make templates of the Shepherd Treat Holder patterns. Trace and cut out the shepherds' heads and feet from light brown craft foam. Trace and cut out the shepherds' arms from light brown felt. Trace the patterns for the shepherds' robes and headdresses onto fabric scraps. Cut out the robe parts with regular scissors and the headdress parts with pinking shears. Trace and cut out the shepherds' noses from pink felt. Measure and cut 15" lengths of raffia for the shepherds' belts. Measure and cut 2" lengths of raffia for the shepherds' sandal ties. Measure and cut 8" lengths of black satin ribbon for the shepherds' headbands. You will need one head, one set of feet, one set of arms, one robe, one headdress, one nose, one belt, one headband and four sandal ties for each Shepherd Treat Holder.

 ## What to Do

1.  Give each child a cardboard toilet tissue tube and shepherd's robe. Tell the children to cover the tubes with craft glue and attach the robes to make the shepherds' bodies.

*continued on next page...*

2. Show how to fold and adjust the side edges of the headdresses as the children attach them to the heads with glue. Have the children position the black satin ribbon headbands across the shepherds' foreheads and glue them into place on the backs of the heads.

3. The children should create their shepherds' faces with movable plastic eyes, pink felt noses and red yarn mouths. Have each child glue a jumbo craft stick onto the back of each shepherd's head, extending down past his neckline. Allow the shepherds heads to dry.

4. Demonstrate how to crisscross raffia for sandal ties and glue them onto the shepherds' feet. Have the children trim excess raffia ends. Allow the shepherds' feet to dry.

5. Help the children attach the shepherds' heads to the bodies by gluing the previously-glued craft sticks to the backs of the fabric-covered cardboard tubes.

6. Show each child how to glue arms on a shepherd's body by wrapping the arms over the craft stick in the back and reaching around to the front on each side.

7. Demonstrate how to tie a raffia belt around the middle of a shepherd's body.

8. Tell the children to apply glue to the bottom circumferences of the cardboard tube bodies and attach them to their shepherds' feet.

9. As you are working, say, **Shepherds were the first people to hear about Jesus' birth. They were taking care of their sheep on a hillside at night when an angel surprised them with the news. Jesus knows that it takes a special person be a shepherd. He calls Himself the "Good Shepherd."**

10. When the Shepherd Treat Holders are dry, fill them with candy cane "shepherd's staffs." Have the children write their names on the bottoms of their shepherds.

 # Star of Bethlehem Pencil Topper

❄ ❄ ❄ ❄ ❄ ❄ ❄ ❄ ❄ ❄ AGES 3-12

**Bible Reference:** The star leads the wise men to Jesus / *Matthew 2:2*

 Overview

The children will make stars as reminders that God wants everyone to find Christ.

 Helpers: 1

one for every 3-4 children

 What You Need

❋ poster board
❋ Star of Bethlehem pattern, page 233
❋ metallic, foil or glitter pencils
❋ foil or metallic gift wrap
❋ 1-ounce chip or snack bags
❋ spring-type clothespins
❋ sequins and rhinestones
❋ pencil          ❋ glitter glue
❋ craft glue      ❋ scissors
❋ clear tape      ❋ masking tape

 Preparation

Make a template of the Star of Bethlehem pattern. Trace and cut stars from foil or metallic gift wrap. You will need two stars for each child. Slit open a chip bag along the back and bottom seams and trim the bag's edges. Lay it flat. Clean the inside of the bag. Allow the bag to dry. Trim the edges. You will need one chip bag per child.

 What to Do

1. Have each child lay one foil star face down on a work surface. Give each child a foil, metallic or glitter pencil. Show how to place the pencils' eraser ends in the centers of the stars. Let the children use clear tape to attach their pencil ends to the centers of the stars.

2. Give each child another pencil and a clean, flattened chip bag. Demonstrate how to roll the bag around the pencil, shiny side out, to fashion a small tube. The children can then remove the pencils from the centers of their tubes. Let each child fringe one end of the shiny tube. This becomes the star's "tail."

3. Have the children use clear tape to attach the un-fringed ends of their stars' tails to the centers of the foil stars, on top of the pencils' erasers. The fringed ends will extend out the sides of the stars to resemble "shooting sparks."

4. Each child should glue a second foil star on top of the first one. Let the children use spring-type clothespins to clamp the star arms together to dry.

5. When the glue is dry, remove the clothespins. Allow the children to decorate their stars with glitter glue, sequins and rhinestones.

6. Say, **The Star of Bethlehem led the wise men to baby Jesus. God wants us to find Jesus, know Him and worship Him, too.**

7. Have the children write their names on masking tape and stick the tape on their pencil toppers. Allow the decorated pencils to dry.

# Walnut Mouse

 AGES 3-12

**Bible Reference:** God made all creatures / *Psalm 104:24*

 ## Overview

The children will make mice from walnut shells as reminders
that God loves and cares for even His smallest creatures.

 ## Helpers: 1

one for every 4-6 children

 ## What You Need

❄ poster board
❄ Walnut Mouse patterns,
    page 233
❄ walnuts in shells
❄ nutcracker
❄ light brown felt
❄ 7 mm movable plastic eyes
❄ 5 mm pink pompons
❄ natural-colored raffia    ❄ fabric glue
❄ ruler    ❄ craft glue
❄ scissors    ❄ masking tape

 ## Preparation

Make a template of the Walnut Mouse pattern using poster board. Trace and cut out the
mouse ears and tails from light brown felt. You will need two ears and one tail for each
mouse. Use a nutcracker to break the walnuts into halves. Remove the nutmeats and extra
shell parts from the insides. Cut thin strands of raffia into 2" lengths (mouse "whiskers").
You will need three strands of raffia for each mouse.

## What to Do

1. Give each child a walnut shell half, felt tail and felt ears. Show how to apply fabric glue
   to half of each felt ear, fold the glued surface in half and leave the unglued half of the ear
   unattached so that it sticks up. The children should hold the glued ear sections in
   between their thumbs and forefingers for a few minutes until the glue adheres to the felt.

2. Help each child position the ears and tail onto a walnut shell mouse "body" and attach
   them with craft glue.

3. The children should use craft glue to affix movable plastic eyes, raffia whiskers and
   pink pompon noses to their mice.

4. Say, **Mice are some of the smallest animals in God's kingdom. But they are still
   important to the Lord. God made all creatures, both great and small. He loves
   you just as much as He loves adults.**

5. Have the children write their names on masking tape and stick inside their mice.
   When the Walnut Mice are dry, the children can use them to play Race Down the
   Chimney (page 120).

# Gifts

# Bouncy Balls

 AGES 3-12

**Bible Reference:** Elizabeth bears John the Baptist / *Luke 1:39-44*

 Overview

The children will make a set of colorful balls out of modeling compound as reminders of John leaping inside Elizabeth when she saw Mary.

 Helpers: 1

one for every 5-6 children

 What You Need

✳ modeling compound
✳ wax paper
✳ mesh produce bags
✳ resealable plastic sandwich bags
✳ twist ties
✳ scissors
✳ Holiday Heart Gift Tag, page 201
✳ Bouncy Ball Gift Tag, page 202

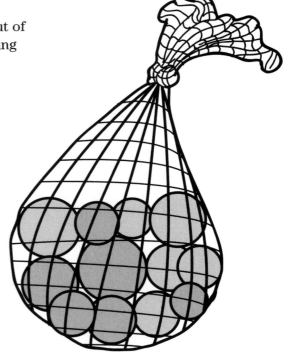

 Preparation

Examine the mesh bags and locate the openings where the produce was removed. Trim the edges around the openings. Duplicate the Holiday Heart Gift Tags and Bouncy Ball Gift Tags from pages 201 and 202 for each child.

## What to Do

1. Set out modeling compound. Show how to roll the compound in the palms of your hands to make round balls. Explain that rolling two or more colors together creates swirled patterns on the balls.

2. Have the children write their names on sheets of wax paper and set their Bouncy Balls on the paper to dry for 24 hours (or as long as the manufacturer packaging instructs).

3. Ask, **What makes Bouncy Balls so fun?** Allow the children to respond. Say, **Yes, they bounce and leap and move all around. That reminds me of Elizabeth, John the Baptist's mother, while she was pregnant. She was filled with the Holy Spirit. The baby inside Elizabeth began to leap and bounce around when she saw Mary. She learned that Mary was going to have baby Jesus.**

4. Distribute resealable plastic sandwich bags. Explain that the balls will bounce and retain shape after being squeezed, but only if they are not allowed to dry out completely. Encourage the children to store the balls in the plastic bags when they are not used. (The bag interiors will display some condensation when the balls are stored.)

5. Show how to let the filled plastic bags act as liners when inserted into the mesh bags. Let the children use twist ties to secure the trimmed edges of the bags. Help the children make Holiday Heart Gift Tags and attach them to their bags.

6. Suggest that they give the Bouncy Balls to siblings or friends.

# Celebration Soap Bar

 AGES 3-12

**Bible Reference:** God cleanses us from sin / *Psalm 51:1-2*

 Overview

Children understand that washing gets their bodies clean. This gift shows that when we ask forgiveness, God cleans us on the inside, too.

 Helpers: 1

one for every 3-4 children

 What You Need

❊ soap bars
❊ vegetable peeler
❊ acrylic paints
❊ paraffin wax or white candles
❊ paper plates
❊ paint brushes
❊ small bowls
❊ double boiler

❊ wax paper
❊ ½"-wide ribbon
❊ ruler or tape measure
❊ smocks (men's long-sleeved shirts work well)
❊ Holiday Heart Gift Tag, page 201
❊ Celebration Soap Bar Gift Tag, page 202

 Preparation

Unwrap soap. Use a vegetable peeler to scrape off the logo and create a smooth surface. Cut 10" sheets of wax paper for wrapping. Cut ribbon into 15" lengths. Duplicate the gift tags from pages 201 and 202 for each child. You will need one soap bar, one sheet of wax paper, one strand of ribbon and one set of gift tags for each Celebration Soap Bar. Before the children begin, pour several paint colors onto plates. Three or four children can work from each plate. Set out bowls of water for rinsing paintbrushes. Use a double boiler to melt wax.

 What to Do

1.  Have the children wear smocks for this activity. Give each child a clean paper plate and bar of soap. Say, **Let's paint these bars of soap with festive Christmas designs.** Let the children use acrylic paints to add Christmas trees, candles, border designs and short words such as "Joy!" and "Ho, Ho, Ho!" to their soap bars. Remind the children to rinse their paintbrushes when they change colors. Allow the paint to dry.
2.  Make sure the wax in the double boiler is melted. Remove it from the stove.
3.  Work with older children individually as they select clean paintbrushes to dip in the melted wax, and brush the wax across the soap surfaces to seal their painted designs. Younger children should not work with melted wax, so an adult should seal their soap bars for them. (The wax will keep the designs on the soap intact when they make contact with water.)
4.  Ask, **When do you use soap?** Allow the children to respond. Say, **Yes, we use soap to get our bodies and hands clean. And when we confess our sins to God, He forgives us and cleans us on the inside, too.**
5.  When the wax has cooled, help the children wrap their soap bars with wax paper and tie them with ribbons. Have the children make gift tags and attach them to their Celebration Soap Bars.

# Christmas Card Roundabout

❋ ❋ ❋ ❋ ❋ ❋ ❋ ❋ ❋ **AGES 7-12**

**Bible Reference:** Early Christians send greetings / *3 John 1:14*

 ## Overview

The children will make a clever Christmas card holder from an oatmeal container.

 ## Helpers: 1

one for every 3-4 children

 ## What You Need

- ❋ cylindrical cardboard container, as for oatmeal
- ❋ Christmas gift wrap or old Christmas cards
- ❋ blank Christmas cards
- ❋ yarn
- ❋ craft glue
- ❋ clear tape
- ❋ scissors
- ❋ ruler or tape measure
- ❋ kitchen knife
- ❋ Holiday Heart Gift Tag, page 201
- ❋ Christmas Card Roundabout Gift Tag, page 202

 ## Preparation

Prepare the cylindrical containers by removing the labels and plastic rings from the top edges (if applicable). Wipe out the containers and allow them to dry. (Save the plastic lids.) You will need one container and one set of gift tags for each cardholder.

 ## What to Do

1. Let the children decorate the containers by gluing on cards or gift wrap. Allow to dry.
2. Show how to make an even number of cuts around the top edge. The cuts should be ½" deep and about ½" apart. The children should make the same cuts on the bottom edge.
3. Show how to insert the end of a yarn strand in one of the bottom notches. Make sure the children leave at least 1" tails of yarn.
4. Help the children thread the yarn across the outsides, securing the yarn firmly in each notch and pulling it taut. They should continue weaving until all notches are threaded.
5. Show how to tie the two yarn tails together. The children can trim the ends and attach yarn knots to the bottoms of the Roundabouts with clear tape.
6. Help each child place a plastic lid on top of a Roundabout. This will secure the yarn notches on the upper edge and give the holder a clean finish.
7. As the children are working, say, **In Bible times, Christians communicated with others who lived far away by sending them letters of love and encouragement. We do something similar today. We send our families and friends special cards at Christmastime to show that we care about them.**
8. Let each child select a Christmas card and use pens or markers to record appropriate greetings to recipients. Demonstrate how to hook the Christmas cards through the yarn strands.
9. Have the children make gift tags to attach to their Roundabouts.

# Confetti Treat Tin

❄ ❄ ❄ ❄ ❄ AGES 7-12

**Bible Reference:** Mary stored good thoughts in her heart / *Luke 2:19*

 ## Overview

People received the shepherds' good news about the Savior with joy and amazement. Mary stored that encouragement in her heart, just as we can store good snacks in this treat tin.

 ## Helpers: 1

one for every 3-4 children

 ## What You Need

❄ empty cans with lids (such as coffee cans)
❄ 2"-wide clear packaging tape
❄ colored poster board
❄ construction paper
❄ used or new Christmas cards
❄ tape measure
❄ scissors
❄ craft glue
❄ clear, adhesive-backed plastic
❄ rubber cement
❄ hot glue gun
❄ paper plates
❄ craft sticks or toothpicks
❄ Holiday Heart Gift Tag, page 201
❄ Confetti Treat Tin Gift Tag, page 202

 ## Preparation

Wash and dry the cans and lids thoroughly. For safety purposes, attach a strip of clear packaging tape around the top edge of each can. Measure the depth and circumference of the cans, adding ½" to the lengths of the circumferences for overlap. Cut pieces of colored poster board to fit this measurement. Cut pieces of clear, adhesive-backed plastic that measure ½" larger on each side than the corresponding pieces of poster board. Cut construction paper into confetti-like squares. Be sure to cut different sizes (½", ¾" and 1" squares) in a variety of colors. Duplicate the Holiday Heart Gift Tags and Confetti Treat Tin Gift Tags from pages 201 and 202 for each child. Set out Christmas cards so that children can refer to them. Just before the children begin working, pour puddles of craft glue onto paper plates. Set out craft sticks or toothpicks.

 ## What to Do

1. Pass out pre-cut poster board. Explain that the children will decorate the poster board first, then attach it to the tins.

*continued on next page...*

2. Tell the children that they can make Christmas scenes on the poster board using confetti. If the children struggle for ideas, encourage them to look at the Christmas card pictures, or use their imaginations.

3. Suggest that the children arrange the confetti pictures before beginning to glue them. (To minimize sticky fingers, the children can apply the glue to the confetti with craft sticks or toothpicks.)

4. Allow the glue to dry.

5. Have older children apply clear, adhesive-backed plastic to their pictures and turn the excess edges to the backs of the poster board. Younger children will need assistance applying the plastic.

6. Help the children spread rubber cement on the poster board backs and attach the boards to the cans, smoothing down the edges.

7. With a glue gun, apply a bead of hot glue along the back seam of each poster board to seal the edges. (Only adults should use the hot glue gun!)

8. Say, **This tin can be used to store treats and keep them fresh. Mary, Jesus' mother, received some special treats, too. The shepherds and people around her praised God for sending baby Jesus. Those words were a special encouragement to Mary. She stored them up in her heart, just like we can store goodies in the Confetti Treat Tin.**

9. The children can fill their Confetti Treat Tins with prepared snacks such as Cheesy Popcorn (page 131) or John the Baptist's Snack Mix (page 136).

10. Have the children make gift tags to attach to their Confetti Treat Tins.

# Cookie Mix in a Jar

 AGES 3-12

**Bible Reference:** The Magnificat / *Luke 1:46-55*

 ## Overview

The children will assemble cookie mix in quart jars, and learn that God wants to fill us with every good thing.

 ## Helpers: 1

one for every 3-4 children

 ## What You Need

❄ Cookie Mix in a Jar lid pattern, page 235
❄ poster board
❄ quart-size canning jars with lids

| | |
|---|---|
| ❄ bowls | ❄ crushed nuts |
| ❄ flour | ❄ funnel |
| ❄ baking soda | ❄ wooden spoons |
| ❄ salt | ❄ Christmas fabric |
| ❄ brown sugar | ❄ pinking shears |
| ❄ granulated sugar | ❄ pencil |
| ❄ chocolate chips | ❄ raffia or ribbon |

❄ measuring cup and spoons
❄ Holiday Heart Gift Tag, page 201
❄ Cookie Mix in a Jar Gift Tag, page 203

## Preparation

Make a template of the pattern from poster board. Trace the pattern onto fabric and cut it out with pinking shears. You will need one for every jar. Duplicate the tags and the "Cookie Mix in a Jar" instructions to include on the tags for each child.

 ## What to Do

1. Instruct the children to wash their hands before handling food. Ask, **What is your favorite kind of cookie?** Allow the children to respond. Say, **Cookies are fun to eat. Today we are going to assemble a Cookie Mix in a Jar for you to give as a gift.**

2. Set a canning jar in front of each child. Have them remove the lids. Help each child, one at a time, to measure out and mix together 1½ cups of flour, ½ teaspoon of baking soda and ½ teaspoon of salt in a bowl. Have each child place the funnel in the mouth of the jar and pour the flour mixture into the jar.

3. Show the children how to gently shake the jars so the flour mixture settles evenly.

4. Have each child layer ½ cup packed brown sugar, ⅓ cup granulated sugar, 1 cup chocolate chips and ½ cup crushed nuts in a jar.

5. Show how to separate the lid's disk and ring, place the fabric liner in between them, and replace the disk inside the ring. The children should screw the lids onto the jars.

6. Help the children tie raffia or ribbon around their lids. Say, **Mary, Jesus' mother, said a special prayer that reminds me of cookies. She praised God for filling us with good things.**

7. Each child should attach a handmade gift tag and the cookie instructions to his or her jar.

# Cozy Cocoa Kit

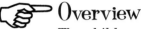 AGES 3-12

**Bible Reference:** God loved us and sent His Son / *1 John 4:10*

 ## Overview

The children will make this tasty gift to show the warmth and sweetness of God's love.

 ## Helpers: 1

one for every 3-4 children

 ## What You Need

❋ round, plastic containers
  (such as frosting cans)
❋ Cozy Cocoa Kit patterns, page 236
❋ Cozy Christmas Cocoa mix, page 133
❋ computer or printer paper
❋ clear, adhesive-backed plastic
❋ poster board ❋ glitter glue
❋ fabric scraps ❋ yarn
❋ tape measure ❋ mini marshmallows
❋ pencil ❋ sandwich-size resealable plastic bags
❋ scissors ❋ snack-size resealable plastic bags
❋ pinking shears ❋ Holiday Heart Gift Tag, page 201
❋ craft glue ❋ Cozy Cocoa Kit Gift Tag, page 203

 ## Preparation

Remove the labels from the containers, then wash and dry the containers. Measure the depth and circumference of each container, adding ½" to the circumference for overlap. With pinking shears, cut a piece of fabric for each container to fit this measurement. Make a template of the patterns. Trace and cut out teacups and saucers from fabric. Duplicate and cut out the labels and cover them with clear plastic. Duplicate the tags and the "Cup of Cocoa Instructions" to include on the gift tags.

## What to Do

1. Give each child a container and fabric. Show how to glue the fabric so it overlaps the edges.
2. Have the children arrange the teacups and saucers on their containers and glue them on.
3. Allow the children to use glitter glue to create twists of "steam" from the teacups.
4. The children should glue the "Cozy Cocoa Kit" labels to their container lids.
5. Show how to create yarn swirls. First, apply glue to the uncovered part of a lid. Then attach the end of the yarn to a label's edge, wind it around the label and continue circling until the lid is covered. Have the children set aside their lids and containers to dry.
6. Meanwhile, the children can assemble the cocoa mix in plastic bags (one per kit). Also have them put some mini marshmallows in snack-size plastic bags (one per kit).
7. Say, **God gave us Jesus because He loves us. You can give this Cozy Cocoa Kit to show the warmth and sweetness of God's love.**
8. Let each child place the cocoa mix and marshmallows in his or her container and cover it with a lid. Have the children attach the "Cup of Cocoa Instructions" and handmade gift tags to their kits.

# Cranberry Grapevine Wreath

✳ ✳ ✳ ✳ ✳ ✳ ✳ ✳ AGES 7-12

**Bible Reference:** The crown of thorns / *Matthew 27:28-29*

 **Overview**

The children will decorate a wreath with cranberries as reminders of Jesus' crown of thorns and the blood He shed for us.

 **Helpers: 1**

one for every 3-4 children

 **What You Need**

✳ grapevine wreaths
✳ fresh cranberries
✳ ½" woven gold ribbon
✳ fishing line
✳ tape measure
✳ blunt needles
✳ upholstery or quilting thread
✳ paper plates ✳ hot glue gun
✳ 5" piece of cardboard ✳ newspapers
✳ scissors ✳ Holiday Heart Gift Tag, page 201
✳ spring-type clothespins ✳ Cranberry Grapevine Wreath Gift Tag, page 204

 **Preparation**

Cut fishing line into 10" lengths and ribbon into 5" lengths. You will need one fishing line, one ribbon and one copy of the tag patterns for each wreath. Spread newspapers over the work area. Set out fresh cranberries on paper plates.

**What to Do**

1. Let each child select a wreath and measure its circumference with a tape measure. Help each child calculate the thread length by doubling the wreath circumference and adding 12 inches. The children should cut upholstery or quilting thread to those lengths.
2. Show how to thread a needle and tie a knot six inches from the end. The children should string cranberries through the needles and down the threads to the knots. Tell the children to leave six inches free at the threads' ends.
3. Show how to hold the needle and string in one hand so the berries don't slip off. Then hold the knotted string end against the wreath. Show how to weave the string on the wreath with the needled end. When the thread ends meet, the children can adjust the lengths by adding or removing a few berries. Have the children tie the ends and clip the excess.
4. Show how to make a wreath bow by wrapping ribbon around a 5" piece of cardboard five times, clipping the ribbon, slipping it off and securing the middle with a clothespin. Let the children use 5" ribbon lengths to tie the bow centers, then remove the clothespins. Have an adult use the hot glue gun to attach the bows to the wreaths.
5. The children should loop fishing line through the wreath backs and knot for hangers.
6. Say, **This wreath reminds us of the crown of thorns Jesus wore on the cross. The cranberries represent the blood He shed for our salvation. The gold bow reminds us that He is King.**
7. Have the children make gift tags to attach to their Cranberry Grapevine Wreaths.

# Hand Towel for a King

 AGES 3-12

**Bible Reference:** No room in the inn / *Luke 2:7*

 ## Overview

Mary gave birth to Jesus in the humblest of circumstances, yet she still had cloths in which to wrap the new baby. These hand towels the children will decorate remind us that God always provides us with what we need.

 ## Helpers: 1

one for every 3-4 children

## What You Need

❄ new hand or kitchen towels
❄ assorted lace, ribbon, rickrack, trims and buttons
❄ scissors
❄ fabric glue
❄ small safety pins
❄ Holiday Heart Gift Tag, page 201
❄ Hand Towel for a King Gift Tag, page 204

 ## Preparation

Set out lace, ribbons, trims and glue in work area.

 ## What to Do

1.  Give each child a hand towel. Explain that they will decorate the towels by adding assorted lace, ribbon and trims.
2.  Show how to layer trims across the widths of the towels to create appealing combinations. Let the children experiment before choosing which trims they want to cut and use.
3.  Remind the children to add 1" to the trim lengths before cutting to allow for ½" turn-under on each side.
4.  The children can cut trims and attach them to their towels with fabric glue. Help them turn and glue under the raw ends of the trims at the edges of their towels. The children can add buttons and bows as final touches, if desired.
5.  As the children are working, say, **When Mary and Joseph traveled to Bethlehem, they expected to stay in the inn, but it was full. Have you ever stayed in a hotel? What was it like?** Allow the children to respond. Say, **Yes, a hotel room has beds, sheets and towels. It's comfortable. You can get a good rest. But Mary and Joseph had to stay in a stable. That's where baby Jesus was born. Yet even though Mary was in an uncomfortable place, the Bible tells us that she still had special cloths in which to wrap her baby. God provided for her needs and for the baby's needs.**
6.  Say, **Your hand towels are beautiful. They are fit for a King! They remind us that as with Mary, God will always provide for our needs.**
7.  Have the children make gift tags. When the fabric glue is dry, have them use safety pins to attach the gift tags to their Hand Towels for a King.

# Holiday Heart Gift Tag

※ ※ ※ ※ ※ ※ ※ ※ ※ ※ **AGES 3-12**

**Bible Reference:** For unto us a Son is given / *Isaiah 9:6*

 **Overview**

The children will make gift tags that demonstrate the love of God through Christ.

 **Helpers: 1**

one for every 3-4 children

 **What You Need**

※ Santa Stamps, page 100
※ Holiday Heart Gift Tags pattern, page 201
※ red and green ink pads
※ card stock, colored and white
※ decorative-edge scissors, pinking shears or regular scissors
※ glue           ※ hole punch
※ metallic thread   ※ ruler
※ sandwich-size resealable plastic bags, optional

 **Preparation**

Make Santa Stamps following the directions on page 100. Include heart and cross designs on your stamp. Make a template of the tag pattern. Cut white card stock into 6" x 3" rectangles. Cut 12" lengths of metallic thread. You will need one rectangle and one metallic thread for each tag. If desired, reproduce gift tag poems and Bible verses from pages 202-207.

 **What to Do**

1. Ask, **When you see Christmas gifts under the tree, how do you know who is to open them?** Allow the children to respond. Say, **Yes, gifts are labeled with tags.**
2. Give each child a pre-cut white rectangle. Show how to use the inkpads and stamps to stamp a red heart and a green cross close together.
3. Ask, **Why are the heart and the cross important symbols at Christmastime?** Allow the children to respond. Say, **Yes, the heart shows that God loves us. He sent us the most wonderful gift of all – baby Jesus, His own Son. And the cross shows us how much Jesus loves us. He gave His life for us.**
4. Allow the ink to dry. Have the children trim around the heart/cross designs with decorative-edge scissors, pinking shears or regular scissors.
5. Have the children use the tag pattern template to trace tags on colored card stock. Let them cut out their tags with decorative or regular scissors.
6. Help the children fold the gift tags in half to make 3" squares. Have them glue the heart/cross designs to the fronts of the tags. If a tag is for a specific gift, help the child glue a poem and Bible verse to the inside of the tag.
7. The children can use hole punches in the upper left corners of the gift tags. Have them loop the metallic thread through the holes and knot the thread ends together.
8. Say, **When you use these tags to label your presents, remember the gift God gave you: baby Jesus.**
9. If a child chooses to make a set of gift tags to give as a present, help him or her group the completed tags in resealable plastic bags and attach a gift tag.

# Holly Door Stopper

❄ ❄ ❄ ❄ ❄ ❄ ❄ ❄ ❄ **AGES 3-12**

**Bible Reference:** The Suffering Servant / *Isaiah 53:3-5*

## Overview
The children will decorate a brick to use as a doorstopper – and a reminder of Jesus' gift of salvation to us.

## Helpers: 1
one for every 3-4 children

## What You Need
❄ Holly Door Stopper patterns, page 237
❄ poster board
❄ bricks
❄ natural or brown-colored fleece
❄ natural-colored burlap
❄ red and green felt          ❄ fabric glue
❄ red rickrack                ❄ scissors
❄ ruler or tape measure       ❄ Holiday Heart Gift Tag, page 201
❄ craft glue                  ❄ Holly Door Stopper Gift Tag, page 204

## Preparation
Measure and cut two fleece pieces, 8" x 10" and 2½" x 15½", to pad the brick. The larger piece will wrap around the three largest sides of the brick. The smaller strip will attach around the three remaining sides. Cut burlap into 13" x 15" pieces. Make templates of the Holly Door Stopper patterns. Trace and cut holly leaves from green felt and holly berries from red felt. Copy the gift tag patterns. You will need one set of fleece pieces, one piece of burlap, four holly leaves, four holly berries and one set of gift tag patterns for each Holly Door Stopper.

## What to Do
1. Give each child a brick. Ask the children to hold the bricks. Ask, **What can you tell me about these bricks?** Allow the children to respond. Say, **Yes, these bricks are heavy. They are strong, like Jesus.** Distribute the fleece sets. Help the children wind fleece around their bricks and attach it with craft glue.
2. Hand out burlap pieces. Say, **Let's pretend that these bricks are gift boxes. The burlap pieces are the gift wrap.** Help the children wrap bricks with burlap as if wrapping gift boxes, attaching edges and seams to the fleece bases with fabric glue.
3. Let the children use fabric glue to add rickrack in crisscross patterns to the fronts of the bricks. Show how to attach holly leaves and berries where the rickrack intersects.
4. Ask, **Can you describe how holly leaves feel to the touch?** Allow the children to respond. Say, **Yes, holly leaves' surfaces are smooth. But the tips of the leaves are sharp. They can poke and pierce us.**
5. Point to the top of a stopper. Say, **Your Holly Door Stoppers are strong like Jesus is. The rickrack intersects like a cross. The holly leaves remind us that He wore a crown of thorns. Jesus shed drops of blood, red like the holly berries, so that we can be forgiven for our sins. What a wonderful gift Jesus has given us – salvation!**
6. Help the children make gift tags to attach to their Holly Door Stoppers.

# Im-pastable Canister

❄✳❄✳❄✳❄✳❄✳❄ AGES 3-12

**Bible Reference:** Nothing is impossible with God / *Luke 1:37*

 ## Overview

The children will decorate jars to fill with dry pasta as a reminder that "nothing is impossible ["im-pastable"] with God."

 ## Helpers: 1

one for every 3-4 children

 ## What You Need

❇ large, clean glass jars with screw lids
   (such as mayonnaise or pickle jars)
❇ pencils
❇ heat-setting paints
   (also called thermo-hardening paints)
❇ smocks (men's long-sleeved shirts work well)
❇ oil-based thinner (mineral spirits or turpentine)
❇ paintbrushes
❇ toothpicks     ❇ cotton swabs
❇ newspapers     ❇ paper plates
❇ cookie sheet     ❇ paper towels
❇ dry pasta     ❇ spray paint
❇ Holiday Heart Gift Tag, page 201
❇ Im-pastable Canister Gift Tag, page 204

 ## Preparation

Spread newspapers over your work area. Remove the lid from the jar. Spray the outside of the lid with spray paint. (Do not spray the inside of the lid.) Allow the lid to dry. You will need one jar, one lid and one set of gift tags for each canister. Set out heat-setting paints on paper plates. Place paintbrushes, cotton-tipped swabs and toothpicks nearby.

 ## What to Do

1. Have the children wear smocks for this activity. Give each child a jar and a pencil. Have the children sketch pasta shapes and patterns on the jars (not the plastic lids). Remind them to outline the word, "pasta" on the jar. Younger children may need help sketching designs.
2. Have the children paint over their pencil designs with heat-setting paints. They should use a different brush for each color. Cotton swabs and toothpicks are helpful in painting smaller designs.
3. As the children are working, say, **Mary was confused when the angel Gabriel told her she was going to have a baby. She couldn't see how this would happen. But Gabriel reminded her: "Nothing is impossible with God." The word "pasta" sounds like the word "impossible."** Have the children repeat both words to hear how similar they sound. Say, **When you are confused, remember, "Nothing is im-pastable with God."**
4. Let the children clean their hands and the paintbrushes with oil-based thinner and paper towels. Allow the canisters to dry for 24 hours.
5. Follow the manufacturer's instructions to heat-set the paints.
6. After the canisters cool, let the children fill them with pasta and attach gift tags.

# Jingle Bell Gloves

❄ ❄ ❄ ❄ ❄ ❄ ❄ **AGES 7-12**

**Bible Reference:** Clap and shout praise to God / *Psalm 47:1-2*

 ## Overview

These gloves – decorated with fabric and bells – are reminders to praise God.

 ## Helpers: 1

one for every 3-4 children

 ## What You Need

- ❋ Jingle Bell Gloves pattern, page 237
- ❋ poster board
- ❋ gloves or mittens
- ❋ felt or Christmas fabric
- ❋ 10 mm jingle bells
- ❋ ½"-wide satin craft ribbon
- ❋ fabric paint pens   ❋ needle and thread
- ❋ scissors   ❋ fabric glue
- ❋ pencils   ❋ safety pins
- ❋ Holiday Heart Gift Tag, page 201
- ❋ Jingle Bell Gloves Tag, page 205

 ## Preparation

Make a template of the Jingle Bell Gloves pattern. Trace and cut out the bells from felt or Christmas fabric. Cut 4"-5" lengths of satin ribbon. You will need two bells, two ribbon lengths and a set of tags for each pair of gloves.

 ## What to Do

1. Have each child select a pair of gloves (or mittens) and two pre-cut fabric bells. Show how to spread fabric glue on the fabric bell backs and attach them to the glove forehands. Let the children use fabric paint pens to outline the bell appliqués.
2. Help the children tie ribbon lengths into bows and trim the bow ends. Have the children use fabric glue to attach the bows to the bell tops. Allow the bells to dry.
3. Show how to thread a needle. Have the children tie knots at the ends of the doubled thread.
4. Demonstrate how to fold back the glove cuffs and insert the needle from the inside to the outside of the glove so the needle emerges at the bottom of the bell appliqué. The knot will secure the thread on the inside of the glove.
5. Let each child sew a jingle bell on the center bottom of a bell (as in sewing a button).
6. Have each child make a knot in the thread about ½" from his or her jingle bell. Tell each child to pass the needle to the inside of the glove, gently tugging the knotted thread through the fabric to secure, and clip any threads.
7. Say, **These gloves will jingle when they are worn. They help us praise God for all His mighty deeds.**
8. Have the children make gift tags for their Jingle Bell Gloves, then attach the tags to the gloves with safety pins.

# Night of Wonder Headband

❋ ❋ ❋ ❋ ❋ ❋ ❋ ❋ ❋ **AGES 3-12**

**Bible Reference:** The glory of the Lord / *Luke 2:8-14*

 ## Overview

The children will decorate headbands that reflect God's glory.

 ## Helpers: 1

one for every 3-4 children

 ## What You Need

❋ 1" wide fabric-covered black or dark blue headband
❋ 15 mm rhinestone stars
❋ 10 mm sequin stars
❋ small rhinestones
❋ sequins
❋ fabric glue
❋ glitter glue
❋ newspapers
❋ Holiday Heart Gift Tag, page 201
❋ Night of Wonder Headband Gift Tag, page 205

 ## Preparation

Make a set of gift tags for each child. Spread newspapers over your work area.

 ## What to Do

1. Give each child a headband. Say, **On the night Jesus was born, shepherds were in the fields nearby taking care of their sheep. Suddenly, the angel of the Lord appeared to them. The sky lit up. The angel choir began singing.**

2. Have each child select a large rhinestone star, position it on a headband, and attach it with fabric glue. Say, **There was one large star in the sky that marked the place where Jesus was born.**

3. Let the children decorate the rest of their headbands with rhinestones, sequins and glitter glue. Say, **The sky was bright with the glory of the Lord. It was a night of wonder.**

4. Allow the headbands to dry. Have the children make gift tags to attach to their completed Night of Wonder Headbands.

# Noel Coffee Mug

❄ *❄* ❄ *❄* ❄ *❄* ❄ *❄* ❄ AGES 3-12

**Bible Reference:** The shepherds praise God / *Luke 2:20*

 Overview

The children will paint mugs with praise messages.

 Helpers: 1

one for every 3-4 children

 What You Need

❄ plain, oven-safe mugs
❄ pencils
❄ heat-setting paints (also called thermo-hardening paints)
❄ paintbrushes
❄ cotton swabs
❄ toothpicks
❄ newspapers
❄ smocks (men's long-sleeved shirts work well)
❄ oil-based thinner (mineral spirits or turpentine)
❄ paper towels
❄ cookie sheet
❄ Holiday Heart Gift Tag, page 201
❄ Noel Coffee Mug Tag, page 205

 Preparation

Spread newspapers over your work area. Copy a set of tags for each child. Be sure to use the mineral spirits or turpentine in a well-ventilated area, as suggested by the manufacturer.

 What to Do

1. Have the children wear smocks for this activity. Give each child a mug and pencil. Say, **Christmas is a time of joy. The shepherds praised God. We can praise God, too.**
2. Explain to the children that they will decorate the mug with heat-setting paints that will not wash off. Say, **"Noel" means "Christmas." Your mug will be a message of praise throughout the Christmas season.**
3. The children can use pencils to sketch designs on their mugs. Encourage them to include joyful messages, such as "Sing Noel!" or "Rejoice!" Stars, music notes, dots, dashes and repeated patterns are good design choices.
4. Have the children paint over their pencil designs with heat-setting paints. They should use different brushes for each color. Cotton swabs and toothpicks work well for painting small details.
5. Let the children clean their hands and the paintbrushes with oil-based thinner and paper towels.
6. Allow the mugs to dry for 24 hours.
7. Follow the manufacturer's instructions to heat-set the paints. The typical directions are to place the mugs on a cookie sheet and bake for 35 minutes in a 300°F oven.
8. Have the children make gift tags for their Noel Coffee Mugs. When the mugs have cooled, let the children attach gift tags.

# Rock Trivet

✳ ✳ ✳ ✳ ✳ ✳ ✳ ✳ ✳ ✳ AGES 3-12

**Bible Reference:** Jesus is our Rock / *Matthew 7:24-27*

 ## Overview

This trivet made from ceramic tile is a good reminder to build our lives on Jesus Christ.

 ## Helpers: 1

one for every 3-4 children

 ## What You Need

❄ 6" square cork tiles (found at hardware and craft stores)
❄ 6" square plain ceramic tiles
❄ assorted small or broken ceramic tile pieces
❄ jumbo craft sticks
❄ spray paint           ❄ craft glue
❄ rulers                ❄ newspapers
❄ pre-mixed tile grout  ❄ pencils
❄ smocks (men's long-sleeved shirts work well)
❄ Holiday Heart Gift Tag, page 201
❄ Rock Trivet Gift Tag, page 205

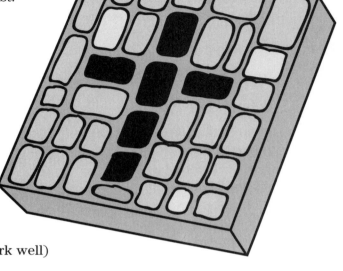

 ## Preparation

Spread newspapers on your work surface. Paint jumbo craft sticks with spray paint. You will need four pre-painted craft sticks and a set of gift tags for each trivet. Cover the children's work area with newspapers.

 ## What to Do

1. Have the children wear smocks for this activity. Give each child a 6" cork tile and a 6" ceramic tile. Have each child use an unpainted craft stick to spread glue over one side of a cork tile, then show how to align the ceramic tile on top of the cork and press it down to create a trivet base.

2. Give each child four pre-painted craft sticks. Let each child apply glue to one side of each stick, center the sticks along the trivet's sides and press to attach them. Allow the glue to dry.

3. Have the children use pencils and rulers to sketch 6" squares on the newspaper work surface for arranging ceramic tile pieces in patterns. Remind the children to leave small spaces (⅛") in between the tile pieces.

4. Show how to use an unpainted craft stick to scoop tile grout onto the prepared trivet base. The children can spread the grout evenly across the tiles.

5. Tell the children to transfer the tile pieces from their pre-arranged patterns onto the grouted trivet bases. Allow the grout to dry.

6. As the children work, say, **Tile and grout start as crushed rock, or sand. They are strong and hard. You can set hot dishes on this trivet, and the trivet will protect the table. Jesus is our Rock. When we build our lives on Jesus, we have security and protection.**

7. Have the children make gift tags to attach to their Rock Trivets.

# Santa Stamps

 AGES 3-12

**Bible Reference:** Believers are marked with a seal / *Ephesians 1:13*

 Overview

The children will make sets of rubber stamps with Christmas symbols, and learn that God marks us with a special stamp: the Holy Spirit.

 Helpers: 1

one for every 3-4 children

 What You Need

❄ Santa Stamps patterns, page 238
❄ blank paper
❄ washable ink pads
❄ poster board
❄ craft foam           ❄ scissors
❄ 1" wooden blocks     ❄ paper plates
❄ sandpaper            ❄ craft glue
❄ spray paint          ❄ nylon netting
❄ pencil               ❄ ribbon
❄ Holiday Heart Gift Tag, page 201
❄ Santa Stamps Gift Tag, page 206

 Preparation

Use sandpaper to sand the wooden blocks. Paint the blocks with spray paint. Allow the blocks to dry. Make templates of the Santa Stamps patterns. Make a sample set of Santa Stamps for the children to try out. Copy a set of gift tags for each child.

## What to Do

1. Let the children experiment with your sample set of stamps, using ink pads and blank paper, so they can choose which designs they want to make.
2. Give each child a paper plate on which to work.
3. Let older children trace and cut out stamp designs from craft foam. Or they might want to create their own original designs. Younger children will need help tracing and cutting out designs.
4. The children should glue the foam stamps to the blocks. Have them attach one design on each side of the block. Or, they could attach just one design per block and leave the remaining sides free for gripping. Allow the blocks to dry.
5. As the children work, ask, **What kinds of things do you like to decorate with stamp designs?** Allow the children to respond. Say, **God likes to stamp His favorite design on people! The Bible says that when we believe in Jesus, God marks us with a special seal: the Holy Spirit.**
6. Let the children tie netting and ribbon around their Santa Stamps, and make gift tags to attach to them.

# Shining Light Votive Holder

❄❄❄❄❄❄❄❄❄❄ AGES 7-12

**Bible Reference:** Let your light shine / *Matthew 5:14-16*

 ## Overview

The children will decorate votive holders to represent the beauty of Christ's light.

 ## Helpers: 1

one for every 3-4 children

 ## What You Need

* ❄ glass votive holders
* ❄ tissue paper, various colors
* ❄ disposable paintbrushes
* ❄ decoupage medium
* ❄ scissors ❄ old newspapers
* ❄ ruler ❄ votive candles
* ❄ glitter ❄ nylon netting
* ❄ paper plates ❄ ribbon
* ❄ smocks (men's old long-sleeved shirts work well)
* ❄ Holiday Heart Gift Tag, page 201
* ❄ Shining Light Votive Holders Gift Tag, page 206

 ## Preparation

Cut tissue paper into ½" squares. Spread newspaper on the work surface. Copy one set of gift tag patterns for each child. Just before the children begin to work, pour small puddles of decoupage medium onto paper plates. Two or three children can work from one plate.

 ## What to Do

1. Have the children wear smocks for this activity. Give each child a votive holder and a paintbrush. Demonstrate how to use the brushes to spread thin coats of the decoupage medium over a small area of the votive holders. The children should attach tissue squares over the medium, smoothing with their fingertips. Squares can overlap.

2. Let the children continue to work until the holders are covered with tissue.

3. On a separate paper plate, mix together small amounts of decoupage medium and glitter. Have the children use this mixture to apply final coatings to their votive holders.

4. As the children are working, say, **Each votive holder is beautiful, yet they are all different. Jesus said something similar about us. He said that we are the light of the world. Jesus' light shines through each of us, just like candlelight will shine through each of these votive holders.**

5. Allow the votive holders to dry. Place a votive candle in each holder.

6. Let the children tie netting and ribbon around their Shining Light Votive Holders, and make gift tags to attach to them.

# Shoelace Elves

**Bible Reference:** Jesus calls the disciples / *Matthew 4:18-22*

 ## Overview

The children will make Santa's elf decorations that attach to shoelaces, and learn that Jesus had helpers, too: the disciples.

 ## Helpers: 1

one for every 3-4 children

 ## What You Need

❄ Shoelace Elves pattern, page 239
❄ poster board
❄ pink, green and light brown craft foam
❄ children's shoelaces
❄ 15 mm movable plastic eyes
❄ 13 mm jingle bells
❄ 10 mm red pompons
❄ red rickrack scraps
❄ ½"-wide red satin ribbon
❄ craft glue
❄ scissors
❄ hole punch
❄ ruler
❄ pencil
❄ Holiday Heart Gift Tag, page 201
❄ Shoelace Elves Gift Tag, page 206

 ## Preparation

Make templates of the Shoelace Elves patterns. Trace and cut elf faces from pink craft foam, elf hats from green craft foam and elf ears from light brown craft foam. Be sure to cut shoelace openings on the elf faces where shown. Cut individual arcs from rickrack to create elves' mouths. Cut red ribbon lengths 1" longer than shoelaces. You will use the extra length to tie knots on the ribbons' ends. Trace and cut out the shoe pattern from poster board. Use a hole punch to make the shoelace eyelets on the shoes. The children will lace their Shoelace Elves onto these poster board shoes to present them as gifts. (You do not need poster board shoes if the children plan to keep and wear their Shoelace Elves themselves.) You will need two faces, two hats, four ears, two mouths, two ribbon lengths, two poster board shoes and one set of gift tags for each pair of Shoelace Elves.

 ## What to Do

1. Distribute the elf faces, hats and ears. Show how to attach the hats and ears to the faces with craft glue.

2. The children can decorate the elf hats with red pompons along the bottom edges of the hats and at the hat tips.

*continued on next page...*

3. Point out where the children can attach movable plastic eyes and rickrack mouths to their elf faces.

4. Help each child thread a jingle bell onto red ribbon, centering the bell halfway down the ribbon length.

5. Have the children weave the shoelaces, then the ribbons, through the shoelace openings on the elves' faces. (The jingle bell becomes the elf's nose.)

6. Demonstrate how to lace a Shoelace Elf onto a poster board shoe, positioning the elf on the front of the shoe and weaving the shoelace and ribbon together through the shoelace eyelets. Help the children "tie" the shoes and knot the ribbon ends to prevent fraying.

7. As the children are working, say, **Elves are Santa's helpers. Jesus had helpers, too. They were called His "disciples."**

8. Have the children make gift tags to attach to their Shoelace Elves. Say, **We can be Jesus' helpers by loving Him, obeying Him, serving Him and loving others.**

# Silver and Gold Sachet

 AGES 3-12

**Bible Reference:** God's law is precious / *Psalm 119:72*

 ## Overview

The children will make sachets from soap, sequins and fabric, and learn that the Bible is more precious than silver or gold.

 ## Helpers: 1

one for every 3-4 children

 ## What You Need

* perfumed bar soap
* scissors
* measuring spoons
* fabric glue
* spring-type clothespins
* sequins, silver and gold (mixed)
* nylon netting, silver or gold
* woven sheer fabric, silver or gold
* ½"-wide silver ribbon and gold lamé ribbon
* Holiday Heart Gift Tag, page 201
* Silver and Gold Sachets Tag, page 206

* wax paper
* pinking shears
* bowls
* ruler or tape measure

 ## Preparation

Use pinking shears to cut the fabric into 9" squares. Use scissors to cut the netting into 9" squares. Cut ribbons into 15" lengths. You will need one fabric square, one nylon netting square, one length silver ribbon, one length gold ribbon and one set of tags for each sachet.

## What to Do

1. Let the children work over wax paper. Give each child a fabric square. Have the children use fabric glue and sequins to decorate their squares. Allow the glue to dry.
2. Give each child a bar of soap. Let the children unwrap the bars and discard the paper.
3. Have the children place their decorated fabric squares on the work surface, wrong side up. Show how to center the soap at one end of the square, hold the fabric to the bar, and flip over the bar until it is covered with fabric, as if rolling together into a tube.
4. Help the children glue the edges of the overlapped fabric into place. Allow the glue to dry.
5. Give each child a netting square. Have the children place the squares flat on the work surface. Help the children gently lift the fabric sachet bar "tubes" and place them in the centers of the netting squares. They should overlap the netting around the fabric bar tubes, creating second layers. Point out that the fabric and sequins appear through the netting.
6. Distribute clothespins. Show how to pinch the fabric at both ends of the soap bars and secure with clothespins. Each child should tie a silver ribbon bow on one end of his or her sachet and a gold ribbon bow on the other, trimming the ends as desired. The children can remove the clothespins after tying the bows.
7. As you are working, say, **Silver and gold are called "precious metals" because they are very costly. But the Bible is more precious than thousands of pieces of silver and gold. The Bible is God's Word.**
8. Have the children make gift tags to attach to their Silver and Gold Sachets.

# Snowflake Fleece Scarf

 AGES 7-12

**Bible Reference:** Put on love / *Colossians 3:12-14*

 ## Overview

The children will make winter scarves from polar fleece as reminders of what we should also put on to stay close to God.

 ## Helpers: 1

one for every 3-4 children

 ## What You Need

❅ polar fleece, 60" wide
❅ snowflake patterns, page 236
❅ white felt
❅ poster board
❅ yardstick
❅ ruler
❅ scissors
❅ fabric glue
❅ safety pins
❅ Holiday Heart Gift Tag, page 201
❅ Snowflake Fleece Scarf Gift Tag, page 207

 ## Preparation

Measure and cut 9" widths of polar fleece. You will need one 9" x 60" piece of fleece for each scarf. Make templates of the snowflake patterns. On white felt, trace and cut out six snowflakes for each scarf that a younger child will make. Older children can trace and cut their own snowflakes. Provide one set of gift tags for each child.

## What to Do

1. Give each child a pre-cut piece of fleece. The children should use scissors to fringe both ends of their fleece with ½"-wide and 6" deep cuts.
2. Demonstrate how to curl the fringe: grasp one piece at a time, twist until it is completely coiled, pull it away from the scarf to stretch the fabric, and let go. As it is released, the fringe curls into a spiral. The children can continue twisting and stretching each piece until all of their fringes are curled.
3. Older children can use white felt and patterns to cut out snowflakes.
4. Show the children how to arrange snowflakes on the scarves and attach them with fabric glue.
5. Ask, **Why do we wear scarves in the winter?** Allow the children to respond. Say, **Yes, we put on scarves to keep warm. In the same way, the Bible says we should put on forgiveness, compassion, patience, kindness and love. They help us keep close to the warmth of God.**
6. Allow the scarves to dry.
7. Have the children make gift cards and use safety pins to attach them to the scarves.

# Spicy Scented Coasters

 AGES 3-12

**Bible Reference:** We are the aroma of Christ / *2 Corinthians 2:15*

 ## Overview

These spice-scented coasters are a reminder that we are the aroma of Christ.

 ## Helpers: 1

one for every 3-4 children

 ## What You Need

- ❄ Spicy Scented Coaster patterns, page 240
- ❄ poster board
- ❄ Christmas fabric
- ❄ ground cinnamon, nutmeg, cloves and allspice
- ❄ muslin
- ❄ ⅛"-wide satin ribbon
- ❄ measuring spoons
- ❄ pinking shears
- ❄ fabric glue
- ❄ safety pins
- ❄ felt
- ❄ pencils
- ❄ bowls
- ❄ scissors
- ❄ rulers
- ❄ Holiday Heart Gift Tag, page 201
- ❄ Spicy Scented Coasters Gift Tag, page 207

 ## Preparation

Make templates of the Spicy Scented Coaster patterns using poster board. Trace the coaster pattern onto Christmas fabric and cut it out with pinking shears. Trace the lining pouch square pattern onto muslin and cut it out with pinking shears. Trace the lining pouch square pattern from felt and cut it out with scissors. Trace and cut out the heart patterns from felt. Cut 10" lengths of satin ribbon. You will need two squares of Christmas fabric, two muslin lining pouch squares, one felt square, one set of hearts, one length of satin ribbon and one set of gift tags for each coaster.

## What to Do

1. Have the children mix the spices. In a bowl, they should measure 2 tablespoons of ground cinnamon with two teaspoons each of nutmeg, ground cloves and allspice. They should mix the spices thoroughly.

2. Give each child two squares of muslin lining pouch. Have each child lay one square on a work surface. Help each child measure 1 tablespoon of mixed spices and pour it carefully in the center of his or her muslin square. Say, **The three wise men brought baby Jesus special gifts: gold, frankincense and myrrh. Frankincense and myrrh were expensive spices in Bible times. They were used as perfumes and in oils.**

3. Show how to squeeze a bead of fabric glue around the edges of the muslin square. Each

*continued on next page...*

child should then place his or her second muslin square on top of the first, gently tapping down the edges to create a pouch of spices. Allow the pouches to dry.

4. Tell each child to place one square of Christmas fabric face down on the work surface. Help each child center the felt square on top of the Christmas fabric, then layer a muslin spice pouch on top of the felt.

5. Have the children squeeze beads of fabric glue around the edges of the Christmas fabric squares. Help them place their second Christmas fabric squares on top, gently tapping down the edges to secure the coasters. Say, **The spices in this coaster have a wonderful smell. In the same way, the Bible says that we can be "God's aroma." What do you think that means?** Allow the children to respond. Say, **Yes, we are God's aroma in the world when we show His love and kindness to others. That kind of fragrance is especially noticeable!**

6. The children should position the felt hearts on top of their coasters and glue the hearts into place.

7. Help the children tie satin ribbons into bows and trim the ends. Show how to glue bows on top of the felt hearts.

8. The children can repeat steps 1-7 to make additional coasters.

9. Let each child tie a ribbon around his or her coaster set, and make a gift tag to attach with a safety pin.

# Games

# Build a Stable Relay

 AGES 3-12

**Bible Reference:** Jesus was born in a stable / *Luke 2:7*

 ## Overview

Jesus was born in the humblest of surroundings – a stable! In this relay race, the children will learn how buildings were constructed in Bible times.

## Helpers: 2

one person to give instructions, referee the race and award prizes

one person to restack the blocks

 ## What You Need

❄ brown paper grocery bags
❄ newspapers
❄ masking tape or chalk
❄ beach towels
❄ prizes

 ## Preparation

To make a "mud brick block," fill a brown paper grocery sack with 5 to 6 loosely crushed pages of newspaper. Insert the filled sack, top side down, into a second, empty grocery sack – creating a block. Make 32 blocks (16 for each team). Use masking tape or chalk to create two parallel lanes – each 24" x 12-16 feet – leading to the "construction zone." Mark a starting line at one end of the lanes and a finish line at the other end. Place the pile of mud brick blocks and beach towels at the starting line.

## What to Do

1. Divide the children into two teams. Have them line up behind the starting line.

2. Say, **In Bible times, many buildings were constructed of stones or mud bricks. It took hard work to build a house. When Mary and Joseph arrived in Bethlehem, the town was so crowded that there was no place for them to stay. They ended up spending the night in a stable with the animals. Let's see which team can build a stable first using these "mud bricks."**

3. At your signal, the first child in each line should select a brick, carry it down the lane and place it in the construction zone. When that child returns to the starting line, the second child can take a turn.

4. Play should continue until each team has constructed a U-shaped "mud brick" stable, and placed a beach towel on top for the roof.

5. Every participant should receive a prize.

# The Call from King Herod

❄*❄*❄*❄*❄*❄* AGES 3-12

**Bible Reference:** King Herod summons the Wise Men / *Matthew 2:7-8*

 ## Overview

This beanbag toss game shows how King Herod sent for the wise men so he could find out more about Jesus, the baby King.

 ## Helpers: 2

one person to explain the rules and hand out beanbags

one person to retrieve beanbags and award prizes

 ## What You Need

❄ 3 Gingerbread Magi Men (page 68) or 3 beanbags
❄ large cardboard box
❄ brown grocery-size paper sacks or brown mailing paper
❄ clear or brown packaging tape
❄ compass          ❄ pencil
❄ glitter          ❄ craft glue
❄ black marker     ❄ ruler
❄ scissors         ❄ masking tape
❄ prizes

 ## Preparation

Tape the bottom of the box to secure it. Open one top flap. Use the compass and pencil to draw a semi-circle on the flap, creating a palace "dome." Cut away the excess. Fold the remaining top flaps into the box and tape them. Use tape and paper sacks or mailing paper to cover the outside of the box, including the dome. Decorate the front by using the ruler and pencil to outline a crossbar and front columns. Go over the pencil with black marker. Fill in the columns, crossbar and dome with craft glue and glitter. Set King Herod's Palace in your play area. With masking tape, mark two tossing lines: one closer to the palace for younger children, and one farther away for older children. Note: Wipe up stray glitter immediately so that it does not pose a safety risk to very young children.

 ## What to Do

1. Have each child stand behind a line. Say, **King Herod was a Roman leader in Israel. He heard that wise men were in Jerusalem. They knew where to find the new baby King, Jesus. So Herod sent for the three wise men. They went to see him.**
2. Explain that the object of the game is to toss all three wise men (or beanbags) into Herod's palace for a "visit." Let the player toss the wise men into the palace.
3. Once the wise men have "visited" the palace, say, **The wise men discovered that King Herod wanted to harm Jesus. They decided they would not tell Herod where to find Jesus. God used the wise men to protect baby Jesus. God protects you, too.**
4. Each child should receive a prize.

# Camels and Donkeys

**Bible Reference:** Traveling to Bethlehem / *Luke 2:4-5*

## Overview

Mary and Joseph likely traveled from Nazareth to Bethlehem on a donkey. When the wise men went to find Jesus, they probably traveled on camels. In this race, the children will "ride" balloon donkeys and camels to Bethlehem.

## Helpers: 1

one person to give instructions, referee the race and hand out prizes

## What You Need

❋ 10" brown and 10" gray (or black) helium-quality balloons
❋ masking tape
❋ prizes

## Preparation

With masking tape, create two parallel "roads" on the floor, each about 24" wide and 12-16 feet long. Mark a start line at one end of the roads and a finish line at the other. Inflate several balloons of each color. Place the brown balloons at the beginning of one lane and the gray (or black) balloons at the other one.

## What to Do

1. Divide the children into two teams. Have them line up behind the starting lines.
2. Hold up a gray (or black) balloon. Say, **Mary and Joseph traveled to Bethlehem on a donkey.**
3. Hold up a brown balloon. Say, **The wise men traveled to Bethlehem on camels.**
4. Say, **We are going to ride camels and donkeys to Bethlehem, too.** Explain that the brown balloons represent camels and the gray (or black) balloons represent donkeys.
5. At your signal, the first child in each line should straddle a balloon between the legs or knees, and jump down the "road" to Bethlehem. If the balloon falls during the trip, the child should pick it up and "climb back on" to finish the journey.
6. As each child crosses the finish line, the next child in that line can begin the trip.
7. The team whose players finish first wins.
8. When everyone has had a turn, say, **We've traveled to Bethlehem to worship baby Jesus!**
9. Each participant should receive a prize.

# The Census in Bethlehem

❄ ✳ ❄ ✳ ❄ ✳ ❄ ✳ ❄ ✳ ❄ AGES 3-6

**Bible Reference:** Joseph and Mary register in Bethlehem / *Luke 2:1-5*

 Overview

This variation of "Duck, Duck, Goose" shows how Joseph and Mary traveled to Bethlehem to be counted in the Roman census.

 Helpers: 1

one person to give instructions and award prizes

 What You Need

❄ prizes

 Preparation

None.

 What to Do

1. Have the children form a line. Say, **At the time Jesus was to be born, the Roman rulers decided to take a census in Israel. What is a census?** Allow the children to respond. Say, **A census is a counting of all the people.**

2. Say, **The rulers said that everyone had to go to his or her hometown to register. Joseph's family was from Bethlehem. So Joseph and Mary had to travel from where they were living, in Nazareth, to Bethlehem.**

3. Have the children walk in a line around the room, into the hallway, into other rooms if possible, and back to the original starting point.

4. Have the children sit on the floor or sit on chairs in a circle. Say, **Once Joseph and Mary arrived in Bethlehem, they had to register and be counted.** Explain that each child will have a turn as a "census counter."

5. Have the first census counter stand and walk around the outside of the circle, tapping each player on the head and counting aloud while walking. The census counter can continue counting heads as long as desired. When the census counter taps the last person he or she wants to count in the census, the census counter should say, "People in Bethlehem!"

6. The last person tapped by the counter should stand up and race the counter around the circle. Whichever player reaches the vacated slot first is "safe." The unseated player becomes the census counter.

7. Continue play until everyone has had the chance to be the census counter.

8. Each child should receive a prize.

# Christmas Story Match-up

❄*❄*❄*❄*❄*❄* AGES 3-12

**Bible Reference:** The Christmas Story / *Luke 2:1-35*

  **Overview**

The children will match cards to review important symbols in the Christmas story.

**Helpers: 1**

one person to set out the cards, explain the symbols and award prizes

 **What You Need**

❄ Christmas Match-up patterns, page 241
❄ crayons or markers
❄ clear, self-stick plastic
❄ scissors
❄ prizes

 **Preparation**

Reproduce two copies of the Christmas Match-up Lotto patterns for each game set you want to make. Color the symbols on the cards. Be sure to color each pair of symbols identically so they match each other. Cover both pages with clear, self-stick plastic for durability. Cut out the cards.

 **What to Do**

1. Place the cards face down on the table or floor and mix them up. For younger children, use only two or three pairs. Older children will enjoy the challenge of more cards to match.

2. Have the children take turns turning cards over two at a time. Encourage them to remember where each symbol is located in the arrangement

3. When a child makes a match, ask, **Why is this symbol important in the Christmas story?** If the children have difficulty answering, help them with the following review:

   • 1, 2, 3…: Mary and Joseph traveled to Bethlehem to be counted in the Roman census. (Luke 2:1-5)
   • Manger: Baby Jesus was placed in a manger after He was born. (Luke 2:7)
   • Angel: Angels announced Jesus' birth to the shepherds. (Luke 2:9-14)
   • Shepherd's crook: Shepherds were the baby Jesus' first visitors. (Luke 2:8, 15-20)
   • Star: The star led the wise men to the house in Bethlehem. (Matthew 2:9-10)
   • Gifts: The wise men brought gifts of gold, frankincense and myrrh. (Matthew 2:11)
   • Temple: Mary and Joseph presented Jesus at the temple for dedication. (Luke 2:22)
   • Pair of doves: Mary and Joseph offered doves as a sacrifice on behalf of Jesus, their firstborn. (Luke 2:24)

4. When the children have uncovered and matched all the cards, award prizes.

114

# Escape to Egypt

AGES 3-12

**Bible Reference:** Joseph, Mary and Jesus flee from Judea / *Matthew 2:13-15*

 ## Overview

This obstacle course is a reminder that Jesus and His family fled to Egypt for safety during the reign of King Herod.

 ## Helpers: 2

one person to give instructions, monitor the players and award the prizes

one person to time the players

 ## What You Need

* assorted tables, chairs, large boxes, Hula Hoops® and pillows
* flashlight
* masking tape or chalk
* stopwatch or watch with second hand
* prizes

 ## Preparation

Set up an obstacle course in the play area so the children can crawl under tables, climb over chairs, wriggle through large boxes, hop through consecutive hoops and jump on pillows. Close the curtains or blinds in the play area to make it as dark as possible. Mark a start line and a finish line with masking tape or chalk.

## What to Do

1. Have the children line up behind the start line. Say, **King Herod was looking for baby Jesus and wanted to hurt Him. So God told Joseph to leave Bethlehem with Mary and baby Jesus and take them to Egypt instead. The family left Bethlehem at night so they wouldn't be noticed.**

2. Give the first player a flashlight. Explain that the object of the game is to escape from Bethlehem in Judea (the starting line) and travel to Egypt (the finish line) as quickly as possible.

3. At your signal, the first player should move through the obstacles. If desired, use a stopwatch or watch with a second hand to calculate the player's time.

4. When the player crosses the finish line, say, **You have escaped safely to Egypt! Let's give thanks to God.**

5. Repeat steps 2, 3 and 4 for each player.

6. Each player should receive a prize.

# Fields of Snow

✳ ✳ ✳ ✳ ✳ ✳ ✳ AGES 3-12

**Bible Reference:** The fields are white for harvest / *John 4:34-35*

 ## Overview

The children will cover a "field" with newspaper "snow" to represent hearts that are ready to harvest for God's kingdom.

 ## Helpers: 2

one person to give instructions and award prizes

one person to keep the newspapers replenished and clear the "fields"

 ## What You Need

✳ newspapers
✳ masking tape
✳ snow shovels
✳ large cross
✳ prizes

 ## Preparation

With masking tape, mark off the boundaries for two identical "fields," each approximately 6-8 feet square. With masking tape, mark two tossing lines for each field: one for older children, about 3-5 feet from the field, and one for younger children, immediately adjacent to the field. Set a stack of newspapers next to each field's tossing lines. Set up the cross in an area away from the fields that is still easily accessible.

 ## What to Do

1. Divide the children into two teams. Explain that the object of the game is for each team to cover their "field" with snow.
2. Demonstrate how each player should stand at the tossing line, wad up a sheet of newspaper and toss it onto his or her team's field.
3. Have the children line up at the tossing lines. At your signal, the first player on each team should begin the "snowstorm" to cover the field.
4. Let play continue, with team members taking turns, until one team covers their field with snow and is declared a winner.
5. Say, **These fields are completely white. Let's gather up the snow!** Distribute snow shovels. Have the children help remove the snow to the area where the cross is situated.
6. Say, **Jesus said that the people we know are like fields that are white for harvest. We can gather up the people we know and introduce them to Christ.**
7. Each participant receives a prize.

116

# Grow a Beard

✳ ✳ ✳ ✳ ✳ ✳ ✳ ✳ ✳ AGES 3-12

**Bible Reference:** John the Baptist was a Nazirite / *Num. 6:1-8 & Luke 1:13-16*

 ## Overview

The children will learn about Nazirite vows when they apply shaving cream beards to their faces.

 ## Helpers: 1

one person to give instructions, monitor shaving cream application and award prizes

 ## What You Need

※ shaving cream
※ paper cups
※ small mirrors
※ smocks (men's long-sleeved shirts work well)
※ plastic mat or tarp
※ plastic tablecloth
※ paper towels or wipes
※ prizes
※ table and chairs

 ## Preparation

Spread a plastic mat or tarp in the play area, underneath the table and chairs. Cover the table with a plastic tablecloth. Set out mirrors. Just before play begins, fill paper cups with shaving cream. Note: This game will be messy! Keep paper towels handy.

 ## What to Do

1. Have the children wear smocks for this activity.
2. Invite the children to be seated at the table. Provide each child with a hand mirror.
3. Ask, **Why do men wear beards?** Allow the children to respond. Say, **In Bible times, certain people called "Nazirites" made a special pledge to be different for God. As part of that pledge, they never ate grapes or raisins, and they never shaved their beards or cut their hair. You are going to grow beards, just like the Nazirites did. Your beard will be white.**
4. Give each child a cup of shaving cream. On your signal, the children should use their fingertips to dip into the shaving cream and spread it on their faces. Remind the children that they are to apply the cream to *their own faces only*. Let the children check their beards in the mirrors.
5. The first child to cover his or her face with shaving cream wins.
6. Say, **John the Baptist had a beard, too. He was a Nazirite. John the Baptist had a special job to do for God. He prepared the Israelites for Jesus.**
7. Help the children wipe off their faces and hands with paper towels.
8. Each participant should receive a prize.

# The Land Where Jesus Was Born

 AGES 3-12

**Bible Reference:** The Christmas story's setting / *Matthew 2:13-15, Luke 2:4, 22*

 ## Overview

This variation of Twister® will help the children learn geography that is significant in the Christmas story.

 ## Helpers: 1

one person to give instructions and award prizes

 ## What You Need

❋ large plastic mat, tarp or shower curtain liner
❋ red, blue, yellow and green construction paper
❋ clear, self-stick plastic
❋ self-stick plastic squares
❋ The Land Where Jesus Was Born cards, pages 242-243
❋ compass
❋ pencil
❋ ruler
❋ scissors
❋ prizes

 ## Preparation

Use a compass, pencil and scissors to draw and cut out 7" circles from red, blue, yellow and green construction paper. You will need six circles of each color. Cover the construction paper circles with clear, adhesive-backed plastic for durability. Measure and cut out 24 10" squares of clear, self-stick plastic to attach circles to the mat. Arrange the circles in four rows of six on the mat, with 2-3" of space between circles. Make sure there is one row of each color. Attach the circles to the mat with adhesive-backed plastic squares. Spread out the mat in the play area. Duplicate The Land Where Jesus Was Born Cards. Cover the sheets of cards with clear, self-stick plastic. Cut apart the cards, shuffle them and place them in a stack near the play area.

## What to Do

1. Gather 1 to 4 players near the mat. Say, **There are some important places to know as we celebrate Jesus' birth.**
   • Nazareth: Jesus' parents, Mary and Joseph, lived in the town of Nazareth.
   • Bethlehem: Mary and Joseph traveled from Nazareth to Bethlehem for the Roman census. Jesus was born in Bethlehem.

*continued on next page...*

- Jerusalem: When Jesus was eight days old, His parents took Him to the temple in Jerusalem to dedicate Him to the Lord.
- Egypt: Joseph, Mary and Jesus escaped to Egypt because their lives were in danger.

2. Explain that the children will play a game to review these important places. Each location is represented by a color on the game mat.
   **Red:** Nazareth
   **Blue:** Bethlehem
   **Yellow:** Jerusalem
   **Green:** Egypt

3. Have the children assemble around the edges of the mat.

4. Select a card and read it aloud. After you ask the significance of the location on the card, the children should follow the card's instructions. For example, when the card reads, "Right foot Bethlehem (blue)," ask, **Why is Bethlehem significant in the Christmas story?** After the children respond, each child should place his or her right foot on a blue circle.

5. When all circles of one color are full, the children may double up their hands and feet on individual circles.

6. When a child is unable to balance solely on his or her hands and feet, he or she is "out."

7. The last child remaining is the winner.

8. Each child should receive a prize.

# Race Down the Chimney

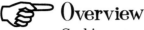 AGES 7-12

**Bible Reference:** God's Omnipresence / *Psalm 139:7-10*

 ## Overview

God is everywhere. In this game, the children will learn that no matter where they go, God is near.

 ## Helpers: 2

one person at the top of the "chimney" to help the children arrange the mice

one person below the "chimney" to determine the winner and hand out prizes

 ## What You Need

* Walnut Mice, page 82
* marbles
* plywood or sturdy cardboard (at least 3' x 3')
* books or blocks
* masking tape
* prizes

 ## Preparation

Make Walnut Mice as instructed on page 82. Or you could have the children make their own mice to use in the race. Set up a "chimney" in your play area: elevate one end of a sheet of plywood or sturdy cardboard with books or blocks. Determine a satisfactory incline angle so that it is not too steep (so the mice don't speed out of control) or too level (so the mice don't roll too slowly). With masking tape, mark a start line along the top of the chimney. Note: For safety purposes, do not let very young children handle marbles.

## What to Do

1. Assemble 2 to 4 children across the chimney start line. Make sure the children have their Walnut Mice, and give each one a marble. Show how to place the marble inside the walnut shell so the mouse can "run."
2. Say, **Mice are living in the chimney. On Christmas Eve, they hear noises on the roof. Suddenly, they realize that Santa is coming down the chimney. What do you think the mice will do?** Allow the children to respond. **Yes, the mice are going to get out of Santa's way as quickly as they can! On the count of three, let go of your mice so that they can race down the chimney. One-two-three!** Have children release the mice down the incline.
3. The mouse that travels the farthest wins the race.
4. Say, **The mice were afraid. They ran away. But we never have to be afraid of God or run away from Him. He promises to be with us and help us wherever we are.**
5. Each participant should receive a prize.

# Santa's Belly

❋ ❋ ❋ ❋ ❋ ❋ ❋ ❋ ❋ AGES 3-12

**Bible Reference:** Overflowing love / *1 Thessalonians 3:12*

 **Overview**

The children will stuff balloons in a sweatshirt to demonstrate a heart overflowing with love.

 **Helpers: 2**

one person to give instructions and use the stopwatch

one person to replenish balloon supplies, count stuffed balloons and award prizes for each team

 **What You Need**

❋ large or extra-large adult sweatshirts, red
❋ balloons
❋ large plastic trash bags
❋ stopwatch or watch with second hand
❋ prizes

 **Preparation**

Inflate the balloons and place them in large trash bags in the play area.

 **What to Do**

1. Divide the children into teams of 2 to 5 (mixed ages can be on the same teams).
2. Have one person on each team volunteer to be "Santa." Each Santa should put on a red sweatshirt.
3. Say, **Santa wears a red jacket. When he leaves the North Pole on Christmas Eve, his jacket is loose. But along the way, he eats the snacks and treats that children leave out for him. By the end of the night, Santa's belly is ready to burst out of his jacket.** Explain that the object of the game is for each team to fill their Santa's belly with balloons.
4. On your signal, team members should take balloons, one at a time, out of a trash bag and stuff them into their Santa's sweatshirt.
5. Allow play to continue for 60 seconds.
6. At your signal, play should stop. Helpers can count the balloons in each Santa's belly. The team with the highest number wins.
7. Say, **Santa has eaten lots of cookies and milk. His belly is filled until it is bursting. It reminds me of God working in our lives. God wants to fill us with an overflowing love for Him and for each other.**
8. Each participant should receive a prize.

# Sheep on the Hillside

❄❄❄❄❄❄❄❄ AGES 3-12

**Bible Reference:** Shepherds watch their flocks / *Luke 2:8*

 ## Overview

The children will use candy cane "shepherd staffs" to guide their flocks to safety.

 ## Helpers: 1

one person to give instructions, distribute staffs and flocks of sheep, and award prizes

 ## What You Need

❄ large, individually-wrapped candy canes (about 6" long)
❄ cotton balls
❄ masking tape
❄ prizes

 ## Preparation

Use masking tape to mark two parallel lanes in your play area, each about 18" wide and 8 feet long. Use masking tape to mark a start line and a finish line for each lane.

 ## What to Do

1. Give each child a candy cane. Say, **Shepherds use staffs to guide their sheep to water and pastures. Sometimes sheep stray from the group. Then they are in danger of being attacked by other animals or injured on the rocky hillsides. The shepherd rescues a sheep by hooking it with the curved end of the staff and pulling it to safety.**

2. Explain that the object of the game is for each "shepherd" to guide his or her "sheep" from the danger of the start line to the safety of the finish line. Shepherds will use their candy canes as staffs.

3. Divide the children into two teams. Have the teams line up behind the start line.

4. Place a pile of cotton balls at each team's start line (same number of balls in each). Tell the children that these are the "flocks." Say, **You are going to watch your flocks of sheep and keep them safe, just like the shepherds on the hillside of Bethlehem did on the night Jesus was born.**

5. At your signal, the first participant in each line should use his or her staff to free a "sheep" from the pile, then prod the sheep down the lane to the finish line. Remind the shepherds that they cannot use their fingers to touch the sheep – only their staffs – and that they should gently nudge their sheep to the finish line, not throw or push them.

6. The first shepherd to get his or her sheep to safety wins the round.

7. Teams can continue play until all sheep are safely with the rest of the flock at the finish line.

8. Each participant should receive a prize.

# Snow Shoveling in the Dark

❋ ❋ ❋ ❋ ❋ ❋ ❋ ❋ ❋ AGES 3-12

**Bible Reference:** Walk in the light / *John 12:35-36*

 ## Overview

The children will shovel popcorn "snow" while blindfolded to show how much better it is to walk with Jesus, the Light, than to live in darkness.

 ## Helpers: 2

one person to give instructions, blindfold players, operate stopwatch and distribute prizes

one person to replenish popcorn "snow"

 ## What You Need

- ❋ popped popcorn
- ❋ large plastic bowls
- ❋ children's shovels or large serving spoons
- ❋ blindfolds
- ❋ stopwatch or watch with second hand
- ❋ table and chairs
- ❋ plastic mat or tarp
- ❋ prizes

 ## Preparation

Spread the plastic mat in your play area underneath the table and chairs. Set up the shoveling station with two large bowls and a shovel or large spoon. Fill one bowl with popcorn. If you plan to have the children race against each other, set up stations for two teams.

 ## What to Do

1. If the children will race against each other, divide them into two teams.
2. Have the first participants sit at snow shoveling stations. Explain that there was a big snowstorm during the day. It is dark now, but it is important to clear the snow so families can get out the next day.
3. Blindfold the players. (Note: If younger children are afraid to be blindfolded, have them play with their eyes closed.)
4. At your signal, each player should use a shovel or spoon to transfer the popcorn "snow" from the first bowl into the second. Remind the players that they cannot pour the snow. They should only move it by using a "shovel." Allow play to continue for 60 seconds.
5. The player who has moved the most snow from the first bowl into the second is the winner.
6. Ask, **Why is it difficult to shovel snow in the dark?** Allow the children to respond. Say, **When we walk in the darkness, we don't know where we are going. Jesus is the Light. When we walk with Him, we become children of light. The road of life becomes clearer.**
7. Each participant should receive a prize.

# Stocking Stuffers

 AGES 3-6

**Bible Reference:** The filling of the Holy Spirit / *Luke 1:15, 41, 67*

 ## Overview

The children will race to stuff stockings, then learn how people can be "stuffed" with the Holy Spirit.

 ## Helpers: 2

one person to give instructions, referee the race and award prizes

one person to keep the stocking stuffer pieces organized

 ## What You Need

❄ men's white athletic crew socks
❄ permanent markers
❄ fabric paints
❄ empty potato chip cans or tennis ball cans
❄ craft glue
❄ tissue paper
❄ assorted blocks or small toys
❄ heavy twine
❄ thumbtacks or packaging tape
❄ brown lunch-size paper sacks
❄ stopwatch or watch with a second hand
❄ prizes

## Preparation

You will need two "stockings" if you plan to have the children race against each other. One stocking will be enough if the children simply race against the clock. Wipe out the inside of a potato chip or tennis ball can. Allow can to dry. Use permanent markers to decorate the sock with stripes. Outline the stripes with beads of fabric paint. Allow sock to dry. Stuff the toe, foot and heel of the sock with crumpled tissue paper. Insert the can into the sock, aligning the top edges of the can and sock. Fold back the top edge of the sock to reveal the top rim of the can. Apply a bead of craft glue along the outer rim of the can. Fold the sock back and smooth it in place. Allow the glue to dry. To see how much your stocking will hold, select assorted blocks or small toys and stuff them into the can. Remove the blocks or toys from your stocking and count them, making note of how many pieces the children must stuff in order to complete the game. If you plan to have children race against each other, make sure that there are an equal number of toys for each team. Wrap a two-foot length of heavy twine around each stocking. Tie to secure. Use thumbtacks or packaging tape to hang the stockings on a bulletin board or wall at children's height. Place the toys for each stocking in a brown lunch-size paper sack. Set the sacks on the floor underneath the stockings.

*continued on next page...*

**What to Do**

1. Position a child in front of each stocking.
2. Point to the brown bag of toys and say, **Let's pretend you are Santa's helper. Here is Santa's sack of toys. When I say, "Go!," take out one toy at a time and stuff it in the stocking. Keep filling the stocking as quickly and quietly as you can. Remember, you don't want to wake up anybody who might be asleep while the stockings are being filled!**
3. At your signal, the children can begin filling the stockings. You can keep track of their time with a stopwatch or a watch with a second hand, if desired.
4. When the children are finished, say, **That stocking was empty, but now it is filled with treats and fun things! It reminds me of how God fills us with the Holy Spirit. That's what happened to a very special family in the Bible. Zechariah and Elizabeth were faithful to God. God sent them a baby whom they named John. Zechariah, Elizabeth and John were filled with the Holy Spirit – just like your stockings are completely filled. They served God in special ways. God used John to announce Jesus' birth to the Hebrew people.**
5. Each child should receive a prize. Say, **God can fill us with the Holy Spirit and use us when we are faithful to Him.**

# Snacks

# Angel Clouds

❄ ❄ ❄ ❄ ❄ ❄ ❄ ❄ ❄ AGES 3-12

**Bible Reference:** Angels are God's messengers / *Mark 13:26-27*

 ## Overview

The children will make a dip for fruit and cake chunks that allows for a discussion of God's angels.

 ## Helpers: 1

one for every 5-6 children

 ## What You Need

❋ 8-ounce container of non-dairy whipped topping
❋ 6-ounce container strawberry or raspberry yogurt
❋ red food coloring
❋ spoon
❋ mixing bowl
❋ angel food cake
❋ fresh fruit
❋ toothpicks
❋ knife

 ## Preparation

Cut the angel food cake and fresh fruit into chunks.

 ## What to Do

1. If the children are helping, instruct them to wash their hands before preparing food.
2. To make the Angel Clouds, combine the whipped topping and yogurt in a mixing bowl.
3. Add 5-6 drops red food coloring to the yogurt dip. Mix thoroughly.
4. Say, **Angels do special work for God. Do you know what it is?** Allow children to respond. Say, **Angels are God's messengers. The angel Gabriel told Mary she was going to have a baby – the Messiah. Angels announced Jesus' birth to the shepherds in Bethlehem. And when Jesus comes back to earth on the clouds, angels will gather people from all over the world to go to heaven.**
5. Let the children spear angel food cake and fresh fruit chunks with toothpicks and dip them into the Angel Clouds.

# Animals in the Stable

 AGES 3-12

**Bible Reference:** Jesus was born in a stable / *Luke 2:7*

 Overview

The children will make animal-shaped crackers from
flour tortillas and discuss the animals in the stable
where Jesus was born.

 Helpers: 1

one for every 5-6 children

 What You Need

❄ flour tortillas
❄ animal-shaped cookie cutters
  (sheep, donkeys, cows or goats)
❄ vegetable spray
❄ granulated sugar
❄ cinnamon
❄ cutting board or plate
❄ cookie sheets
❄ measuring cup and spoons
❄ bowl
❄ salt or sugar shaker
❄ spoons
❄ spatula

 Preparation

In a bowl, mix together ½ cup of granulated sugar and 1 teaspoon of cinnamon. Pour the
mixture into a salt or sugar shaker.

What to Do

1. If the children are helping, instruct them to wash their hands before preparing food.

2. To make tortillas easier to manipulate, just before cutting heat them in a microwave
   oven for 30 seconds on high setting. Lay the warmed tortillas on a cutting board or plate.

3. Let the children use cookie cutters to cut out animal shapes from the tortillas.

4. Have pairs of children share cookie sheets in order to keep track of their animals. Place
   the animals on a cookie sheet. Coat the animals with vegetable spray.

5. Sprinkle cinnamon sugar onto the animals.

6. Bake the animals for 8-10 minutes at 350° F.

7. Remove the animals from the tray with a spatula.

8. Say, **When Mary and Joseph arrived in Bethlehem, there was no place for them
   to spend the night except at a stable. Cows, goats, sheep and donkeys lived in
   stables in Bible times.**

# Bright Morning Stars

 AGES 3-12

**Bible Reference:** Jesus is the Bright Morning Star / *Revelation 22:16*

 Overview

The children will make a snack out of orange slices and citrus topping that is a reminder of Jesus, the Bright Morning Star.

 Helpers: 1

one for every 5-6 children

 What You Need

* oranges
* non-dairy whipped topping
* lemon flavoring
* yellow food coloring
* yellow sugar crystals
* knife
* plate
* bowl
* spoon
* measuring cup
* measuring spoons
* paper plates

 Preparation

Cut the oranges around the middle into circular slices. Leave the rind intact. Cut the orange slices into pie-shaped segments. You will need five orange segments for each snack.

## What to Do

1. If the children are helping, instruct them to wash their hands before preparing food.
2. On a paper plate, arrange five orange segments in the shape of a star, with points facing out and rind facing in.
3. To make the citrus topping, measure ½ cup of non-dairy whipped topping, ½ teaspoon of lemon flavoring and 4-5 drops of yellow food coloring in a bowl. Fold the ingredients together until well blended.
4. With a spoon, place a dollop of citrus topping in the center pentagon of each orange star. Sprinkle yellow sugar crystals on the citrus topping.
5. Say, **There are many names for Jesus in the Bible. Can you say some of them?** Allow the children to respond. Say, **Yes, Jesus is called "Savior," "Son of God," "Messiah" and "Teacher." He is also called "The Bright Morning Star."**
6. Let the children dip the orange segments into the citrus topping.

# Cheesy Popcorn

 AGES 3-12

**Bible Reference:** Jesus and the disciples eat grains / *Luke 6:1*

 ## Overview

The children will make a variation of a party favorite – popcorn – and learn that raw kernels of grain were a common food in Bible times.

 ## Helpers: 1

one for every 5-6 children

 ## What You Need

❋ popcorn kernels
❋ hot air popper
❋ cheese sauce seasoning packet (from boxed macaroni and cheese)
❋ vegetable oil cooking spray
❋ large bowl
❋ large spoon
❋ measuring cup and spoons

 ## Preparation

None.

 ## What to Do

1. If the children are helping, instruct them to wash their hands before preparing food.
2. Set up the hot air popcorn popper and a bowl for popped corn.
3. Measure ½ cup of popcorn kernels and add them to the popper. Say, **People in Bible times ate fresh grains. Jesus and His disciples picked kernels and ate them in the fields.** Turn on the popper and let the corn pop.
4. Measure 8 cups of fresh popcorn. Spray the warm popcorn with vegetable oil cooking spray.
5. Measure 4 tablespoons of cheese sauce seasoning. Sprinkle the seasoning over the warm, sprayed popcorn, stirring to coat.
6. The children can snack on Cheesy Popcorn or pack it into Confetti Treat Tins (page 87) for gifts.

# Cornflake Wreaths

❄ ❄ ❄ ❄ ❄ ❄ AGES 3-12

**Bible Reference:** Jesus never changes / *Hebrews 13:8*

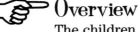 Overview

The children will make a cereal treat in the shape of a festive Christmas wreath.

Helpers: 1

one for every 3-4 children

 What You Need

- ❄ cornflake cereal
- ❄ 40 large marshmallows
- ❄ 3 tablespoons butter or margarine
- ❄ green food coloring
- ❄ candy cinnamon dots
- ❄ microwave-safe bowl
- ❄ wax paper            ❄ vegetable spray
- ❄ large mixing bowl   ❄ measuring cup
- ❄ wooden spoon        ❄ tray or plate
- ❄ 13" x 9" pan         ❄ drinking glass or biscuit cutter

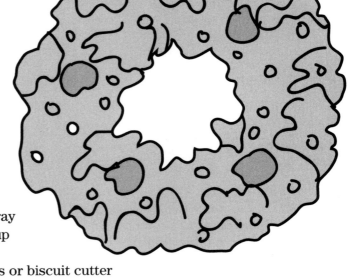

 Preparation

None.

 What to Do

1. If the children are helping, instruct them to wash their hands before preparing food.
2. Place butter or margarine in microwave-safe bowl. Cover it with wax paper. Microwave on high for 30 seconds and stir. Repeat until butter or margarine is melted.
3. Toss the marshmallows in the melted butter or margarine to coat. Microwave them on high for 30 seconds and stir. Repeat until marshmallows are melted and smooth.
4. Add 10-12 drops of green food coloring to the marshmallow mixture. Stir thoroughly.
5. In a large mixing bowl, measure 8 cups of cornflakes. Pour the marshmallow mixture into the cornflakes and mix until all the flakes are coated.
6. Spray a 13" x 9" pan with vegetable spray. Press the cornflake mixture into pan.
7. Use a drinking glass or biscuit cutter to cut out the cornflake "wreaths." (Dip the glass in cold water for a cleaner cut.) Place the wreaths on a tray or plate.
8. Use the handle end of a wooden spoon to press a hole in the center of each wreath.
9. Say, **At Christmastime, many people decorate their homes with evergreen wreaths. Wreaths are round, like circles. How does that remind us of Jesus?** Allow the children to respond. Say, **Yes, a circle is never-ending. In the same way, Jesus' love for us is never-ending. He will never change. The Bible says, "Jesus Christ is the same yesterday and today and forever."**
10. The children can decorate their cornflake wreaths with cinnamon candies.
11. Store extra Cornflake Wreaths in an airtight container.

# Cozy Christmas Cocoa

 AGES 3-12

**Bible Reference:** God's Word is sweet / *Psalm 119:103*

 ## Overview
The children will follow this easy recipe to make a cold weather favorite – hot cocoa – and learn that the Bible is also "sweet" to taste.

 ## Helpers: 1
one for every 5-6 children

 ## What You Need
- ❄ dry milk
- ❄ powdered sugar
- ❄ non-dairy creamer
- ❄ cocoa powder
- ❄ malted milk mix
  (such as Ovaltine®)
- ❄ salt
- ❄ measuring cups
- ❄ measuring spoons
- ❄ resealable plastic sandwich bags
- ❄ hot water
- ❄ mugs
- ❄ teaspoons
- ❄ miniature marshmallows

 ## Preparation
None.

## What to Do
1. If the children are helping, instruct them to wash their hands before preparing food.
2. Measure ½ cup each of dry milk and powdered sugar and pour them into a plastic bag.
3. Measure 1 tablespoon each of non-dairy creamer, cocoa powder and malted milk mix and pour them into the plastic bag.
4. Add a dash of salt to the plastic bag.
5. Seal the plastic bag. Shake the ingredients to mix thoroughly. This recipe makes 3-4 servings.
6. Measure 3 heaping teaspoons of cocoa mix into a mug. Add 5-6 ounces of hot water. Stir. Top with miniature marshmallows.
7. Say, **Cocoa is a warm, sweet drink. The Bible is like cocoa. Why?** Allow the children to respond. Say, **Psalm 119:103 says, "How sweet are your words to my taste!"**

# Crunchy Shepherd's Staffs

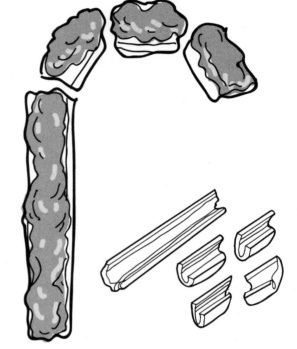

AGES 3-12

**Bible Reference:** The Lord is my Shepherd / *Psalm 23*

 ## Overview

Stuffed celery sticks in the shape of shepherd's staffs will remind the children that Jesus is the Good Shepherd.

 ## Helpers: 1

one for every 5-6 children

 ## What You Need

❄ celery stalks
❄ peanut butter or cream cheese
❄ paring knife
❄ cutting board or plate
❄ plastic knives
❄ paper plates

 ## Preparation

Wash the celery. Cut the celery stalks into 4-5" pieces to make staff shafts. Cut 1" pieces of celery to make curved staff ends. You will need one 4-5" shaft and four 1" pieces for every Crunchy Shepherd's Staff. Cut off one end of each piece of celery at a 45° angle (see diagram above right).

 ## What to Do

1. If the children are helping, instruct them to wash their hands before preparing food.
2. Use a plastic knife to fill the celery pieces with peanut butter or cream cheese.
3. Place a staff "shaft" on a paper plate.
4. To make the staff's hook, arrange four 1" pieces of stuffed celery in a curve by matching the straight end of one piece with the pre-cut angled end of the previous piece, beginning with the staff shaft.
5. As the children eat their Crunchy Shepherd's Staffs, say, **Shepherds used their staffs to keep the sheep close by and out of danger. Jesus is our Shepherd. He wants us to be safe and to stay close to Him.**

# Donkey Biscuits

❄❄❄❄❄❄❄❄ AGES 3-12

**Bible Reference:** Mary and Joseph travel to Bethlehem / *Luke 2:4-5*

 **Overview**

Tradition holds that Mary rode on a donkey when she and Joseph traveled from Nazareth to Bethlehem to register for the census. The children can assemble this sandwich that resembles a donkey.

 **Helpers: 1**

one for every 5-6 children

 **What You Need**

❄ canned biscuits
❄ hot dogs
❄ baby carrots
❄ leafed celery stalks
❄ cookie sheet
❄ knife
❄ spatula
❄ plate
❄ paper plates

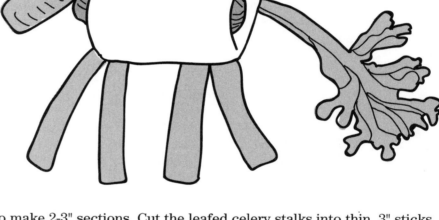

 **Preparation**

Cut the hot dogs in half to make 2-3" sections. Cut the leafed celery stalks into thin, 3" sticks, keeping the leaves intact. These sticks will become the donkeys' tails. Cut the remaining celery into thin, 2½" sticks. These sticks will become the donkeys' legs. Slice carrots in 1" triangles, which will become the donkeys' ears. Reserve some whole baby carrots for the donkeys' heads. You will need one hot dog half, one head, one tail, four legs and two ears for each Donkey Biscuit.

 **What to Do**

1. If the children are helping, instruct them to wash their hands before preparing food.
2. Open the canned biscuits. Stretch each biscuit until it is an oval, 5" long x 1" wide. Wrap each biscuit around a hot dog half. Press the biscuit ends together to seal.
3. Place the "donkey bodies" (wrapped biscuits) on a cookie sheet, seams down.
4. Bake the wrapped biscuits according to the package directions, typically 10 minutes at 400° F.
5. Allow the donkey bodies to cool for two minutes on the tray. Use a spatula to remove the donkeys from the tray and place them on individual paper plates.
6. Position a whole baby carrot at one hot dog end. This will be the donkey's head.
7. Add two triangle carrots (ears), a celery leaf stick (tail) and four celery sticks (legs).
8. Say, **Mary was pregnant with baby Jesus when she and Joseph traveled to Bethlehem to register for the census. She rode a donkey because it was a long, long trip.**

# John the Baptist's Snack Mix

❄ ❄ ❄ ❄ ❄ ❄ ❄ ❄ ❄ **AGES 3-12**

**Bible Reference:** John the Baptist preaches repentance / *Matthew 3:1-6*

 **Overview**

The children will prepare a snack mix that teaches about John the Baptist.

 **Helpers: 1**

one for every 5-6 children

 **What You Need**

- ❄ pretzel sticks
- ❄ shredded, sweetened coconut
- ❄ cinnamon
- ❄ whole, pitted dates
- ❄ honey-roasted peanuts
- ❄ table knife
- ❄ plate or cutting board
- ❄ small mixing bowl
- ❄ large mixing bowl   ❄ measuring spoons
- ❄ measuring cup   ❄ wooden spoon

 **Preparation**

Cut whole, pitted dates into length-wise strips.

 **What to Do**

1. If the children are helping, instruct them to wash their hands before preparing food.
2. Say, **God sent John to tell people that Jesus was coming. John preached to the people who lived in a desert area called "Judea." What is the desert like?** Allow the children to respond. Say, **Yes, the desert is dry and hot. John needed a walking stick for his travels. Let's pretend these pretzel sticks are walking sticks.**
3. Help the children break pretzel sticks into 1" or 1½" pieces. Have them measure one cup of broken pretzel sticks and pour into the large mixing bowl. Say, **These pretzel sticks represent John's time in the desert.**
4. Help the children measure one cup of shredded coconut and one teaspoon of cinnamon into a small bowl, and blend together. Say, **John wore unusual clothing. It was made of camel's hair, which is brown and coarse. This cinnamon coconut looks like camel's hair.** Have the children pour the coconut mixture into a large bowl.
5. Help the children measure one cup of pre-cut date strips and pour them into the large bowl. Say, **John wore a leather belt. These dates are leathery like his belt.**
6. Say, **John knew God would provide food for him. And God did!** Help the children measure one cup of honey-roasted peanuts and pour them into the large bowl. Say, **John ate locusts and wild honey. These peanuts look like the locusts. They are covered with honey.**
7. Have the children take turns mixing the snacks in the bowl. As they eat the snack, say, **When the people heard John preach, they felt sorry for their sins. They wanted to know about Jesus and be ready when He came. John baptized them. That is why people called him "John the Baptist."**

# The King's Cupcakes

❄ ❄ ❄ ❄ ❄ ❄ ❄ ❄ ❄ ❄ AGES 3-12

**Bible Reference:** Rejoice in the King / *Psalm 149:2*

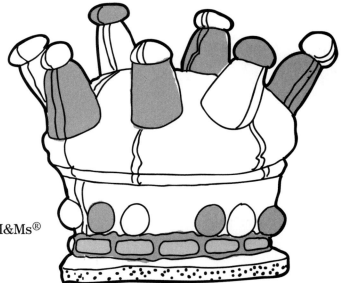

## Overview

The children will make cupcakes that resemble kings' crowns.

## Helpers: 1

one for every 3-4 children

## What You Need

❄ cupcakes
❄ graham crackers
❄ yellow frosting
❄ yellow sugar crystals
❄ gumdrops
❄ miniature chocolate candies, such as M&Ms®
❄ small breath mints, such as Tic-Tacs®
❄ knife
❄ paper plates
❄ birthday candles and matches (optional)

## Preparation

Remove the paper liners from the cupcakes. Break the graham crackers into halves.

## What to Do

1. If the children are helping, instruct them to wash their hands before preparing food.
2. Say, **Christmas is Jesus' birthday. Let's make cupcakes to celebrate.**
3. Place a graham cracker on a paper plate. With a knife, spread frosting on the bottom of cupcakes. Attach a cupcake to the graham cracker. Say, **Jesus is the King of kings. We will decorate His cupcakes to look like crowns.**
4. Frost the cupcake. Add extra frosting around the top edge to accommodate decorations.
5. Sprinkle yellow sugar crystals on the crown to make it "shimmer like gold."
6. To prepare "crown jewels," apply a small dab of frosting to gumdrop ends. Attach miniature chocolate candies to the gumdrop ends.
7. Arrange the crown jewel gumdrops around the top of the cupcake.
8. Use small breath mints to make a border around the bottom of the crown where it attaches to its graham cracker "presentation tray."
9. Decorate the rest of the crown with miniature chocolate candy "jewels."
10. Refrigerate The King's Cupcakes to allow the frosting and decorations to set.
11. Remove the cupcakes from the refrigerator. Place a birthday candle in the center of each one.
12. Say, **Let's sing "Happy Birthday" to Jesus!**
13. Light the candles. Lead the group in singing.
14. Let the children blow out the candles and enjoy The King's Cupcakes.

# Mangers with Straw

❋ ❋ ❋ ❋ ❋ ❋ ❋ ❋ ❋ ❋ **AGES 3-12**

**Bible Reference:** Shepherds find Jesus in a manger / *Luke 2:16*

 ## Overview
The children will make snacks that represent mangers filled with straw.

 ## Helpers: 1
one for every 3-4 children

 ## What You Need
❋ white chocolate chips
❋ butterscotch or peanut butter chips
❋ chow mein noodles
❋ graham or Club® crackers
❋ microwave-safe bowl
❋ measuring cup
❋ spoon
❋ measuring spoon
❋ wax paper
❋ cookie sheet

 ## Preparation
None.

 ## What to Do
1.  If the children are helping, instruct them to wash their hands before preparing food.
2.  Line the cookie sheet with wax paper. Say, **Baby Jesus was born in a stable. There was no crib for Him, but there was a manger filled with straw for the animals.** Set out 12-15 Club® crackers or graham cracker quarters on the sheet to represent mangers.
3.  Say, **We're going to fill these mangers with straw.** Measure 1 cup white chocolate chips and 1 cup butterscotch or peanut butter chips into the microwave-safe bowl.
4.  Microwave the baking chips on high for 30 seconds. Stir. Repeat this procedure several times until the chips are melted and smooth.
5.  Measure 1½ cups of chow mein noodles. Add them to the chip mixture. Gently stir the "straw" until all the noodles are covered.
6.  Drop tablespoonfuls of chow mein "straw" onto the top of each cracker "manger." Use the spoon to create a small indentation in the middle of the straw. Say, **When the shepherds came to Bethlehem, they found baby Jesus lying in a manger.**
7.  Place the cookie sheet in the freezer for five minutes to allow the mangers to set.
8.  If desired, prepare Swaddled Dates (page 145) and place them in the Mangers with Straw.

# Shepherd's Dip

❄ ❄ ❄ ❄ ❄ ❄ ❄ ❄ **AGES 3-12**

**Bible Reference:** Shepherds keep watch over their sheep / *Luke 2:8*

 ## Overview

The ingredients in this snack dip represent elements of a shepherd's trade.

 ## Helpers: 1

one for every 5-6 children

 ## What You Need

❄ 8-ounce package of cream cheese, softened
❄ marshmallow cream
❄ brown sugar
❄ toffee bits
❄ pretzels
❄ bowl
❄ measuring cup
❄ measuring spoons
❄ fork

 ## Preparation

Transform pretzels into shepherd's staffs: grasp pretzels with your thumbs in the center, crack in half, and break off the inside pieces.

 ## What to Do

1. If the children are helping, instruct them to wash their hands before preparing food.
2. Unwrap the cream cheese and place it in the bowl.
3. Measure 3 tablespoons of marshmallow cream and add it to the cream cheese. Say, **Shepherds watch over sheep. Most sheep have white wool – white, like these ingredients. Shepherds brush sheep's wool to keep it from getting tangled. We'll use this fork to pretend we are brushing the sheep's wool.** Use the fork to combine the two ingredients together.
4. Measure ⅓ cup of packed brown sugar. Say, **The hills in Bible lands have sandy, rocky soil.** Add the brown sugar to the cream cheese mixture and use the fork to combine thoroughly.
5. Measure ½ cup of toffee bits. Say, **Shepherds must watch their sheep carefully. Sheep can get caught in rocky crags, ravines and crevices. Let's pour these "rocks" into our mixture.** Use the fork to combine the toffee bits with the other ingredients.
6. Say, **Shepherds use staffs to guide sheep along mountain paths and to retrieve sheep when they are in danger.** Let the children use the pretzel "staffs" to eat the Shepherd's Dip.
7. Refrigerate leftover Shepherd's Dip.

# Snowman Sticks

**Bible Reference:** God created man / *Genesis 1:27*

 **Overview**

The children will make snacks that resemble snowmen, and learn that God made us in His own image.

 **Helpers: 1**

one for every 5-6 children

 **What You Need**

❄ large marshmallows
❄ 10" wooden skewers
❄ jumbo gumdrops
❄ gumdrop jelly rings
❄ fruit leather
❄ miniature chocolate candies
❄ white frosting
❄ knife
❄ plastic knives

 **Preparation**

Cut fruit leather into ½"-wide strips to make snowmen's scarves. Cut orange gumdrops into ½" triangles to make snowmen's noses.

 **What to Do**

1. If the children are helping, instruct them to wash their hands before preparing food.
2. Thread three marshmallows onto a wooden skewer to create each snowman's head and body.
3. Make snowmen's top hats: with white frosting "glue" attach jumbo gumdrops to gumdrop jelly rings.
4. Spread additional frosting onto the bottom of each jelly ring "hat." Thread the hats onto the skewers, spearing through to the jumbo gumdrops. The frosting will secure the hats to the snowmen's marshmallow "heads."
5. Wrap fruit leather strips around the marshmallows to make the snowmen's scarves.
6. Use frosting to attach chocolate candies and orange gumdrop triangles to the snowmen, creating eyes, noses and buttons.
7. Say, **It's fun to build snowmen during the winter. The Bible says that God enjoyed making us, too. He created man in His own image.**
8. Refrigerate extra Snowman Sticks.

# Spicy Hot Cider

❄ ❄ ❄ ❄ ❄ ❄ ❄ ❄ ❄ ❄ **Ages 3-12**

**Bible Reference:** Jesus quenches our thirst / *John 7:37*

 **Overview**

This warm fruit drink, with juices and spices, contains
a good lesson on how Jesus works in our lives.

 **Helpers: 1**

one for every 5-6 children

 **What You Need**

❄ apple juice or cider
❄ orange juice
❄ lemon juice
❄ oranges
❄ brown sugar
❄ cinnamon sticks
❄ whole cloves
❄ allspice
❄ ground cloves
❄ nutmeg
❄ saucepan
❄ measuring cup and spoons
❄ kitchen knife
❄ cutting board or plate
❄ wooden spoon
❄ ladle

 **Preparation**

Cut an orange into ½"-thick round slices. Cut the large circles into semi-circles.

 **What to Do**

1. If the children are helping, instruct them to wash their hands before preparing food.
2. Measure one quart (4 cups) of apple juice or cider, ½ cup of orange juice and 2 tablespoons of lemon juice into a saucepan. Stir.
3. Add ½ cup of packed brown sugar, ½ teaspoon of allspice and ½ teaspoon each of ground cloves and nutmeg to the cider mixture. Stir.
4. Press two to three whole cloves into each orange slice. Add the orange-clove slices and two cinnamon sticks to the cider.
5. Set the saucepan on medium-low heat. Allow the cider to warm slowly, stirring occasionally.
6. Say, **This Spicy Hot Cider shows how Jesus works in our lives. Like the cider, Jesus satisfies our thirst. The cider warms us on the inside, just as the Holy Spirit warms our hearts. The spicy scent fills the room, just as Jesus wants us to spread His love to others. The cider is made from fruit, just as Jesus wants our faith in Him to produce fruit for His kingdom.**
7. Ladle the Spicy Hot Cider into cups or mugs.

# Sprinkle Spoons

❄ ❄ ❄ ❄ ❄ ❄ ❄ ❄ ❄ ❄ **AGES 3-12**

**Bible Reference:** Add virtue to your faith / *2 Peter 1:5-8*

 ## Overview

These chocolate-covered spoons add extra flavor to cocoa, just as adding certain behaviors adds "flavor" to our faith.

 ## Helpers: 1

one for every 4-5 children

 ## What You Need

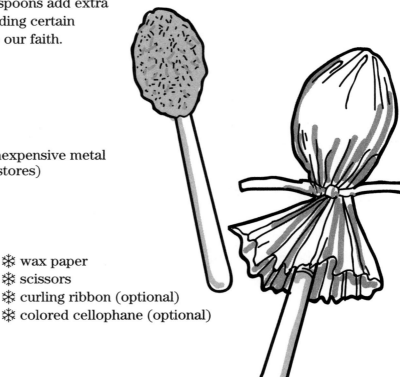

❄ teaspoons (purchase inexpensive metal teaspoons at discount stores)
❄ chocolate chips
❄ margarine or butter
❄ mixing spoon
❄ measuring cup
❄ microwave-safe bowl    ❄ wax paper
❄ chocolate decors    ❄ scissors
❄ bowl    ❄ curling ribbon (optional)
❄ cookie sheet    ❄ colored cellophane (optional)

 ## Preparation

None.

 ## What to Do

1. If the children are helping, instruct them to wash their hands before preparing food.
2. In a microwave-safe bowl, measure one cup of chocolate chips and two tablespoons of margarine or butter. Microwave on high for 30 seconds. Stir. Repeat this procedure until the chocolate is melted and smooth. One cup of chocolate chips coats about 8-12 teaspoons.
3. Pour the chocolate decors into a separate bowl. Spread wax paper on a cookie sheet.
4. Dip teaspoons one at a time into the melted chocolate. Lift out each spoon and let the excess chocolate drip off.
5. Roll the chocolate-covered spoon in chocolate decors, allowing the candies to cover the chocolate. Transfer the decorated spoon to a wax paper-covered tray.
6. When all of the teaspoons have been dipped and decorated, set them in the refrigerator to harden.
7. Have the children use their Sprinkle Spoons as they mix and drink servings of Cozy Christmas Cocoa (page 133).
8. Say, **These spoons add flavor to cocoa. We can add "flavor" to our faith, too. When we practice kindness, goodness and love, we grow closer to Jesus.** If the children plan to give Sprinkle Spoons as gifts, help them wrap each spoon with colored cellophane and tie with curling ribbon bows.

# Stained Glass Candies

❄❄❄❄❄❄❄❄❄ AGES 3-12

**Bible Reference:** The house of God / *Luke 2:22-28*

## Overview

The children will make candies that resemble colored glass, as in stained glass church windows.

## Helpers: 1

one for every 3-4 children

## What You Need

❄ colored hard candies
❄ metal cookie cutters
❄ rubber mallet
❄ freezer bags
❄ cookie sheets
❄ aluminum foil
❄ vegetable oil cooking spray
❄ paper towels

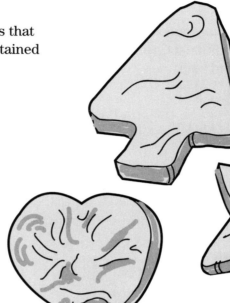

## Preparation

Spread aluminum foil on cookie sheets. Spray lightly with vegetable oil cooking spray. Spray see-through cookie cutters with vegetable spray. Line the cupped cutters with aluminum foil, being careful to press the foil into the corners and crannies of the cutter. Spray the lined cutters with vegetable spray and place them on cookie sheets. Set aside an extra cookie sheet to be used for crushing candies.

## What to Do

1. If the children are helping, instruct them to wash their hands before preparing food.
2. Say, **A church is called, "The House of the Lord." Let's name some of the things in our church that honor God.** Assist the children in listing architectural items such as the altar, communion rail, cross and stained glass windows. Say, **Stained glass windows are a beautiful feature in churches. Let's make candies that are like colored windows in the house of the Lord.**
3. Separate and unwrap candies of one color, place them in a freezer bag and set the sealed bag on the extra, uncovered cookie sheet. Use the rubber mallet to crush the candies.
4. Sprinkle the crushed candies in the cutters.
5. Bake the candies for 8-10 minutes at 350° F.
6. Let the candies cool. Break off pieces that have seeped through the cutter edges. Carefully peel away the foil. Blot any excess vegetable spray on paper towels.
7. As the children enjoy their Stained Glass Candies, say, **Mary and Joseph dedicated baby Jesus to God at the house of the Lord in Jerusalem. Their house for God was called a "temple," and it was very beautiful.**

# Sugarplums

 AGES 3-12

**Bible Reference:** Joseph has a dream / *Matthew 1:20-21*

 ## Overview

The children will make a modified version of sugarplums – a traditional Christmas delicacy – using dried fruit and nuts.

 ## Helpers: 1

one for every 3-4 children

 ## What You Need

- ❄ ½ cup chopped dates
- ❄ ½ cup chopped dried apricots
- ❄ ½ cup raisins
- ❄ ½ cup walnuts
- ❄ ½ cup almonds
- ❄ orange juice
- ❄ ½ cup miniature chocolate chips
- ❄ powdered sugar
- ❄ food processor
- ❄ measuring spoons
- ❄ wooden spoon
- ❄ tray or plate
- ❄ candy paper liners (optional)

 ## Preparation

None.

## What to Do

1. If the children are helping, instruct them to wash their hands before preparing food.
2. Place the dried fruit and nuts into a food processor with a steel blade. Pulse the ingredients until they are finely chopped.
3. Measure three tablespoons of orange juice into the fruit and nut mixture. Pulse until the mixture begins to stick together and pull away from the sides of the processor bowl.
4. Stir ½ cup of miniature chocolate chips into the mixture with a wooden spoon.
5. Form the fruit and nut mixture into 1" balls. Roll them in powdered sugar. Place the balls in candy paper liners, if desired.
6. Ask, **Is it difficult for you to go to sleep on Christmas Eve?** Allow the children to respond. Say, **You might have dreams about the surprises you'll find on Christmas morning. Years ago, snacks like these sugarplums were a favorite Christmas treat. Remember the poem called "'Twas the Night Before Christmas"? In it, we hear about children dreaming of sugarplums while they tried to go to sleep. God used a dream to tell Joseph that his wife, Mary, would have a baby who would be our Savior – Jesus!**
7. Refrigerate extra sugarplums.

# Swaddled Dates

 **AGES 3-12**

**Bible Reference:** Jesus was wrapped in swaddling cloths / *Luke 2:12*

 ## Overview

The children will make a variation of stuffed dates that represents baby Jesus draped in swaddling cloths.

 ## Helpers: 1

one for every 3-4 children

 ## What You Need

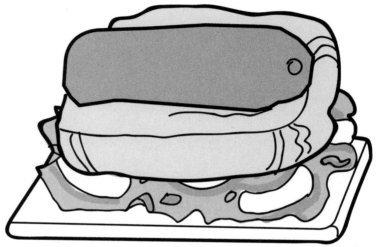

- ❉ whole, pitted dates
- ❉ large marshmallows
- ❉ powdered sugar
- ❉ knife
- ❉ kitchen scissors
- ❉ spoons
- ❉ bowl
- ❉ paper plates

 ## Preparation

Use a knife to cut open the pitted dates lengthwise, along one side only. With kitchen scissors, cut the large marshmallows lengthwise into sixths.

## What to Do

1. If the children are helping, instruct them to wash their hands before preparing food.
2. Work on paper plates. Place a marshmallow slice inside the pitted date. Squeeze the sides of the date together to secure the treat.
3. Pour the powdered sugar into a bowl. Roll the stuffed dates in the sugar with spoons, shake off the excess and set the Swaddled Dates on paper plates.
4. Say, **Today, newborn babies are wrapped in blankets. In Bible times, babies – including Jesus – had their arms and legs wrapped in "swaddling cloths."**
5. If desired, place the Swaddled Dates on Mangers With Straw (page 138).

# More Activities

# Caroling Fun

**Bible Reference:** Sing praises to God / *Psalm 47:6*

## Overview

Children and families will sing Christmas carols together and praise God for sending His Son.

## Helpers: varies

one person to prepare songbooks and candleholders

several people to chaperone carolers (if children)

## What You Need

❆ Caroling Songbooks, see below

❆ Caroling Candleholders, page 149

❆ flashlights

❆ your church's brochure and Advent schedule of events

❆ refreshments (see Snacks, pages 127-145)

## Preparation

Decide what kind of Caroling Activity is appropriate for your situation (see ideas on the following pages). Determine a date and time. Be sure to allow enough time at the beginning of your party so that participants can gather, practice singing the carols and make Caroling Candleholders, if desired. Estimate how many participants you will have. Prepare Caroling Songbooks, allowing at least one songbook for every two singers. If you elect to prepare Caroling Candleholders prior to the party instead of during the event, make one for each participant. Recruit a volunteer with a strong singing voice to lead the carols.

# Caroling Songbooks

## What You Need

❆ Caroling Songbook cover and lyrics, pages 244-252

❆ card stock

❆ stapler

❆ scissors

❆ ruler

*Christmas Caroling Songbook*

## What to Do

1. Reproduce the Caroling Songbook lyrics.

2. You can supplement the songbook with additional selections. Be sure that the carols

*continued on next page...*

you choose are familiar, easy to sing and communicate the message of Christ's birth. Also, be sure that the songs are in the public domain, or ask your music minister for help with copyright permissions.

3. Reproduce the Caroling Songbook covers on card stock.

4. Layer each set of carol sheets and songbook covers in a stack, ending with the cover. Staple along the songbook spines. (Be sure to check the lyric sheets before stapling to make sure they are arranged in numerical order.)

5. Fold each Caroling Songbook along its spine.

## Caroling Candleholders

### What You Need

❊ 2-liter soda bottles, washed and dried, labels removed
❊ 6-8" candle tapers
❊ black electrical tape
❊ kitchen knife
❊ scissors
❊ ruler or tape measure
❊ fire starter

### What to Do

1. Measure, mark and cut a line around the bottle's middle, 8" from the neck. Discard the bottle bottom.

2. Turn the bottle upside down and hold it by the neck. Slip the candle taper, wick first, up through the bottleneck and into the body of the pre-cut bottle. Leave the lower end of the candle taper hanging below the bottleneck. If the taper is too thick to insert into the bottleneck, trim its sides with a kitchen knife.

3. Use electrical tape to secure the candle to the bottleneck and wrap the exposed lower end of the taper.

4. Carolers can carry the candleholders by grasping the lower, taped portion of the candles extending from the bottlenecks, allowing the inverted bottles to catch dripping wax.

5. Have an adult light the candles with a fire starter. Extinguish the flames when the candles burn to 1" above the bottlenecks.

## Door-to-door Caroling

This traditional form of caroling is best suited for evenings. Participants walk from door to door, stopping at each home to sing carols and to wish the occupants a Merry Christmas.

### What to Do

1. Select an area or neighborhood in which to carol.

*continued on next page...*

2. If your destination is farther than walking distance from your church, recruit drivers to provide transportation.

3. Remind participants to dress appropriately for the weather.

4. Designate a meeting time at your church.

5. When the group gathers, distribute songbooks, candleholders and flashlights. Practice the carols as a group.

6. Give the song leader copies of your church's brochure and Advent schedule of events.

7. Have each caroler select a "buddy" to walk with and watch over.

8. Once you arrive at a caroling destination, have the participants assemble on the sidewalk, step or front porch outside the first home. Light the candles and extinguish the flashlights. If desired, ring the doorbell or knock on the door just as the group begins singing. Have the song leader lead the group in one or two carols, ending with "We Wish You a Merry Christmas."

9. When the group has finished, the song leader can give the house's occupants copies of church literature and invite them to join you for worship.

10. Continue caroling through the neighborhood.

11. Return to your church for refreshments.

## Indoor Caroling

Have your group carol door-to-door for the residents of a retirement home, nursing facility or apartment complex. This option works well both in the daytime and in the evening, and is especially good for younger children, who might be difficult to watch on dark streets.

 ### What to Do

1. Select a location at which to carol.

2. If your destination is a retirement home or nursing facility, contact the director in advance. Secure permission to visit, ask about special requirements and find out if candleholders are allowed.

3. If your destination is farther than walking distance from your church, recruit drivers to provide transportation.

4. Designate a meeting time at your church.

5. When the group gathers, distribute songbooks and candleholders. Practice singing the carols as a group.

6. Give song leader copies of your church's brochure and Advent schedule of events.

7. Have each caroler select a "buddy" to walk with and watch over.

8. Once you arrive at your destination, have the participants assemble outside a selected doorway. Light your candles. Have the song leader lead the group in one or two carols, ending with "We Wish You a Merry Christmas."

9. If it is appropriate, the song leader can give the listeners copies of your church's literature and invite them to join you for worship.

*continued on next page…*

10. Continue caroling through the building.

11. Return to your church for refreshments.

# Carol Sing

Bring family and friends together for an old-fashioned Carol Sing. This format does not require traveling to another location.

## What to Do

1. Encourage congregation members to invite family, friends and neighbors to the Carol Sing.

2. If desired, plan a meal, games, crafts or gift-making prior to the Sing.

3. Recruit the church's music director, organist or another accomplished keyboardist to provide keyboard accompaniment.

4. Recruit several volunteers to light candles at the start of the Sing. Give each volunteer a fire starter.

5. You might want to supplement the Caroling Songbooks with carols from your church's hymnbook.

6. Participants can gather in a large room, fellowship hall or church sanctuary.

7. Distribute candleholders. Have volunteers light each participant's candle.

8. Participants can request favorite carols from a songbook or hymnal.

9. At some point during the event, the song leader should invite Carol Sing visitors to return and join your congregation for worship.

10. Make sure each visitor receives a church brochure and an Advent schedule of events.

11. Conclude the Sing with an a cappella version of "Silent Night." Participants should exit the building quietly and extinguish candles once outside.

# The Christmas Story

❄*❄*❄*❄*❄*❄*❄*❄ ALL AGES

**Bible Reference:** The Christmas Story / *Matthew 2:1-12, Luke 2:1-20*

 ## Overview

Select from these various ways to present the Christmas story to children and families.

 ## Helpers: varies

varies according to chosen format

 ## What You Need

❄ varies according to chosen format

 ## Preparation

Decide how you and your team will present the Christmas story (see ideas on the following pages). If you choose the Christmas Card Magnet Scene, Crèche Drama, Finger Puppet Presentation or the Pageant With Narration and Carols, prepare the text from Scripture. Combine the accounts of the Christmas story from Luke 2:1-20 and Matthew 2:1-12. Type or copy the script so that it is easy to read. Make copies for participants. Prepare necessary props and costumes. Schedule rehearsals for those involved in the presentation.

## Christmas Card Magnet Scene

Children can take an active role in telling the story by moving the magnetic figures across a metal display surface. This is an excellent choice for classrooms or home.

 ## What to Do

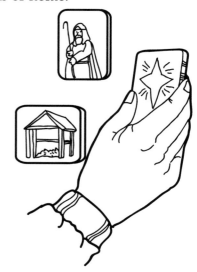

1.  Prepare Christmas Card Magnets (page 66). Make sure to select cards that include the key figures in the Christmas story: Mary, Joseph, baby Jesus, shepherds, sheep, angel, wise men, camels and star. You may also wish to make magnets that show the town of Bethlehem and the nearby hillsides.

2.  Find a metal surface on which to manipulate the figures, such as the side of a metal file cabinet or the front of a refrigerator. Check to see if the prepared magnets will attach to the surface.

3.  Recruit two presenters: one with a clear speaking voice to read the script, and one to manage the magnets.

4.  Have the presenters rehearse the story for clarity and pacing. Time the presentation to make certain that it is 10 minutes or less.

*continued on next page...*

5. Let the children sit in a semi-circle around the presenters.

6. Before the presentation begins, solicit volunteers to handle the magnet figures. Give each volunteer one figure. Cue him or her at the proper time in the story.

# Crèche Drama

This method works well with a small group of children, where participants can help manipulate the figures during the presentation.

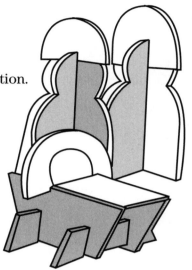

 ## What to Do

1. Prepare the Tabletop Crèche figures (page 61).

2. Recruit two presenters: one with a clear speaking voice to read the script, and one to manage the crèche.

3. Make sure there is a suitable table or flat surface for the crèche.

4. Have the presenters rehearse the story for clarity and pacing. Time the presentation to make certain that it is 10 minutes or less.

5. Arrange chairs so that everyone in the audience will be able to see the tabletop.

6. Before the presentation begins, solicit volunteers from the audience to handle the crèche figures. Give each volunteer one figure. Cue him or her at the proper time in the story.

# Finger Puppet Presentation

Use this option for simple storytelling to very young children. The informal atmosphere will allow youngsters to make comments and ask questions.

 ## What to Do

1. Make the finger Pocket Crèche Puppets (page 73).

2. Recruit several presenters: one with a clear speaking voice to read the script, and 2-4 additional helpers to portray the characters with finger puppets.

3. Have the presenters rehearse the story for clarity and pacing. Time the presentation to make certain that it is 10 minutes or less.

4. Invite audience members to sit in a semi-circle around the presenters.

# Pageant with Narration and Carols

While this choice requires extra planning, it can have significant impact. Familiar carols will impart deep meaning to the audience members when the music is intertwined with a live portrayal of the Christmas story. Also, a pageant is flexible. It is suitable for a large assembly but can be adapted for a small venue.

 ## What to Do

1. Recruit a presenter with a clear speaking voice to serve as narrator for the drama.

*continued on next page...*

Remind him or her to speak slowly and distinctly. If your presentation will be held in a large room or church sanctuary, make sure the narrator has a microphone.

2. Enlist your church's music director, accompanist or another skilled keyboardist to provide keyboard accompaniment for the carols.

3. Use your church's hymnal or songbook to select carols. Consider interspersing a carol at each important juncture in the story. Here are some suitable choices:

   **Prelude:** "Oh, Come, All Ye Faithful"

   **The Manger in Bethlehem:** "Away in a Manger" or "What Child is This?"

   **The Angels:** "Angels From the Realms of Glory," "Angels We Have Heard on High" or "It Came Upon the Midnight Clear"

   **The Shepherds:** "The First Noel" or "While Shepherds Watched Their Flocks"

   **The Wise Men:** "We Three Kings"

   **Personal Commitment:** "In the Bleak Midwinter" or "O Little Town of Bethlehem"

   **Celebration of Christ's Birth:** "Go Tell It on the Mountain," "Hark! the Herald Angels Sing," "I Heard the Bells on Christmas Day" or "Joy to the World"

   **Postlude and Exit Music:** "Silent Night"

4. Mark the place for each carol in the script. Make sure the narrator and the accompanist have copies of the script.

5. Recruit volunteers to enact the drama. Explain to the actors that they will not need to speak, but can merely pantomime along with the narration.

6. Assemble simple Bible-time costumes for the actors, such as sheets draped around the shoulders in earth-tones for Joseph and the shepherds, light blue for Mary, white for the angels and purple for the wise men. Make men's headpieces from dishtowels and headbands. Angels can wear tinsel halos. Make King's Crowns (page 70) for the wise men.

7. Assemble props, such as a doll wrapped in a blanket (baby Jesus), a wooden box (manger), lawn-sized plastic candy canes covered with brown packaging tape (shepherds' staffs) and foil-and-rhinestone wrapped containers (wise men's gifts).

*continued on next page...*

8. Rehearse the drama several times so the actors, narrator and accompanist feel comfortable with their roles.

9. Time the presentation to make sure that the narration portion does not exceed 10 minutes. Carols add more time.

## Story Book

Children love to hear stories and see pictures. This option works well for both large and small groups.

 ### What to Do

1. Choose a storybook with clear text and attractive illustrations. Consult your pastor, local Christian bookstore staff and public library personnel for suggestions.

2. Recruit a volunteer with a clear speaking voice to read the story. Remind the reader to speak slowly and distinctly. If your presentation will be held in a large room or church sanctuary, make sure the narrator has proper amplification. Encourage the reader to show the pictures on each page of the book to the audience after reading that page's text.

3. Arrange chairs around the reader or provide rugs and pillows for seating.

# Gingerbread Houses

✳ ✳ ✳ ✳ ✳ ✳ ✳ ✳ ✳ **AGES 3-12**

**Bible Reference:** God builds everything / *Hebrews 3:4*

 ## Overview

In this simplified version of a traditional favorite, the children will use graham crackers and icing to build houses laden with treats.

 ## Helpers: 1

one for every 2-3 children

 ## What You Need

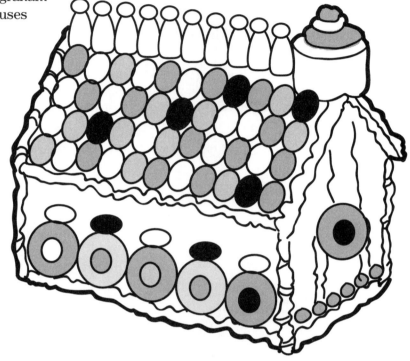

- ✳ empty, washed half-pint cartons (school milk cartons work well)
- ✳ sturdy paper plates
- ✳ bowls
- ✳ graham crackers
- ✳ kitchen knife
- ✳ meringue powder
- ✳ powdered sugar
- ✳ warm water
- ✳ bowl
- ✳ measuring cup and spoons
- ✳ spoon
- ✳ electric mixer
- ✳ resealable plastic sandwich bags
- ✳ plastic knives
- ✳ scissors
- ✳ assorted candies, cake and cookie decorations, colored sugar, miniature marshmallows, pretzels and cereals

## Preparation

Prepare the sides of the house to resemble a roofline: Lay a whole graham cracker flat on your work surface. Use the tip of a knife to score a straight cut beginning at the center top of the cracker and angling to the outside, halfway down. Score a similar cut on the opposite side of the cracker (see illustration at right). Lay the blade of the knife in one of the scored trenches and rock it back and forth to cut the cracker. Repeat the cutting process for the opposite side of the cracker. You will need two house sides for every gingerbread house. Prepare royal icing: Measure three tablespoons of meringue powder, four cups of powdered sugar and six tablespoons of warm water into a bowl. Use a mixer to beat the ingredients on high speed until the icing forms peaks, about 7-10 minutes. Spoon the icing into resealable plastic sandwich bags. Seal the bags. The icing will not spoil or harden if it is kept sealed in the refrigerator until use. Each child will need at least one bag of icing. Just before the children arrive, set out candies and decorations in bowls. (Bring extra for snacking!)

## What to Do

**Diagram 1**

1. Have the children wash their hands.

2. Give each child a half-pint carton, paper plate, plastic knife and plastic bag of icing. Say, **We are going to build Gingerbread Houses.**

3. With the scissors, snip off one corner of each plastic bag so the children can use the icing as "glue" and pipe it onto their crackers (see Diagram 1).

4. Show the children how to lay a carton on its longest side. Let the children lift up their cartons, pipe icing onto the undersides, spread it with plastic knives and attach their cartons to their paper plates to create house "bases."

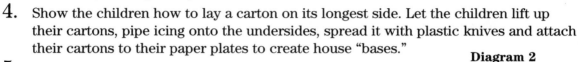
**Diagram 2**

5. Give each child four whole graham crackers and two pre-cut crackers (house sides). Each child can spread icing onto the backside of two whole crackers and attach them to the long sides of the carton (see Diagram 2).

6. Point out where to pipe icing onto the edges of the long house sides to attach the pre-cut crackers (see Diagram 3).

7. Demonstrate how to pipe icing along the upper edges of the "frame" of the house (see Diagram 4).

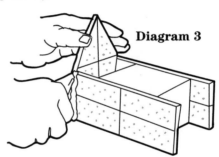
**Diagram 3**

8. Older children can carefully attach two whole graham crackers to the house frames and bring them together at an angle to make a roof point. Roofs can be sealed with beads of icing along the rooflines. Younger children will need help adding roofs to their houses (see Diagram 5).

9. Allow the icing to set for a few minutes.

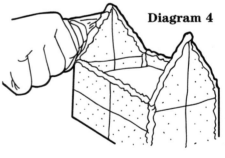
**Diagram 4**

10. Let the children use icing as glue to attach candies, treats and snacks to the house as decorations.

11. As the children are working, say, **God provides everything we need to build houses. He is the Master Builder.**

12. Allow the houses to dry.

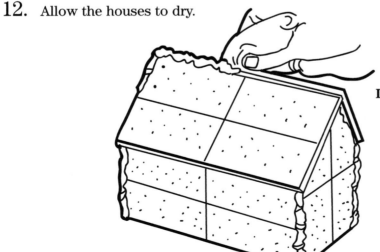
**Diagram 5**

# Hanging the Greens

ALL AGES

**Bible Reference:** Adorn the Lord's Sanctuary / *Isaiah 60:13*

## Overview

God instructed the Israelites to adorn the temple with pine, fir and cypress in His honor. In the same way, decorating the church with greenery glorifies Christ at His birth.

## Helpers: varies

one person to supervise each group of 1-6 participants

## What You Need

* ❄ fresh or artificial greenery, such as pine, spruce, cedar and holly boughs, cut from trees or purchased at garden centers
* ❄ fresh or artificial Christmas tree with stand
* ❄ tree skirt or cloth
* ❄ pine cones
* ❄ red, plastic-backed velvet ribbon
* ❄ foam, wire or straw wreath frames
* ❄ miniature tree lights, white only
* ❄ Chrismons, page 52
* ❄ picture wire, fishing line or floral twist ties
* ❄ garden shears
* ❄ wire cutters
* ❄ scissors
* ❄ ruler or tape measure
* ❄ garden gloves
* ❄ ladder or step stool

## Preparation

Put on garden gloves. Use garden shears to cut greenery into manageable branches, 1-2 feet long.

# Evergreen Swags

## What to Do

1. Have the children wear garden gloves when working with fresh greenery.
2. Let each child select three or more greenery branches. Point out that pine and spruce branches form an attractive base. Cedar and holly provide contrast.
3. Demonstrate how to grip the cut ends together so the greenery cascades down like large bouquets.

*continued on next page...*

4. Older children can use wire, fishing line or twist ties to tie cut ends together. Younger children will need help tying bundles.

5. The children can use wire, fishing line or twist ties to attach pinecones to the swags.

6. Help the children tie red, plastic-backed velvet ribbon into bows around the swags' gathered ends. They can use scissors to trim bow ends.

7. Say, **We gathered and bundled these swags just like a farmer gathers and bundles wheat. Someday God will gather His people and take us to heaven.**

# Evergreen Wreaths
## What to Do

1. Have the children wear garden gloves when working with fresh greenery.

2. Give each child a wreath frame. Say, **We are going to cover these wreath frames with greenery.**

3. Let the children select evergreen branches and lay them on the frames, adjusting as desired (see illustration below).

4. Older children can use picture wire or fishing line to wrap the greenery to the frames. They can tie the wire or line ends together to secure. Younger children will need help attaching greenery to the frame.

5. Have the children use wire, fishing line or twist ties to attach pinecones to the wreaths.

6. Help the children tie red, plastic-backed velvet ribbon into bows. They can use scissors to trim bow ends.

7. Measure and cut 1-foot lengths of picture wire or fishing line. Show how to loop wire or line around the centers of the bows, twist or tie to secure, and attach the bows to the wreaths.

8. Ask, **What kinds of greenery make up your wreaths?** Allow the children to respond. Say, **Pine, spruce, cedar and holly are called "evergreens." They stay green all year long – even in the winter. God's Kingdom is "evergreen." It lasts forever.**

# Twinkling Rope
## What to Do

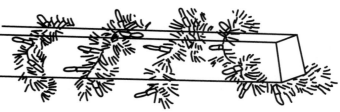

1. Have the children wear garden gloves while they are working with fresh greenery.

2. Help the children cut the greenery branches into small pieces, about one foot in length each.

3. Show how to lay the cut branches end to end, each overlapping slightly with the next, to make long "ropes."

4. Continue laying out greenery until the ropes reach the desired lengths.

5. Cut picture wire or fishing line into 6" lengths. Demonstrate how to attach the branches together at overlaps, using picture wire, fishing line or twist ties to secure.

6. Have the children weave miniature tree light strings around greenery.

*continued on next page...*

7. Hang Twinkling Ropes on railings or in doorways. Say, **God wants us to wrap ourselves in wisdom, just like we are wrapping this Twinkling Rope around this railing (or this doorway).**

8. When each Twinkling Rope is secure, plug in its lights.

## Jesus Tree
### What to Do

1. Set up a fresh or artificial Christmas tree in a prominent location.

2. Have the children arrange a tree skirt or cloth around the base of the tree.

3. Help the children attach miniature tree lights to the tree branches. Use only white lights.

4. Let the children decorate the tree with Chrismons. Ask, **How is this tree like Jesus?** Allow the children to respond. Say, **This tree sprouted roots. The Bible calls Jesus "The Root of Jesse." Jesse was one of Jesus' ancestors.**

5. Say, **The green branches on the Jesus Tree tell us that Jesus is alive. The white lights represent His purity. The gold on the Chrismons represent His majesty.**

# Live Nativity

❄ ✳ ❄ ✳ ❄ ✳ ❄ ✳ ❄ ✳ ❄ **ALL AGES**

**Bible Reference:** Mary treasures the birth of Christ / *Luke 2:19*

 ## Overview

Actors and animals can make the first Christmas come to life in this living tableau.

 ## Helpers: varies

actors to portray Mary, Joseph, shepherds, wise men and angels

dressers to help costume the actors

snack servers to bring or prepare light snacks for actors

animal owners or trained animal helpers to provide stable animals

 ## What You Need

❄ shed or lean-to
❄ straw bales
❄ outdoor spotlights
❄ electric star
❄ outdoor extension cords
❄ live animals, such as donkeys, sheep, goats or cows
❄ costumes (see The Christmas Story: Pageant With Narration and Carols, page 153)
❄ doll wrapped in a blanket (to represent baby Jesus)
❄ wooden box (manger)
❄ lawn-sized plastic candy canes covered with brown packaging tape (shepherds' staffs)
❄ foil-and-rhinestone wrapped containers (wise men's gifts)
❄ flashlights
❄ Luminaries for the Light of the World, page 56 (optional)

 ## Preparation

1. Select a time to feature your Live Nativity. Because of the cost and effort involved in set-up, make the Live Nativity accessible to many viewers by holding it over a two- or three-day period, or on successive weekends during Advent.

2. Find congregation members, friends or local farmers who will bring their animals to your event. Also find out if the animals have any special requirements. For example, owners may allow animals to be petted but not fed.

3. Recruit church members to portray Joseph, Mary, angels, shepherds and wise men. Either designate all children for the actors, or allow children to serve as shepherds and angels only (to avoid a child Joseph standing next to an adult Mary, for example). Post a sign-up sheet with open dates and times in your church's entryway. Group the participants in 30-minute shifts with two teams per night to allow one team to rest and

*continued on next page...*

get warm while the other is outside. Remind the actors to wear extra weather-appropriate clothing under their costumes.

4. Talk with your pastors and suggest that one of them or other designated church leaders plan to be near the Nativity to greet guests and hand out church literature. Viewing a Live Nativity is moving for many people, so be sure to have seasoned greeters on hand who are comfortable praying with visitors if they request it.

5. Decide where to set up the Nativity stable. Choose an outdoor location that is prominent enough to get attention from church guests and passersby, yet set apart so animals will not be distracted.

6. Set up a shed or lean-to for the stable. Arrange bales of straw for seating. Spread loose straw over the stable floor and around the exterior of the building.

7. Place the manger in the stable.

8. Set up spotlights to illuminate the scene. Attach an electric star to the stable roof. Use extension cords to hook the spotlights and star to an electric power source.

9. About an hour before the Live Nativity begin dressing the actors and giving them their props.

10. Help the animal owners set up pens or posts for their animals.

11. If you are planning a nighttime presentation, set out Luminaries for the Light of the World in a ring around the stable or on a path leading to it. Light the luminaries just before the Live Nativity Scene begins.

 ## What to Do

1. Have the actors position themselves at the stable. If your presentation is in the evening, distribute flashlights to participants.

2. Make sure the animal owners or a qualified assistant remain with the animals.

3. Let the children and their families enjoy the Live Nativity and interact with the actors and animals.

# The Mitten Tree

 ALL AGES

**Bible Reference:** Give to the least of these / *Matthew 25:31-40*

 ## Overview

A Christmas tree in a central location is the collection point for donated hats, mittens, gloves, socks and scarves.

 ## Helpers: 2

two people to work together to set up tree, solicit and pack up donations, and deliver them to the receiving charity

 ## What You Need

❄ Christmas tree
❄ boxes
❄ poster board
❄ markers
❄ The Mitten Tree flyer, page 188

 ## Preparation

Set up a Christmas tree in a central location. The tree should be undecorated. Contact local charities to find one in need of winter wear: ask if they need winter wear for their clients, and if so, the particular kinds or sizes of winter wear they can use. Determine a starting and ending date for collecting donations. If you schedule the project early in the season, people in need will receive the winter accessories before the weather gets too cold. Use poster board and markers to make a sign that reads, "The Mitten Tree." Be sure to include a list of needed accessories, the starting and ending collection dates of the project, and Matthew 25:40 on the poster. Or, reproduce The Mitten Tree flyer and fill in the appropriate information. Hang the poster or flyer near The Mitten Tree.

## What to Do

1. About two weeks before your collection project begins, distribute a list of needed accessories to your church newsletter, bulletin, Sunday school classes, youth group and clubs.

2. Visit church classes and groups personally. Say, **Our church family wants to give Jesus a special birthday gift this Christmas. Jesus said that when we show mercy to a person in need, it is as if we are doing it for Him.** Describe the charity and its needs. Share the starting and ending dates of your collection project. Encourage people to participate by bringing donations to your facility and placing them on The Mitten Tree.

3. As part of a Birthday Celebration for Jesus program, you can have children and families make Jingle Bell Gloves (page 96) and Snowflake Fleece Scarves (page 105) to place on The Mitten Tree.

4. Consider asking guests to your Birthday Celebration for Jesus to bring donations for The Mitten Tree.

5. At the conclusion of the collection period, remove the donated items from The Mitten Tree and pack them in boxes.

6. Deliver the items to the charity.

# Lessons

# Ask for Good Gifts

❋ ❋ ❋ ❋ ❋ ❋ ❋ **ALL AGES**

**Bible Reference: *Matthew 7:9-11***

 ## Overview

God wants us to ask Him for good gifts.

 ## What You Need

❋ Santa hat
❋ 5 small sheets of paper
❋ markers
❋ 5 small boxes
❋ gift wrap
❋ clear tape
❋ scissors
❋ gift tags
❋ gift bows
❋ Bible

 ## Preparation

Draw and write one of the following on each of the five sheets of paper:
Page 1: a child pointing to his head with the words "Think before I act"; Page 2: an eye, a book and the words "Read and learn God's Word"; Page 3: an ear and "Be a good listener"; Page 4: a smiley face and "Be cheerful, not grumpy"; Page 5: a hand and "Be helpful, not selfish." Wrap each of the "gifts" above in a small box and add a bow to each. Label and attach a gift tag to each box, marked with the correct number (see above). Set the wrapped gifts out of view. Place a marker at Matthew 7:9-11 in your Bible.

## Presentation

1. Put on the Santa hat. Say, **Let's pretend that I am Santa. I'd like to hear what you want for Christmas.** Allow the children to step up one at a time, sit on your lap if they wish, and name one or two items that they would like to receive on Christmas morning.

2. As the children share their lists, respond with comments like, **That's a wonderful toy; Yes, that is one of my favorites** or **What an excellent choice!**

3. After each child has had a turn, gather the group together. Say, **There is someone else in addition to Santa Claus who wants to give you gifts. Who do you think it is?** (my mom; my grandparents; my brother and sister; my best friend)

4. Read Matthew 7:9-11. Say, **Wow, God wants us to ask Him for special gifts. He promises that He'll give them to us.**

5. Ask, **What does God mean by a "good gift"? Let's find out.** Bring out the wrapped boxes. Let the children open the boxes one at a time, in numerical order.

6. Say, **These show us good gifts that come from God. Our heads, our eyes, our ears, our mouths and our hands remind us what to ask Him. God wants us to think, to learn, to listen, to be cheerful and to be helpful. These are qualities that He will give us when we ask Him!**

7. Say, **Let's pray together.** Have the children bow their heads. Say, **Dear Lord, thank You that You want to give me good gifts. Today, I ask You to help me think before I act, to read and learn Your Word, to be a good listener, to be cheerful and to help others. In Jesus' name, amen.**

# Don't Miss the Party!

❄ ✳ ❄ ✳ ❄ ✳ ❄ ✳ ❄ ✳ ❄ ✳ ❄   ALL AGES

**Bible Reference: *Micah 5:2, Matthew 25:13, John 1:9-11***

 ## Overview

Only God knew when Jesus would be born, and only He knows when Christ will return.

 ## What You Need

❉ construction paper
❉ markers
❉ birthday party invitation, Bulletin Insert or Publicity Postcard, page 192
❉ beanbag
❉ pictures of innkeeper, Bible-time townspeople, shepherds and wise men
❉ Bible

 ## Preparation

If you are planning a Celebration for Jesus' Birthday at your church, present this lesson prior to the event. Reserve a completed Bulletin Insert or Publicity Postcard to use for the lesson. Otherwise, complete a birthday party invitation using information for your church's Christmas Eve service in place of the party information. On a piece of construction paper, write, "God's Party! Savior to be born in Bethlehem. Please come! Micah 5:2." Place markers at Micah 5:2, Matthew 25:13 and John 1:9-11 in your Bible.

 ## Presentation

1. Have the children sit in a semi-circle around you. Toss the beanbag to the first participant and ask, **When is your birthday?** Let the child respond with the date or month of his or her birthday, and toss the beanbag back. Continue through the group until everyone has shared. Say, **It's important to know special dates so you can plan to celebrate.**
2. Say, **Jesus has a birthday, too. When do we celebrate it?** (on Christmas; on December 25)
3. Bring out the completed Bulletin Insert, Publicity Postcard or completed party invitation. Say, **We are having a special birthday party for Jesus, and you are invited. When will the party take place?** Allow the children to respond. Help them refer to the insert, postcard or invitation for correct information. Say, **Yes, it is important to know the date and time of the party so you can make sure to come.**
4. Say, **In Bible times, God told the people that He was sending them a ruler. The Savior was to be born in Bethlehem. But God didn't tell the people the date and time of the Savior's arrival.** Read Micah 5:2.
5. Hold up the construction paper announcement. Say, **God told the people where His**

*continued on next page...*

special party was going to take place. But He didn't tell the people when it would happen.

6. Say, **This was confusing for the people. It can be hard to wait and wait and wait for a party, especially if you don't know when it will be.** Allow the children to respond. Say, **Many people were discouraged. Some gave up waiting. By the time Jesus was born, most people weren't looking for Him. They weren't expecting Him to come anytime soon.** Read John 1:9-11.

7. Hold up the pictures of the innkeeper and townspeople. Say, **These people didn't recognize Jesus. They missed the party!**

8. Hold up pictures of the shepherds and wise men. Say, **But some people were paying attention to God. They recognized Jesus was the new ruler. How?** (they were alert; the angel told them; God sent them to Bethlehem) Say, **Yes, they believed God. They were the first ones to see the Savior. They got to go to the party!**

9. Say, **The Bible tells us that Jesus is coming back to earth again. We don't want to miss the party!**

10. Read Matthew 25:13. Say, **We don't know when Jesus is coming again. But God tells us we can be ready. What instructions does He give us?** (watch; pay attention; be on the alert; be prepared)

11. Say, **Let's pray together.** Have the children bow their heads. Say, **God, thank You that You sent Jesus to earth for us. We want to be ready to meet Him when He comes again. Help us live for You. Help us listen to You. Help us to pay attention to You and Your Word. We don't want to miss the party! In Jesus' name, amen.**

12. If time allows, have the children make invitations to your Celebration for Jesus' Birthday with construction paper and markers. Encourage them to share their invitations with their friends.

# Getting Ready for Christmas

 **Overview**

God wants us to prepare our hearts for Christmas.

 **What You Need**

❄ shopping bags filled with boxes
❄ fresh or artificial garlands and ribbons
❄ gift wrap                    ❄ wooden spoons
❄ children's scissors          ❄ clay dough
❄ clear tape                   ❄ doll and blanket
❄ cookie sheets                ❄ jingle bells
❄ mixing bowls                 ❄ Bible

 **Preparation**

Make three stations in the center of the room: one with shopping bags, boxes, gift wrap, children's scissors and clear tape; a second with garlands and ribbons; and a third with cookie sheets, mixing bowls, wooden spoons and clay dough. Wrap the doll in the blanket and place it in a corner of the room. Have the jingle bells handy. Place a marker at Isaiah 40:3-5 in your Bible.

**Presentation**

1. Say, **Christmas is coming. What do we need to do to get ready?** (trim the tree; shop for presents; bake cookies; hang up decorations; wrap gifts)

2. Say, **Yes, there's a lot to do when Christmas is coming. Let's do some of those jobs right now. But be ready. We won't have much time. See what you can get done. When you hear the jingle bells, stop and freeze.**

3. The children can move to the three stations to wrap boxes, decorate the room with garlands or "bake" cookies out of clay dough. Allow play to continue for several minutes. The play area will become cluttered.

4. Ring the jingle bells. Say, **Freeze! Are you ready for Christmas?** Let the children show their Christmas preparations.

5. Have the children sit down. Say, **God sent a prophet named John the Baptist to help Israel get ready for Jesus.** Read Isaiah 40:3-5.

6. Say, **John the Baptist told the people to prepare a way for the Lord. Do we have a path prepared so we can welcome baby Jesus?** (no, this room is a mess; we've made a lot of things but we're still not ready; we forgot about Jesus)

7. Say, **Being ready for Christmas means more than shopping, decorating, baking and wrapping. Being ready for Christmas means having your heart ready to worship Jesus. Let's prepare the way for the Lord.** Help the children move the play materials to the sides and make a pathway toward the doll in the corner.

8. Lead the children down the pathway. Kneel together around the "manger."

9. Say, **Let's pray together. Have the children bow their heads. Jesus, it's fun getting ready for Your birthday. But the most important thing to get ready is our hearts. Help us to prepare the way for You. In Jesus' name, amen.**

# God's Messengers

❄️❄️❄️❄️❄️❄️ ALL AGES

**Bible Reference:** *Matthew 2:13-15 and Luke 1:26-35, 2:8-15*

 **Overview**

Angels are God's messengers.

 **What You Need**

❄️ instructions and materials for Tabletop Crèche
(page 61), or other crèche figures
❄️ Bible

 **Preparation**

Make the Mary, Joseph, shepherds and angel figures from the Tabletop Crèche, or have other crèche figures ready. You will need more than one angel. If you plan to have the children make their own Tabletop Crèche angels, have the materials ready. Place markers at Matthew 2:13-15 and Luke 1:26-35, 2:8-15 in your Bible.

 **Presentation**

1. Set an angel in front of you. Say, **In Bible times, one way God communicated an extra-special piece of information was by using a messenger.**

2. Set Mary next to the angel. Read Luke 1:26-35. Ask, **Who gave Mary a message?** (an angel; Gabriel) **Why was the message so important?** (she was going to have a baby; the Messiah was coming; God had chosen her) Set Mary aside.

3. Set out the shepherds and additional angels. Read Luke 2:8-15. Ask, **Who gave the shepherds a message?** (the angel of the Lord; a choir of angels; the heavenly host) **Why was the message so important?** (a Savior was born; He came for everyone, not just a few; the angels told them where to look for baby Jesus; the whole choir sang) Set the shepherds and all but one of the angels aside.

4. Set out Joseph next to the remaining angel. Read Matthew 2:13-15. Ask, **Who gave Joseph a message?** (an angel of the Lord; an angel in a dream) **Why was the message so important?** (Joseph, Mary and Jesus needed to escape; their lives were in danger; King Herod wanted to kill baby Jesus)

5. Assemble Mary, Joseph and the shepherds together. Set an angel nearby. Say, **God used His angels to deliver important information.** Move Mary forward slightly. Say, **An angel told Mary to get ready to be Jesus' mother.** Move the shepherds forward slightly. Say, **An angel announced Jesus' birth.** Move Joseph forward. Say, **An angel warned Joseph to escape to Egypt with his family. Angels are God's messengers.**

6. Say, **God speaks to us in other ways, too. He speaks through the Bible. He speaks to us in prayer.**

7. Say, **Let's pray together.** Have the children bow their heads. Say, **Dear God, thank You that You want to communicate with us. We are glad that You used Your messengers to speak to Mary, Joseph and the angels. Help us to hear You when You speak to us through prayer and through the Bible. In Jesus' name, amen.**

8. If time allows, have the children make their own Tabletop Crèche angels.

# Immanuel

❋ ❋ ❋ ❋ ❋ ❋ ❋ ALL AGES

## Bible Reference: *Matthew 1:23*

 ## Overview

Jesus has many names. One of them is
"Immanuel," which means "God With Us."

 ## What You Need

* ❋ instructions and materials for Chrismons, page 52
* ❋ name tag stickers
* ❋ marker or pen
* ❋ doll wrapped in a blanket
* ❋ paper cups and juice
* ❋ Bible

 ## Preparation

Make sample Chrismons: bread, chalice, cross, crown
and shepherd's crook. If you plan to have the children
make their own Chrismons, have materials ready. Put a
marker at Matthew 1:23 in your Bible.

## Presentation

1. Say, **Some of you here may not know my name. I'm going to make myself a name tag. What I should write on the tag? Can you think of any other names someone might call me?** (If you have a special title, be sure to share it with the children.) Write each name on a separate tag. Stick the tags to your shirt.

2. Ask, **Are you surprised that I have so many names?** (Yes, I thought you were just my teacher) Ask, **What do you notice about each of my names?** Say, **Each of my names tells something about me. From my names, you can learn that I** [am married; have children, grandchildren, parents; am a teacher].

3. Ask, **What about you?** Let the children share their names. Write tags for the children and stick them on them.

4. Let one of the children hold the doll. Ask, **Whose birthday do we celebrate at Christmas?** (Jesus) Make name tags for the doll using each appropriate name mentioned by the children. Stick the name tags on the doll's blanket.

5. Say, **The name "Jesus" means "God is our salvation."** Show the children the cross Chrismon. Say, **Jesus died on the cross for our sins. Jesus has other names, too.** Set out the bread, crown and shepherd's crook Chrismons. Ask, **What names for Jesus go with each of these symbols?** (The Bread of Life; The King of Kings; The Good Shepherd) Make tags for the doll and stick them to the doll blanket.

6. Distribute cups of juice. Ask, **How does it feel to drink juice together?** (It's fun being with friends) Say, **That's the idea behind another special name God gave baby Jesus when He sent Him to earth.**

7. Read Matthew 1:23. Set out the chalice Chrismon. Say, **Jesus' other special name is "Immanuel." That means, "God with us." God sent His Son to live with us. That way, people could spend time with Him, eat meals with Him and learn from Him.** Make an "Immanuel" name tag and attach it to the doll blanket.

8. Say, **Let's pray. Father, thank You for sending Jesus so that we can be close to You. We praise You for Immanuel – God With Us. Amen.**

# J.O.Y.

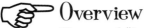 ALL AGES

## Bible Reference: *Mark 12:30-31*

 **Overview**

The word "joy" provides the biblical order for priorities in prayer: Jesus first (J), others second (O) and yourself third (Y).

 **What You Need**

❋ 3 sheets of construction paper
❋ markers
❋ hymnal or Caroling Songbook (page 148)
❋ Bible

 **Preparation**

On the first sheet of construction paper, write the letter "J." On the second sheet of construction paper, write the letter "O." On the third sheet of construction paper, write the letter "Y." Mark the carol "Joy to the World" in a hymnal or your Caroling Songbook. Place a marker at Mark 12:30-31 in your Bible.

**Presentation**

1. Open the hymnal or songbook to "Joy to the World." Say, **One of the most beloved Christmas carols is "Joy to the World." Let's sing the first verse together.** Have the children join in singing.

2. Ask, **Why does this carol tell us we can be joyful?** (the Lord is come; we have a new King; all of nature can rejoice in the Creator) Say, **Yes, those are all good reasons that we can be joyful at Christmas.**

3. Say, **It can be hard to keep that Christmas joy all year long. Why is it difficult for you?** (the rest of the year is predictable; we have parties and celebrations at Christmas)

4. Say, **Let's learn about an easy way to have joy every day, even after Christmas is past.**

5. Read Mark 12:30-31. Say, **These Bible verses tell us what God thinks is important. He wants to come first in our lives, and He wants us to love others. One way we can do both of those things each day is prayer.**

6. Say, **Joy is spelled J-O-Y.** Set out the sheets of construction paper in order.

7. Point to the J. Say, **The J stands for "Jesus." When you put Jesus first in your life and praise Him each day, you discover that remembering His great love brings you joy.**

8. Point to the O. Say, **The O stands for "others." When you put others ahead of**

*continued on next page...*

**yourself and pray for them each day, you discover that helping them brings you joy.**

9.  Point to the Y. Say, **The Y stands for "yourself." When you finally pray for yourself after you have praised Jesus and prayed for others, you discover that all your blessings bring you joy.**

10. Say, **J-O-Y. Jesus, others, yourself. When you pray each day this way, you can have joy all year long.**

11. Say, **Here is a song to help you remember to pray the J.O.Y. way.**

(sing to the tune of "Twinkle, Twinkle Little Star")

| | |
|---|---|
| **Here's an easy way to pray.** | *place hands together in prayer* |
| **It will bring you joy each day.** | *point index fingers at your smile* |
| **Worship Jesus,** | *reach hands up,* |
| **then ask for help,** | *bow down* |
| **first for others** | *point out into the group,* |
| **then yourself.** | *point to self.* |
| **Here's an easy way to pray.** | *place hands together in prayer* |
| **It will bring you joy each day.** | *point index fingers at your smile* |

12. Say, **Let's pray together. Do you know anyone who needs special prayers?** Allow the children to respond. Have the children bow their heads. Say, **Dear God, We praise You for Jesus. We ask that You would help** [name the children's requests]. **We thank You for loving us, and pray that You can help us pray with J.O.Y. each day, all year long. Amen.**

# Jesus Came for Everybody

 ALL AGES

**Bible Reference: *Matthew 2:1-2, Luke 2:10***

 ☞ Overview

Jesus came to earth for all people.

 What You Need

❄ world map
❄ pictures or name tags of missionaries
❄ yarn
❄ push pins
❄ clear tape
❄ scissors
❄ pictures of people from around the world
❄ Bible

 Preparation

Post the world map on the wall or bulletin board. Tape the missionary pictures or name tags around the perimeter of the map. (If your church doesn't sponsor missionaries, check with other local churches or your denomination's headquarters for a list of missionaries.) Place pictures of people from around the world in a stack next to your chair. Mark Matthew 2:1-2 and Luke 2:10 in your Bible.

## Presentation

1. Ask the children to find your city (approximately) and state on the map.
2. Say, **Jesus was born in Bethlehem of Judea, which is in the country of Israel.** Help the children locate Bethlehem, Judea and Israel on the map.
3. Say, **We don't live in Israel. Do you think Jesus came to earth for you and me?**
4. Read Luke 2:10. Say, **In Bible times, the Israelites were waiting for the Messiah. God had promised them a leader. Some Israelites thought that the Messiah was going to be a leader only for them – God's chosen people. But the angel told the shepherds that the Good News was for all the people. Jesus came for everybody!**
5. Read Matthew 2:1-2. Say, **The wise men came from the east. Most Bible teachers think they were from Persia, which is the area now called Iran.** Point to Iran on the map. Say, **The wise men weren't from Israel. But the Bible tells us they worshiped baby Jesus. Jesus came for everybody.**
6. Point to one of the missionary pictures on your map. Say, **[name] lives in [country] and tells people there about Jesus.** Hold up a people group picture from that part of the world. **Did Jesus come to earth for the people in [country]?** (yes, Jesus came for everybody) Have the children help you use yarn and push pins or clear tape to place a locator line from each missionary picture to the area on the map where they serve.
7. Continue to identify all the missionaries on your map as described in Step 6. Reinforce the idea that "Jesus came for everybody" as you mention each missionary group. Label each missionary and country with a yarn locator line.
8. Say, **Let's pray together.** Have the children bow their heads. **Dear Father, thank You for sending Jesus to earth. Your good news is for all the people. Help our missionaries [names of missionaries] share this good news in [names of countries]. And let us share this good news with our friends and families today. In Jesus' name, amen.**

# The Light of the World

✻✻✻✻✻✻✻✻✻✻✻ ALL AGES

**Bible Reference: *Matthew 5:14-16, John 8:12***

 ## Overview

Jesus, the Light of the World, shines through believers.

 ## What You Need

✻ instructions and materials for Luminaries for the Light of the World, page 56
✻ candle and candle holder
✻ flashlight
✻ string of miniature tree lights
✻ camping lantern
✻ matches
✻ black paper or black trash bags
✻ clear tape
✻ Bible

 ## Preparation

Make a sample Luminary for the Light of the World. If you plan to have the children make their own Luminaries, have the materials ready. Darken the classroom by covering the windows with black construction paper or trash bags and clear tape. Set your chair near an electrical outlet. Assemble the candle and candleholder, flashlight, camping lantern, sample Luminary and matches next to your seat. Place a string of miniature tree lights next to the electrical outlet. Place markers at Matthew 5:14-16 and John 8:12 in your Bible.

 ## Presentation

1. Have the children sit in chairs or on the floor in a semi-circle around you.

2. Read John 8:12. Say, **The room is going to get dark.** Close the blinds, shut the door and turn off the lights. Children who are afraid of the dark can move closer to you.

3. As the children get accustomed to the darkness, ask, **What do you notice about being in the dark?** (it is difficult to see; I can't do anything; I'm scared)

4. Light the Luminary candle. Say, **The candle in this luminary represents Jesus. He is the Light of the World. The luminary itself represents people. Notice that when the candle is inside the luminary, the light shines through. When we invite Jesus the Light into our hearts, He shines through us.**

5. Use the matches to light the candle in the candleholder. Ask, **Does this lit candle make the room seem different?** (yes, I can see a few more things; there is more light; the candle makes shadows)

6. Have a volunteer turn on the flashlight and leave it on. Ask, **Does the flashlight help?** (yes, some; when the beam points at something, I can see it)

7. Ask a volunteer near the electrical outlet to plug in the string of miniature tree lights.

*continued on next page…*

As the volunteer works, illuminate the outlet with the candle or flashlight. Ask, **What do these do?** (they are dots of light; we can share the light by unwinding the string)

8. Hand the camp lantern to a volunteer at the back of the group. Have the volunteer turn on the lantern and hold it high. Ask, **Now what do you notice?** (the lantern is powerful; the light spreads)

9. Read Matthew 5:14-16. Say, **Each of these kinds of light adds brightness to the room in different ways. Jesus said, "You are the light of the world." He uses His light in each of us to light up the world in different ways.**

10. Say, **Let's pray together.** Have the children bow their heads. **Dear Lord, You are the Light of the world. Please come into our hearts right now. We want Your love to shine through us. In Jesus' name, amen.**

11. Turn on the room's lights. Extinguish the candles, and turn off the flashlight and lantern. Unplug the tree lights.

12. If time allows, let the children make their own Luminaries for the Light of the World.

# No Room at the Inn

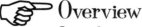 ALL AGES

**Bible Reference: *Luke 2:7, Mark 10:13-16***

 Overview

Jesus knew rejection even before He was born, but He makes room for all children in His kingdom.

 What You Need

❄ table
❄ Bible

 Preparation

Set the table in the center of the room. Place the remaining chairs and furniture along the walls. Place a marker at Luke 2:7 and Mark 10:13-16 in your Bible.

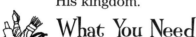

Presentation

1. Designate two volunteers to be Mary and Joseph, and one volunteer to be the innkeeper. Tell the innkeeper to stand next to the table. Explain that his or her job is to let all the other children into the "inn" except for Mary and Joseph.

2. Assemble the children in the hallway or at one end of the room. Say, **The Roman leaders in Palestine took a census. What is a census?** (a count of how many people live in a certain area)

3. Say, **Everyone traveled to his or her hometown in order to be counted. Mary and Joseph traveled to Bethlehem. Many other people traveled to Bethlehem, too.** Have the children form a line, with Mary and Joseph at the end.

4. Say, **We're going to travel to Bethlehem for the census.** Have the children at the front of the line lead the way around the room, into the hall and into other parts of your church, if desired, and then back into the classroom to the table.

5. Say, **When you reach the "inn," ask the innkeeper for a room.** Have the children approach the innkeeper one at a time and seek shelter. When the innkeeper lets them in, the children can crawl under the table. The area under the table will get crowded quickly.

6. When Mary and Joseph ask the innkeeper for entry, the innkeeper can say, **There's no room at the inn.**

7. Have the children come out from under the table and sit around it. Read Luke 2:7. Ask, **How do you think Mary and Joseph felt when there was no room at the inn?** (lonely; afraid; left out) Say, **Jesus knows how it feels to be rejected. But He doesn't want you to feel that way.**

8. Read Mark 10:13-16. Say, **Jesus' arms are open to you. There is always room for you in the Kingdom of God. Let's make a Jesus Welcome Circle.** Have the children stand in a circle, each placing an arm around the shoulders of those on either side. Say, **On the count of three, squeeze the shoulders of the people next to you and say, "Welcome!"** Have the children squeeze and shout several times.

9. Say, **Let's pray together.** Have the children bow their heads. **Dear Lord, We are sorry that there was no room for You at the inn. We welcome You into our hearts right now. And we are thankful that You always make room for us. In Jesus' name, amen.**

# Spread the News

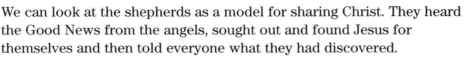

**ALL AGES**

**Bible Reference: *Luke 2:8-18***

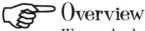 Overview

We can look at the shepherds as a model for sharing Christ. They heard the Good News from the angels, sought out and found Jesus for themselves and then told everyone what they had discovered.

 What You Need

✻ newspaper (front page)
✻ print copy of an e-mail
✻ play telephone or cell phone
✻ Christmas card
✻ Best News Newspaper, page 253
✻ crayons or markers
✻ Bible

 Preparation

Reproduce the Best News Newspaper for each child.
Place a marker at Luke 2:8-18 in your Bible.

 Presentation

1. Set out the newspaper front page, the copy of the e-mail, the phone and the Christmas card. Ask, **Can you tell me what these things are?** Let the children name the items.
2. Ask, **What do we do with them?** (read about the news; receive messages using the computer; talk to family and friends; send greetings and information) Say, **Yes, all of these tools help us communicate and share news with our family and friends.**
3. Ask, **Did people in Bible times use these same kinds of tools to share news with each other?** (No, there were no telephones; computers weren't invented yet; maybe they sent cards) Say, **The most common way they communicated was by telling other people their news in person. Let's see how they did that.** Read Luke 2:8-18.
4. Ask, **What happened to the shepherds?** (they were watching their sheep when the angels came and announced Jesus' birth; the shepherds decided to go see if there really was a new baby; they found the baby; they told everyone about the baby)
5. Say, **Yes, the shepherds heard about the Savior. They went to find Him. Then they told everyone the Good News! The shepherds heard, saw and told.**
6. Ask, **What are some ways you can tell others about baby Jesus?** (talk with them; send them Christmas cards; invite them to church; show them love) Say, **Those are all good ways to share the news.**
7. Say, **Here's another way.** Distribute the Best News Newspapers. Say, **You can make your own newspaper to announce Jesus' birth.** Let the children write a news article or draw a picture of the shepherds and their story.
8. Say, **Give your newspapers to people you know so they can hear the best news of all – God sent us a Savior: baby Jesus.** Ask each child to tell you the name of the person who will receive his or her newspaper.
9. Say, **Let's pray.** Have the children bow their heads. Say, **God, thank You for this wonderful news. You sent a Savior! The shepherds heard it, saw it and told about it. Help us to do that, too. In Jesus' name, amen.**

# Which King Will You Follow?

❄ ❄ ❄ ❄ ❄ ❄ ❄ ❄ ❄ **ALL AGES**

**Bible Reference: *Matthew 2:1-12***

 ## Overview
The wise men chose to listen to God.

 ## What You Need
❄ instructions and materials for King's Crowns, page 70
❄ satin or brightly-colored fabric
❄ 3 beautifully wrapped boxes
❄ doll
❄ old blanket or piece of burlap
❄ worn cardboard box
❄ Bible

 ## Preparation
Make a King's Crown. If you plan to have children make their own King's Crowns, have the materials ready. Use satin or brightly-colored fabric to fashion a king's cape. Wrap the doll in an old blanket or a piece of burlap. Set the doll in the cardboard box. Place a marker at Matthew 2:1-12 in your Bible.

 ## Presentation

1. Ask a volunteer to portray King Herod. Say, **Jesus grew up in Palestine. At the time of His birth, foreigners ruled Palestine. One ruler, King Herod, governed a section called Judea. King Herod was very powerful. People were afraid of him.** Wrap the cape around the king's shoulders and place the crown on his or her head. Have King Herod flex his muscles to show strength.

2. Ask for three volunteers to portray the wise men. Give each wise man a wrapped box to hold. Have them position themselves on the opposite side of the room. Say, **Three wise men heard that there was a new king in Judea. But this king was very special. The wise men traveled from far away to find this baby. When they arrived in Judea, they asked for directions.** Read Matthew 2:1-2. Have the wise men walk across the room to King Herod and ask where they might find the baby king.

3. Set the cardboard box with the doll about 10-15 feet away from King Herod.

4. Say, **King Herod was upset. He thought he was the only king in Judea. But now, these strangers told him that there was another King of the Jews!** Have King Herod make an angry face.

5. Say, **King Herod was very clever. He found out that the Jewish people expected their Messiah to be born in Bethlehem. He told the wise men to go to Bethlehem, find the baby and report back to him. Then he could get rid of the baby! And he would still be king!** Read Matthew 2:3-8. Have King Herod tell the wise men to go to Bethlehem.

*continued on next page...*

6. Say, **The wise men went to Bethlehem, found baby Jesus and gave Him their gifts.** Read Matthew 2:9-11. Have the wise men walk over to the cardboard box, kneel down and place the wrapped boxes there.

7. Say, **The wise men now had a choice. They could go back to King Herod and tell him where to find the baby. Or, they could worship the baby King and return home. Which king would they follow?**

8. Ask, **Why was this a hard choice?** (King Herod was powerful; he could hurt them; he had an army; the Baby didn't look much like a king; they were in a foreign country; they wanted the Baby to be safe; King Herod wanted information) Say, **Yes, it must have been hard to make the choice when they looked at both kings on the surface. King Herod looked wealthy and powerful. He lived in a palace and dressed in fine clothing. King Jesus looked poor and powerless. He was born in a stable and was wrapped in rags.** Have King Herod stand next to the doll in the box to show the contrast.

9. Say, **God helped the wise men make a good choice. He helped them to know that King Herod was dangerous. After the wise men worshiped Jesus, they went home a different way from how they came. They never told King Herod where to find Jesus.**

10. Say, **The next time you are confused, remember the wise men. God helped them make a good choice. Ask God to help you. Ask Him for the courage to do the right thing.**

11. Say, **Let's pray together.** Have the children bow their heads. Say, **Dear Lord, we want to follow You – the King of kings. Help us to make good choices. In Jesus' name, amen.**

12. If time allows, help the children make King's Crowns.

# Why a Baby?

 ALL AGES

**Bible Reference:** *Isaiah 9:6-7, John 1:14*

 ## Overview

God became incarnate as a baby in an ordinary
family, rather than as a temporal king, military
leader or priest.

 ## What You Need

❉ instructions and materials for
   King's Crowns, page 70
❉ instructions and materials for
   The King's Cupcakes, page 137
❉ play helmet, sword, shield or
   other military apparel
❉ white sheet or blanket
❉ 2 yards each of red, blue
   and purple ribbon
❉ doll wrapped in a blanket
❉ 3 sheets of construction paper
❉ markers
❉ Bible

 ## Preparation

Make a sample King's Crown. If you plan to have the children make The King's Cupcakes,
have the materials ready. Braid together red, blue and purple ribbon. Knot the braid at each
end. On the first piece of construction paper, write "Special Leader #1," on the second piece
of paper write "Special Leader #2," and on the third piece of paper write, "Special Leader
#3." Set the doll wrapped in a blanket out of view. Place markers at Isaiah 9:6-7 and John
1:14 in your Bible.

## Presentation

1. Ask three volunteers to portray a king, a military leader and a priest. The king should
   wear the King's Crown. The military leader should wear the helmet and carry the sword
   and shield. The priest should wear the white sheet or blanket as a robe and the braided
   ribbon tied as a belt.

2. Have the three volunteers stand in a row in front of the group. Place the sheet of paper
   marked "Special Leader #1" in front of the king. Place the sheet of paper marked
   "Special Leader #2" in front of the military leader. Place the sheet of paper marked
   "Special Leader #3" in front of the priest.

3. Say, **Before Jesus was born, God told His people that He was sending them
   a very special leader. Here are three examples of leaders from Bible times.
   Let's talk about each of them before you decide which kind of leader God
   would send.**

*continued on next page...*

4. Have the king step forward. Say, **Maybe God would send a king. Describe a king.** (rich; powerful; he sits on a throne; he wears a crown; people obey him; he rules over a kingdom)

5. Have the king step back and the military leader step forward. Say, **Maybe God would send a military leader. Describe a military leader.** (he fights in wars; he is strong; troops do what he says; he is respected)

6. Have the military leader step back and the priest step forward. Say, **Maybe God would send a priest or religious leader. Describe a priest.** (he works in the temple; he has an important job; he has influence)

7. Have the priest step back. Say, **Let's find out what kind of special leader you think God would send.** Have the children vote for one of the volunteers standing in front of them. Tally the results.

8. Say, **God left some clues in the Bible describing this special leader.** Read Isaiah 9:6-7. Let the children explain what the passage says about the special leader. Say, **Yes, it sounds like this leader would be very responsible, successful and good.**

9. Say, **[Number] of you think God would send a king, [number] of you think He would send a military leader, and [number] of you think He would send a priest.** Take out the baby in a blanket. Say, **But God did something different. He sent a baby from a very ordinary family to be the special leader.**

10. Read John 1:14. Ask, **Why would God send an ordinary baby?** (He wanted to become one of us; He knew people might trust an ordinary person more easily than a powerful person)

11. Ask, **But how could an ordinary baby become a special leader?** (because baby Jesus was God; Jesus was God's Son; God worked through Jesus; God can do anything)

12. Say, **This ordinary baby's name was Jesus. He was the special leader God sent. He grew into a man. He is strong and powerful. He rules the Kingdom of God. He is the King of kings and Lord of lords. Yet we can relate to Him. We can talk to Him anytime. God became human like us because He loves us so much.**

13. Say, **Let's pray together.** Have the children bow their heads. Say, **Dear God, thank You for sending us a special leader – baby Jesus. Thank You, Jesus, that You became one of us. In Jesus' name, amen.**

14. If time allows, have the children make The King's Cupcakes. Lead them in singing "Happy Birthday" to Jesus.

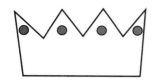

# Worship the King

ALL AGES

**Bible Reference: *Psalm 95:6, Matthew 2:9-11***

 **Overview**

The wise men's visit to the Christ Child demonstrates different ways to worship.

**What You Need**

❊ chairs
❊ rug or mat
❊ Bible

 **Preparation**

Spread a rug or mat on the floor in the lesson area. Place markers at Psalm 95:6 and Matthew 2:9-11 in your Bible. (In preparation, you might want to read more than one translation of Matthew 2:11, noting that some versions render "they bowed down" as "they fell down.")

 **Presentation**

1. Assemble the children. Ask, **In church, do we worship God standing, sitting, kneeling or lying down?** The children can respond according to your denomination's practices.

2. Review the parts of your regular church service, pointing out when the congregation stands, kneels and sits. For example, you might stand for singing, kneel for prayer and sit to hear Scripture reading.

3. Read Psalm 95:6. Say, **This passage teaches about worship. What does it tell us to do?** (bow down, kneel) Ask, **How does bowing our heads or bowing down show worship?** (it demonstrates that you are listening; it shows respect) Ask, **How does kneeling show worship?** (it shows humility; it is an act of reverence)

4. Read Matthew 2:9-11. Say, **In Bible times, "to bow down" meant more than bowing your head or bowing from the waist. When the wise men "bowed down" to baby Jesus, they fell to the ground and extended their hands and arms in front of them.** Have the children practice lying prostrate on the rug or mat.

5. Ask, **How does falling down show worship?** (it shows complete surrender) Ask, **Why did the wise men show such respect and surrender to a tiny baby?** Allow the children to respond. Say, **Yes, they recognized that Jesus was a gift from God. When we worship God, we acknowledge how strong and mighty He is. He is our Creator, our Redeemer and our Savior.**

6. Say, **Let's worship God just like the wise men did.** Have the children stand, then bow their heads, kneel and lie prostrate. Say, **Let's pray together. You can bow your head, kneel or lie down.** Give the children a moment to situate themselves. Say, **God, we worship You this day. We honor and respect You, we reverence You and we surrender ourselves to You. You are King! In Jesus' name, amen.**

# Wrapping Gifts with Jesus

✳❋✳❋✳❋✳❋✳ ALL AGES

**Bible Reference: *Romans 6:23***

 **Overview**

Wrapping a gift demonstrates important elements of God's free gift to us: eternal life in Christ Jesus.

 **What You Need**

✳ boxes
✳ gift wrap
✳ ribbon
✳ gift tags
✳ scissors
✳ clear tape
✳ pen or pencil
✳ Bible

 **Preparation**

Place a marker at Romans 6:23 in your Bible.

 **Presentation**

1. Say, **Christmas is Jesus' birthday. Why did God sent Jesus to the earth?** (to show us how to live; to give us a new chance; to be with us)

2. Say, **There's another important reason. God loves us so much that He wants us to live with Him forever.** Read Romans 6:23b. Say, **God gives us the gift of eternal life in Jesus. But sometimes it's hard to remember Jesus when we get so excited about receiving lots of presents. Let's wrap this gift a special way to remind us about God's gift to us: eternal life in Jesus.** Set the box in front of you.

3. Say, **The first thing we need to do is wrap the box.** Cut a piece of gift wrap and cover the box. Say, **The paper covers the box to hide what is inside. When we admit we have made mistakes and need Jesus, His blood covers our sin.**

4. Say, **We need to seal and secure the box.** Tape the paper and tie a ribbon around the box. Say, **The tape and the ribbon seal and secure the box. When we decide to believe in Jesus, He secures our salvation with the Holy Spirit.**

5. Say, **We need to label this box.** Fill out a gift tag and tape it on the box. Say, **This gift is for** [child's name]. **When we decide to follow Jesus, He begins a relationship with us. We can have Him as our friend forever.**

6. Ask, **Can Jesus give us the gift of eternal life if we don't take it?** (I'm not sure; the gift is still there) Say, **Jesus offers us the gift of eternal life, but we must accept it.** Give the recipient the gift.

7. Say, **Wrapping gifts reminds us of the steps to receive God's gift of eternal life. All He asks is that we receive this free gift.**

8. Say, **Let's pray together.** Have the children bow their heads. Say, **God, thank You for Your free gift in Christ Jesus – eternal life. Help us to remember as we wrap our gifts that You cover our sins, You seal us and You want a personal relationship with us. We receive this gift. In Jesus' name, amen.**

9. Say, **Now when you wrap gifts, you can celebrate Jesus' gift to you: eternal life.** If time allows, have the children each wrap a box. Let them share the steps as they work.

# Reproducibles
# &
# Patterns

# Prayer Checklist

Use this checklist to help you pray for your event from start to finish!

## Praise God for:

- ❑ His exceeding greatness
- ❑ The miracle of the Incarnation
- ❑ The joy and peace that comes with salvation

## Seek from God:

- ❑ Prayer partners who will pray faithfully for the event
- ❑ Wisdom in setting a date and choosing a program
- ❑ Guidance as you choose a leadership team
- ❑ Good judgment as you select activities
- ❑ Insight about which forms of publicity to use
- ❑ The ability to remember many details

## Ask God for:

- ❑ Many willing volunteers
- ❑ Many people to hear about your party and come
- ❑ New families to be reached
- ❑ Sufficient financial resources
- ❑ Your church to grow as a result of this event

## Pray for:

- ❑ A groundswell of enthusiasm in your congregation about your party
- ❑ Unity in your team
- ❑ A smooth set-up
- ❑ Good weather
- ❑ Receptive hearts in guests who are invited to come
- ❑ Safety for all who attend
- ❑ The Holy Spirit to be present throughout your event
- ❑ Changed lives for both participants and helpers

## Thank God for:

- ❑ His great love in sending His Son
- ❑ The opportunity to share the Good News with your community
- ❑ The initiative of those who are organizing your celebration
- ❑ The willingness of your congregation to undertake a new program

## Intercede for:

- ❑ Effective volunteer training sessions
- ❑ A spirit of cooperation and goodwill among your workers
- ❑ Volunteers who greet guests at the registration table
- ❑ Volunteers who help with games, crafts, gifts and activities
- ❑ Helpers who serve snacks
- ❑ Those who present the Christmas story and lead singing
- ❑ Congregation members as they invite family and friends
- ❑ People who receive invitations
- ❑ Your pastors as they greet visitors

## After your celebration:

- ❑ Praise God for the successes of the day
- ❑ Give thanks for your volunteers
- ❑ Ask Him to show you how to improve your program next time
- ❑ Intercede for your visitation team as they follow up with guests
- ❑ Pray that newcomers would join you for worship
- ❑ Ask that the congregation make these future visitors feel welcome and accepted

# The Mitten Tree

## Help us give a very special birthday gift to Jesus!

**We are collecting** (list needed accessories)

**For** (list agency)

**Between** (list starting and ending collection dates)

**Bring in your donations and hang them on the Mitten Tree!**

*I tell you the truth, whatever you did for one of the least of these brothers of mine, you did for me.*
**~ Matthew 25:40**

- - - - - - - - - - - - - - - - - - - - - - - - - - - - - - - - - - - - - - - - - - - - - - - -

# We're Throwing a Birthday Party for Jesus!

…and we need your help.
We're sharing the message of Christmas with the children and families
in our community at a celebration on _____.
(date)

## Can you donate some items?

Please place them in the baskets located _____.

by _____
(date)

## We need:
(list needed supplies here)

_____        _____

_____        _____

_____        _____

_____        _____

## Thank you!

# Help Wanted: Elves!

**We're having a Christmas outreach for the families in our community. Can you help?**

I can help on the day of the event_____.

(event date and time)

| Name | Phone | Job |
|------|-------|-----|
| _____ | _____ | _____ |
| _____ | _____ | _____ |
| _____ | _____ | _____ |
| _____ | _____ | _____ |
| _____ | _____ | _____ |
| _____ | _____ | _____ |
| _____ | _____ | _____ |

I can help set up for the event on _____.

(set-up date and time)

| _____ | _____ | _____ |
|------|-------|-----|
| _____ | _____ | _____ |
| _____ | _____ | _____ |
| _____ | _____ | _____ |

I can help prepare craft, game, gift and decoration materials before the celebration.

| _____ | _____ | _____ |
|------|-------|-----|
| _____ | _____ | _____ |
| _____ | _____ | _____ |
| _____ | _____ | _____ |
| _____ | _____ | _____ |

# Volunteer Training Checklist

Use this checklist to help prepare your volunteers for your event.

## All volunteers need to:

- ❏ Greet guests in a friendly way
- ❏ Know the program schedule
- ❏ Know where the various stations are located

## Registration Table volunteers need to:

- ❏ Know how to fill out the registration form for each guest
- ❏ Show each guest where to go to begin

## Station Leaders need to:

- ❏ Help choose activities for their stations
- ❏ Assemble necessary items
- ❏ Know how to do or make each activity at that station
- ❏ Know how long each activity at that station takes to do or make
- ❏ Meet with the volunteers assigned to that station

## Decorations, Games, Crafts and Gifts volunteers need to:

- ❏ Know how to do or make their activity
- ❏ Know how long their activity takes to do or make
- ❏ Have supplies and prizes ready

## Wrapping Station volunteers need to:

- ❏ Have gift wrap, gift bags, clear tape, bows and scissors ready
- ❏ Be able to wrap gifts neatly

## Santa Claus needs to:

- ❏ Wear his costume
- ❏ Circulate among the participants
- ❏ Carry a sack of candy canes or treats
- ❏ Offer encouragement to children and parents

## Volunteers taking photos need to:

- ❏ Have plenty of fresh film
- ❏ Know the kinds of photos that are wanted
- ❏ Record names of people in photos as they are taken

## Snack volunteers need to:

- ❏ Know how to prepare the snack
- ❏ Show children where to wash their hands

## Volunteers leading Caroling need to:

- ❏ Have songbooks, flashlights, candleholders and matches ready
- ❏ Know what route is planned
- ❏ Sing in strong voices

## Gingerbread House volunteers need to:

- ❏ Know how to assemble a gingerbread house
- ❏ Have icing and decorations ready
- ❏ Be willing to get sticky

## Hanging the Greens volunteers need to:

- ❏ Know how to assemble the greens
- ❏ Know where to hang the decorations
- ❏ Have a vacuum and broom ready to clean up evergreen needles

## The Mitten Tree volunteers need to:

- ❏ Make sure tree is set up in an accessible location
- ❏ Check tree from time to time to keep it neat
- ❏ Collect, package and deliver mittens and hats to the appropriate agency

## Volunteers presenting The Christmas Story need to:

- ❏ Know their parts
- ❏ Rehearse ahead of time
- ❏ Have materials, costumes and props ready

## Volunteers making follow-up visits need to:

- ❏ Thank visitors for attending
- ❏ Ask if there is any way your church can serve them
- ❏ Invite visitors to attend worship
- ❏ Offer to pray with visitors, if appropriate

# Supply Checklist

## Publicity
- ❑ Church Newsletter Article
- ❑ Bulletin Inserts
- ❑ Publicity Flyers
- ❑ Publicity Postcards
- ❑ Mailing List
- ❑ Newspaper Announcement
- ❑ Outside Banner

## Registration
- ❑ Registration Forms and pencils
- ❑ Schedule of Events
- ❑ Setup Map
- ❑ Church Brochure and list of Advent events
- ❑ Visitor Evaluation Forms

## Set-up
- ❑ List of what needs to be done
- ❑ Party decorations
- ❑ Station signs
- ❑ Directional signs
- ❑ Santa costume, treat bag and camera

## Decorations, Games, Crafts, Gifts and Snacks
- ❑ Decoration supplies for activities selected from pages 50-62
- ❑ Game supplies for activities selected from pages 110-124
- ❑ Prizes
- ❑ Prize boxes or baskets for each station
- ❑ Craft and gift supplies for activities selected from pages 64-106
- ❑ Gift wrap and bags, bows, ribbon, clear tape and scissors for wrapping station
- ❑ Snack supplies for activities selected from pages 128-145

## More Activities
- ❑ Caroling books, flashlights, candle holders, candles and candle lighter
- ❑ Gingerbread house supplies
- ❑ Evergreen branches, pinecones, garden clippers, wire, bows, and wire cutters
- ❑ Christmas story materials and supplies
- ❑ Christmas tree for mittens and hats

# A Christmas Celebration for Kids and Families!
## Join Us For...

_____
(type of event)

_____

_____

_____
(date, time, location)

## Decorations • Games • Crafts • Gifts • Prizes • Snacks • Singing • The Christmas Story • FREE!

Pre-registration is encouraged. Please call _____
(church office)

## Christmas is Jesus' birthday – come celebrate!

- - - - - - - - - - - - - - - - - - - - - - - - - - - - - - - - - - - - -

Our Christmas celebration is coming...
and YOU are invited!

Date: _____

Time: _____

Place: _____

### Games • Crafts • Prizes
### Snacks • The Christmas Story
### FREE!

Pre-registration is encouraged:

_____
(phone number)

**Kids, bring your families!**
**Bring your friends!**

### Christmas is Jesus' Birthday...
### Come Celebrate!

# It's a Christmas Celebration for Kids and Families!

Join us for…

_____
(kind of event)

_____

_____

_____
(date, time, location)

## Kids…bring your family! Bring your friends!

Games • Crafts

Gifts• Prizes

Snacks • Singing

The Christmas Story

**FREE!**

Pre-registration is encouraged.
Please call _____.

# Christmas is Jesus' birthday – come celebrate!

# Registration Form

Child's Name:_____

Date of Birth: _____

Grade in School: _____

Parents' Names:_____

Child's Address: _____

Home Phone: _____

E-mail address: _____

May we contact you by e-mail? _____

Person to call in an emergency:_____

Emergency Phone: _____

How did you hear about us? _____

Do you have a home church? _____ **Thank you for joining us!**

- - - - - - - - - - - - - - - - - - - - - - - - - - - - - - - - - - - - - - -

# Welcome to our
# CHRISTMAS CELEBRATION

at _____
(church name)

## Schedule of Events

| | |
|---|---|
| **10:00 a.m.** | Registration |
| | We hope you will participate in the |
| | **Welcome Wreath** and **The Christmas Kindness Tree!** |
| **10:00-11:15 a.m.** | Make decorations, crafts and gifts |
| | Play games |
| **11:15-11:30 a.m.** | Snack Time and Live Nativity |
| | Children will be escorted to the Live Nativity in age groups. |
| **11:30-Noon** | The Christmas Story and Carol Sing |

## Thank you for celebrating Christmas with us!

**Today in the town of David a Savior has been born to you; he is Christ the Lord.**
~ Luke 2:11

*Schedule of Events sample*

| | |
|---|---|
| **GOOD FOR 1 SNACK** | **GOOD FOR 1 SNACK** |
| **GOOD FOR 1 SNACK** | **GOOD FOR 1 SNACK** |
| **GOOD FOR 1 SNACK** | **GOOD FOR 1 SNACK** |
| **GOOD FOR 1 SNACK** | **GOOD FOR 1 SNACK** |
| **GOOD FOR 1 SNACK** | **GOOD FOR 1 SNACK** |
| **GOOD FOR 1 SNACK** | **GOOD FOR 1 SNACK** |
| **GOOD FOR 1 SNACK** | **GOOD FOR 1 SNACK** |

# Set-up Checklist

## Prior to Set-up

❑ Determine station locations

❑ Reproduce instructions for each activity you have chosen

❑ Collect necessary supplies

❑ Construct needed game parts

❑ Reproduce volunteer evaluation forms, visitor evaluation forms, schedule of events and set-up map

❑ Have extra registration forms, church brochures and Advent schedule of events on hand

❑ Make a Happy Birthday Pin (page 69) for each volunteer

## Set-up Time

❑ Set up registration table

❑ Assemble registration packets to include take-home bags, registration forms, church brochures, Advent schedule of events, setup map, party schedule of events and visitor evaluation forms

❑ Post Christmas Kindness Tree (page 35) and Welcome Wreath (page 39)

❑ Arrange tables, chairs and posters at each station

❑ Set up chairs for volunteers and visiting family members

❑ Post set-up map, traffic flow signs and schedule of events

❑ Decorate facility

❑ Assemble Live Nativity scenery (pages 161-162) and The Mitten Tree (page 163)

❑ Complete volunteer training

❑ Give each volunteer written instructions for his or her station

❑ Distribute supplies for each station

❑ Have decorations, crafts and gifts volunteers make samples

❑ Have games volunteers play games

❑ Have snack volunteers make sample snacks

❑ Rehearse the Christmas story

❑ Take photos of stations, decorations and sample activities for Christmas Celebration File

❑ Give each volunteer a Happy Birthday Pin

# Visitor Evaluation

Thank you for joining us for our Christmas celebration! Please take a few minutes and answer the questions below. We would like your feedback so that we can minister effectively to children and families in our community.

1. Which activity did your family enjoy the most? _____

2. Which activity did your family enjoy the least? _____

3. Were you satisfied with the quality and variety of activities? _____

4. Was the message of Christmas evident to you and your family? _____

5. Was the event organized and staffed to your satisfaction? _____

6. Would you come again? _____

7. How did you hear about our event? _____

Additional Comments: _____

_____

Thank you for sharing your thoughts with us. Merry Christmas!

*Today in the town of David a Savior has been born to you; he is Christ the Lord.* ~ Luke 2:11

---

# Volunteer Evaluation

Thank you for helping with our Christmas celebration! Please take a few minutes and answer the questions below. We would like your feedback so that we can effectively minister to children and families.

1. Which activities worked best? Why? _____

2. Which activities were least effective? Why? _____

3. Were you satisfied with the variety, volume and quality of activities presented? Why or why not?

_____

4. Were you satisfied with the organization and preparation put into the event? _____

5. Did you receive adequate training to complete your task?_____

6. What could we do better next year? _____

7. Would you participate again? _____

Additional Comments: _____

_____

Thank you for sharing your thoughts with us. Merry Christmas!

*Today in the town of David a Savior has been born to you; he is Christ the Lord.* ~ Luke 2:11

Dear Friend:

Thank you for attending the Christmas Celebration at [church name]. We were delighted to have you as our guests as we rejoiced together at the coming of our Savior into the world.

We hope you will join us again during Advent for [list other Advent events]. And we extend a special invitation to you and your family to worship with us on Christmas Eve at [times of services].

We also minister to families through our [list family ministry opportunities]. If you and your children enjoyed our Christmas Celebration, then you won't want to miss our [Easter Celebration, vacation Bible school or next children's event]. Check our church's web site [web site address] for regularly updated information.

Our staff is available to answer your questions about these opportunities for you and your family at [church office phone number]. We look forward to seeing you again soon!

In Christ,

[signed]
Christmas Celebration Director

[signed]
Pastor

- - - - - - - - - - - - - - - - - - - - - - - - - - - - - - - - - - - - - - - - - - - - - - -

Dear Friend:

Thank you for attending the Christmas Celebration at [church name]. You modeled the love of Christ by your presence and support.

We hope you will invite your family members, friends and neighbors to join us during Advent for [list other Advent events]. In particular, you may wish to extend them a special invitation to be your guests at worship on Christmas Eve at [times of services].

On behalf of your church family, please accept our deep appreciation for your part in building up the body of Christ.

With gratitude,

[signed]
Christmas Celebration Director

[signed]
Pastor

*Now you are the body of Christ, and each one of you is a part of it.*
~ 1 Corinthians 12:27

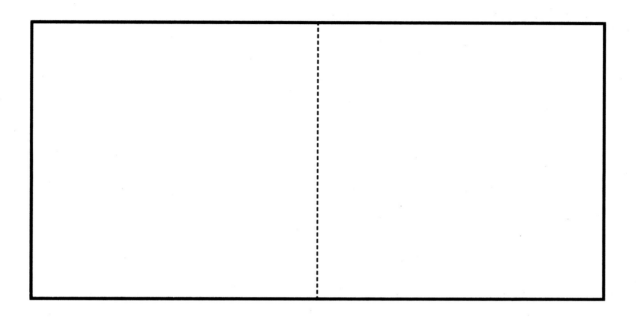

*To use with a set of Holiday Heart Gift Tags as a gift*

Gifts at Christmas
Are so much fun.
But the best gift of all
Is God's own Son!

*For to us a child is born,*
*to us a son is given.*
~ Isaiah 9:6

*Bouncy Balls*

Elizabeth's baby bounced for joy
At the news of Mary's infant Boy.
Let us all now jump and sing;
Our Savior's born – our Lord and King!

*When Elizabeth heard Mary's greeting, the baby leaped in her womb, and Elizabeth was filled with the Holy Spirit.*
~ Luke 1:41

*Celebration Soap Bar*

Get clean on the outside
With this soap bar so fun.
Get clean on the inside
God gets the work done!

*Wash away all my iniquity and cleanse me from my sin.*
~ Psalm 51:2

*Christmas Card Roundabout*

Cards can clutter your countertop,
So put them in this Roundabout
In December, when you hear
From friends you love, both far and near.

*Peace to you. The friends here send their greetings.*
~ 3 John 1:14

*Confetti Treat Tin*

Mary stored good thoughts and joy
At the birth of her baby Boy.
Store some treats in this special tin.
It will remind you of God's good within.

*Mary treasured up all these things and pondered them in her heart.*
~ Luke 2:19

*Cookie Mix in a Jar*

**Instructions**

The jar contains flour, soda, salt, brown sugar, granulated sugar, chocolate chips and nuts.

1. In a large bowl, cream together 2/3 cup softened margarine, one egg, 1 teaspoon water and 1/2 teaspoon vanilla.
2. Add contents of jar. Mix well.
3. Drop by rounded teaspoonfuls onto greased cookie sheets.
4. Bake at 375°F for 8-10 minutes. The mix makes about 3 dozen cookies.

Here is a message
from our God and King:
He wants to fill us
with every good thing.

*He has filled the hungry*
*with good things.*
~ Luke 1:53

*Cozy Cocoa Kit*

**Instructions**

1. Measure 3 heaping teaspoons of cocoa mix into a mug.
2. Add 5-6 ounces of hot water.
3. Stir.
4. Top with miniature marshmallows!

When the world outside
seems dark and cold,
Remember the kit that you now hold.
Pour a cup, and savor this treat:
God's love, like cocoa,
is warm and sweet.

*This is love: not that we loved God,*
*but that he loved us and sent his Son.*
~ 1 John 4:10

*Cranberry Grapevine Wreath*

The crown of thorns on His head,
Pain and suffering did bring.
Yet He bore it for us;
He's our Savior and King!

*[They] twisted together a crown of
thorns and set it on his head.*
~ Matthew 27:29

*Hand Towel for a King*

Mary and Joseph followed God
To a stable He did lead.
When we ask the Lord for help
He'll give us what we need.

*She wrapped him in cloths
and placed him in a manger,
because there was no room for
them in the inn.*
~ Luke 2:7

*Holly Door Stopper*

The brick reminds us
that Jesus is strong.
The trim – like the cross –
has one short arm, one long.
The leaf reminds us
of the sharp crown of thorns.
The berry, like blood,
shows that we are reborn.
Jesus and the Holly Door Stop:
He died for us – so that we will not.

*He was pierced for
our transgressions…
and by his wounds we are healed.*
~ Isaiah 53:5

*Im-pastable Canister*

Are you bewildered and uncertain –
Struggling to understand?
Know this in your confusion:
God always has a plan.

*For nothing is impossible with God.*
~ Luke 1:37

*Jingle Bell Gloves*

If it's hard to share with words
About our God and King,
Then wear these gloves –
they'll shout for you,
The bells His praises sing!

*Clap your hands, all you nations;
shout to God with cries of joy.*
~ Psalm 47:1

*Night of Wonder Headband*

The glory of our God and King
Shone brightly in the sky.
But the wonder of that night is this:
He came for you and I.

*The glory of the Lord
shone around them.*
~ Luke 2:9

*Noel Coffee Mug*

The shepherds worshiped God above
For sending us a King.
Noel, Noel, our voices raise;
Our praise to God we sing.

*The shepherds returned, glorifying
and praising God for all the things
they had heard and seen, which were
just as they had been told.*
~ Luke 2:20

*Rock Trivet*

Set your hot dish on this trivet of rock
To protect a table that's bare.
In just the same way, build your
life on The Rock.
Jesus will keep you –
He'll always be there.

*Therefore everyone who hears these
words of mine and puts them into
practice is like a wise man who
built his house on the rock.*
~ Matthew 7:24

*Santa Stamps*

Are you feeling not-so-special?
Down and out, a little blue?
Ask Jesus to be your Savior.
He'll mark you – you'll be brand-new!

*Having believed, you were marked in him with a seal, the promised Holy Spirit.*
~ Ephesians 1:13

*Shining Light Votive Holder*

The Light of the World
Wants me and you
To let His love
Keep shining through.

*Let your light shine before men, that they may see your good deeds and praise your Father in heaven.*
~ Matthew 5:16

*Shoelace Elves*

Elves give Santa extra help.
They make gifts for girls and boys.
We can be God's helpers, too,
By spreading His love and joy.

*"Come, follow me," Jesus said, "and I will make you fishers of men."*
~ Matthew 4:19

*Silver and Gold Sachet*

These sweet-scented, sparkling sachets
Are treasures of silver and gold.
But you'll find that
riches more precious
The Word of God does hold.

*The law from your mouth is more precious to me than thousands of pieces of silver and gold.*
~ Psalm 119:72

*Snowflake Fleece Scarf*

Wrap this scarf around you
To keep you warm inside.
And dress yourself with God's love.
He will in you abide!

*Over all these virtues put
on love, which binds them
all together in perfect unity.*
~ Colossians 3:14

*Spicy Scented Coasters*

Set down your sweet cocoa
Or your warm cup of tea,
Like the scent of these spices
God's fragrance you can be.

*For we are to God the
aroma of Christ.*
~ 2 Corinthians 2:15

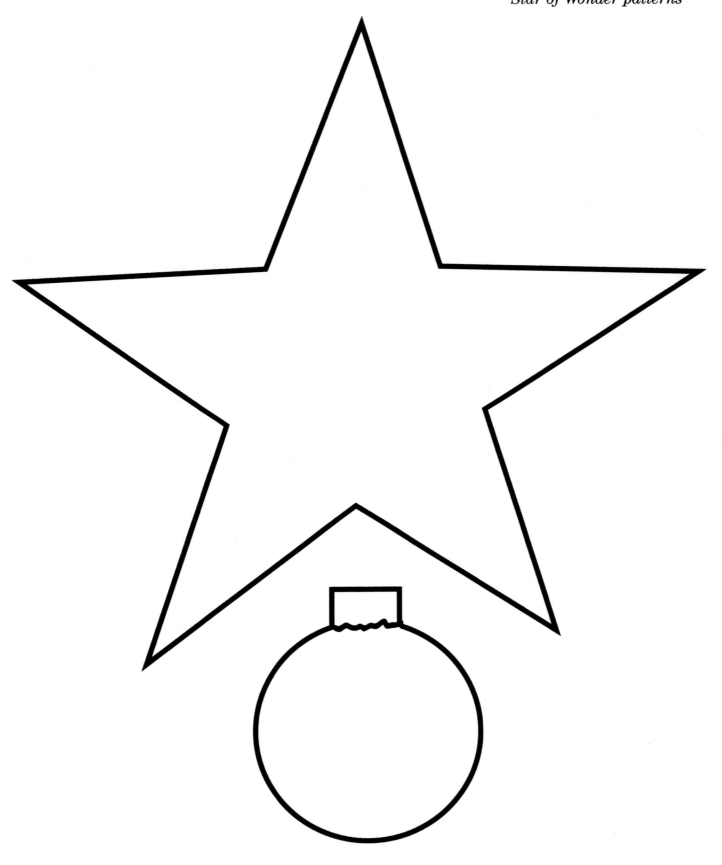

*Sing, Sing, Sing pattern*

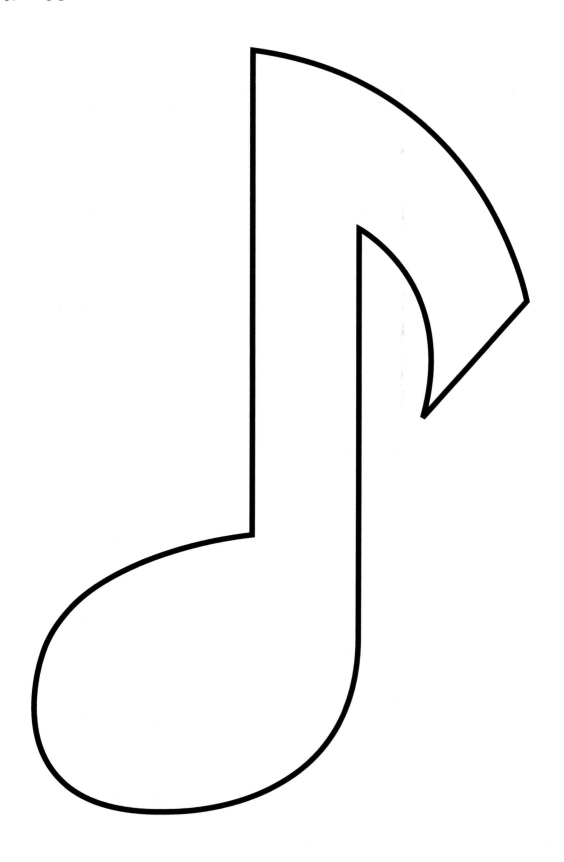

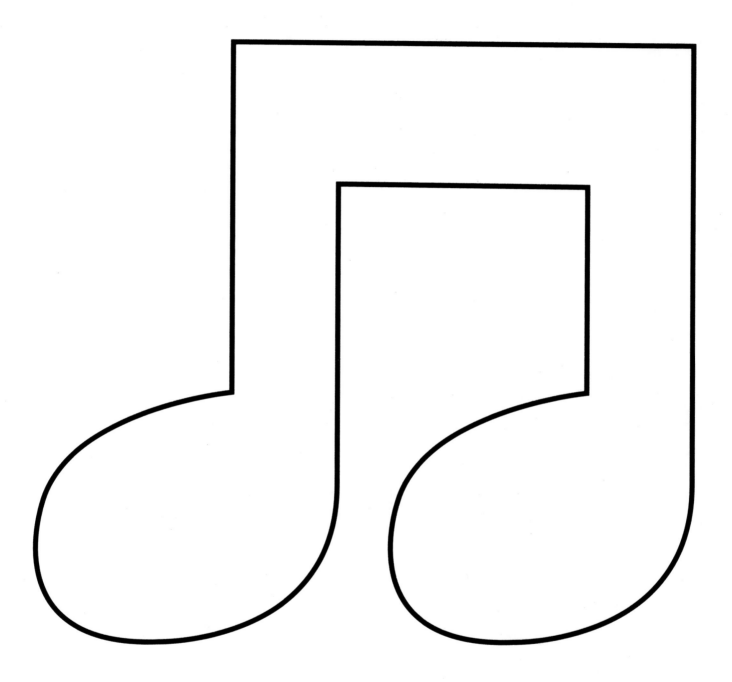

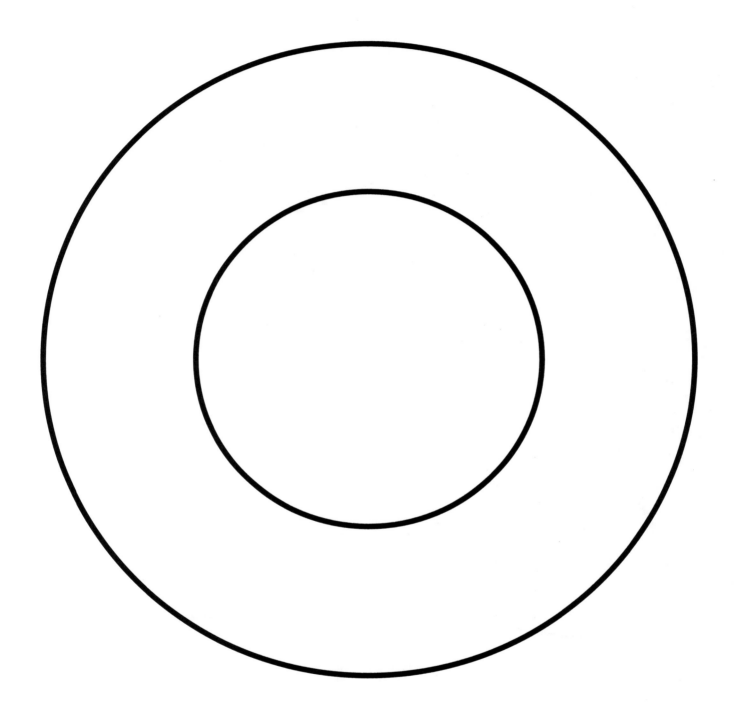

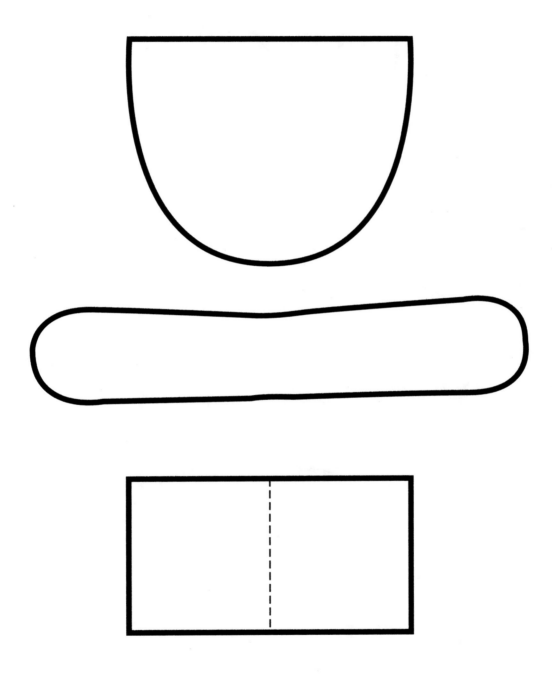

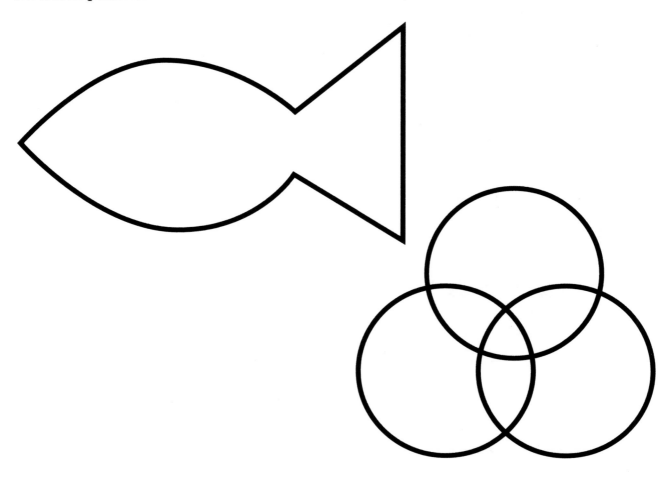

## Chrismons' Symbolic Meanings

Alpha and Omega: Jesus is the First and Last, the Beginning and the End, Revelation 22:13

Bread: Jesus is the Bread of Life, John 6:35

Chalice: Jesus is Immanuel – God with us, Matthew 1:23

Cross: Symbolizes Jesus' work of salvation on the cross, Colossians 1:19-20

Cross and Orb: Symbolizes Christ in the world, John 3:16

Crown: Jesus is the King of Kings, Revelation 19:16

Dove: Symbolizes the presence of the Holy Spirit with Christ, Luke 3:22

Fish (Ichthus): Symbolizes the first letters of Jesus' name in Greek, which are the same as for the Greek word for "fish." Also symbolizes the anointing of the disciples as "fishers of men," Mark 1:17

Shepherd's Crook: Jesus is the Good Shepherd, John 10:11

Triquetra: Symbolizes the Trinity – God in three Persons, Luke 3:21-22

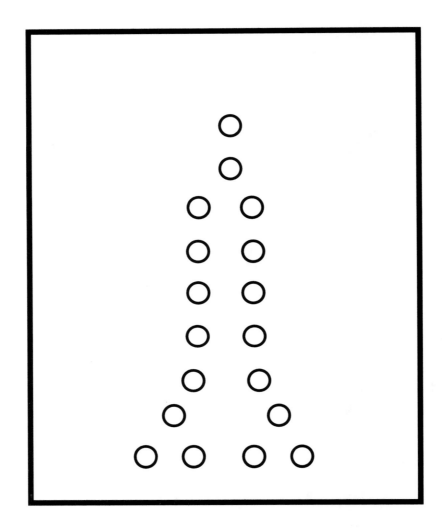

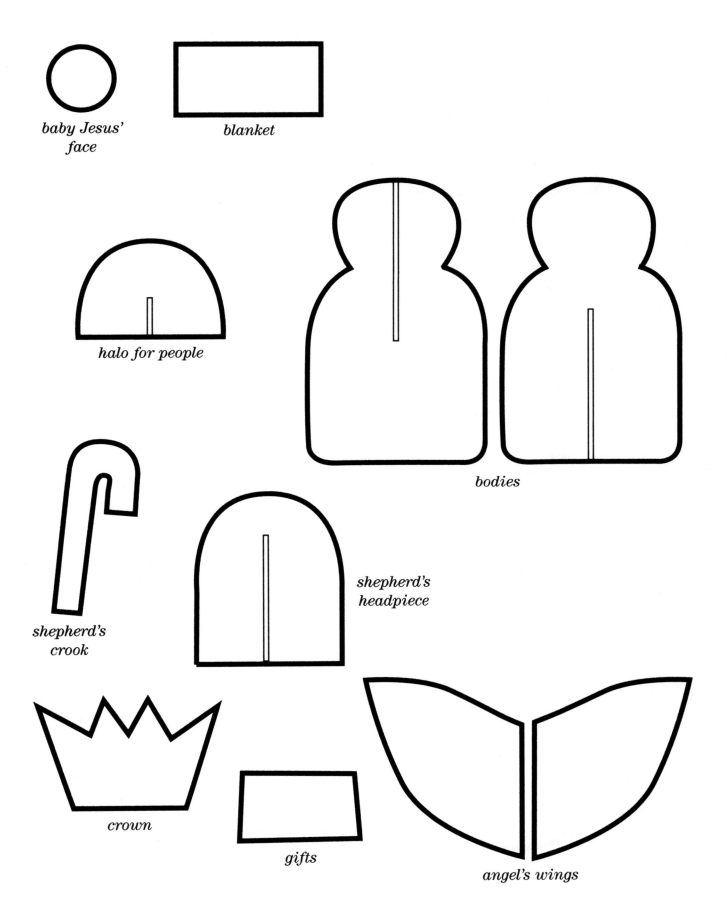

*baby Jesus' face*

*blanket*

*halo for people*

*bodies*

*shepherd's crook*

*shepherd's headpiece*

*crown*

*gifts*

*angel's wings*

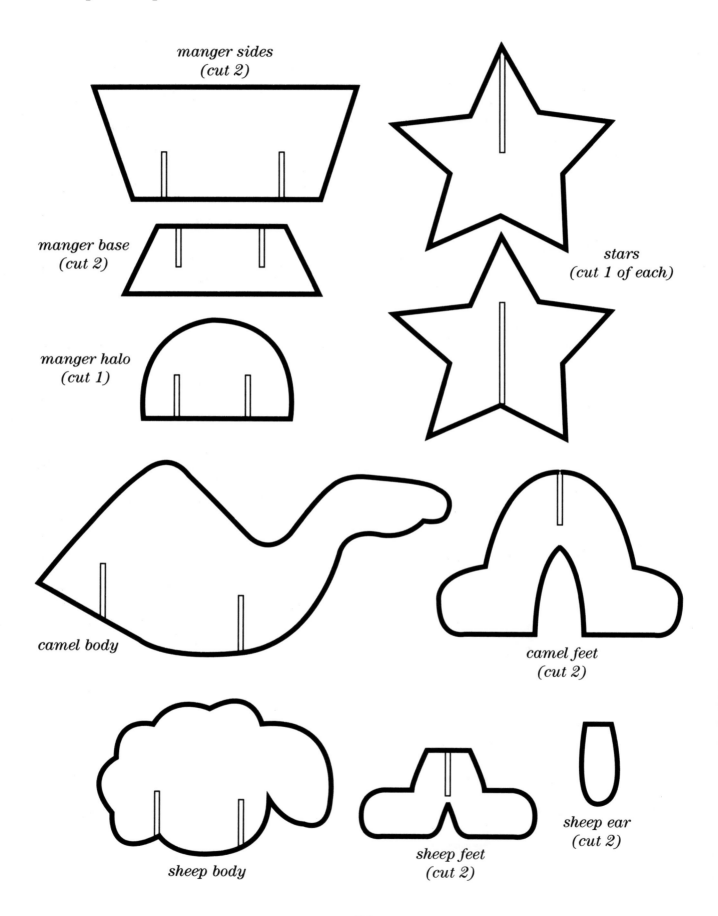

manger sides
(cut 2)

manger base
(cut 2)

manger halo
(cut 1)

stars
(cut 1 of each)

camel body

camel feet
(cut 2)

sheep body

sheep feet
(cut 2)

sheep ear
(cut 2)

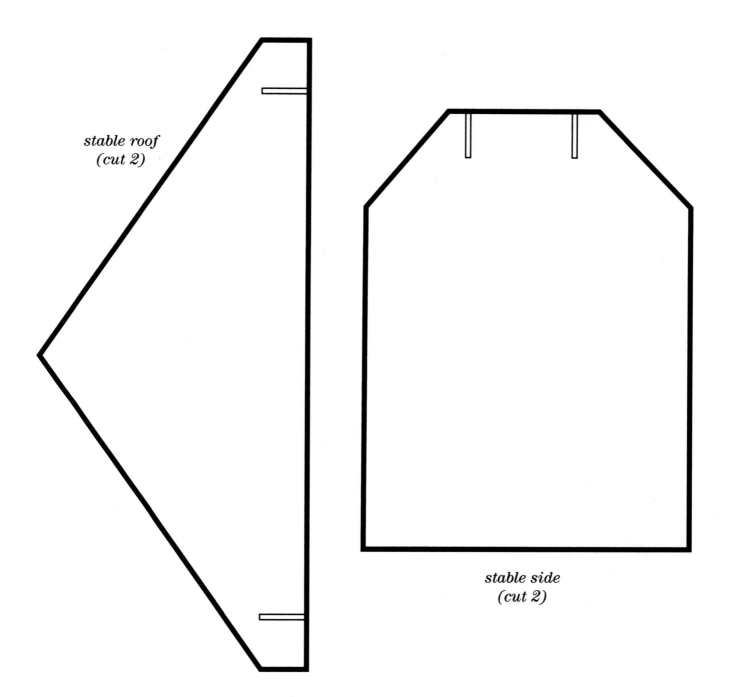

*stable roof*
*(cut 2)*

*stable side*
*(cut 2)*

*Happy Birthday Pin patterns*

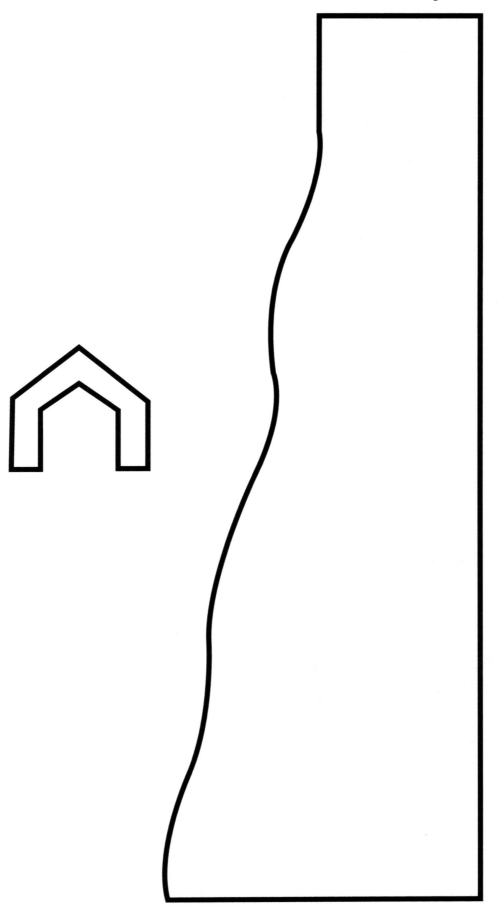

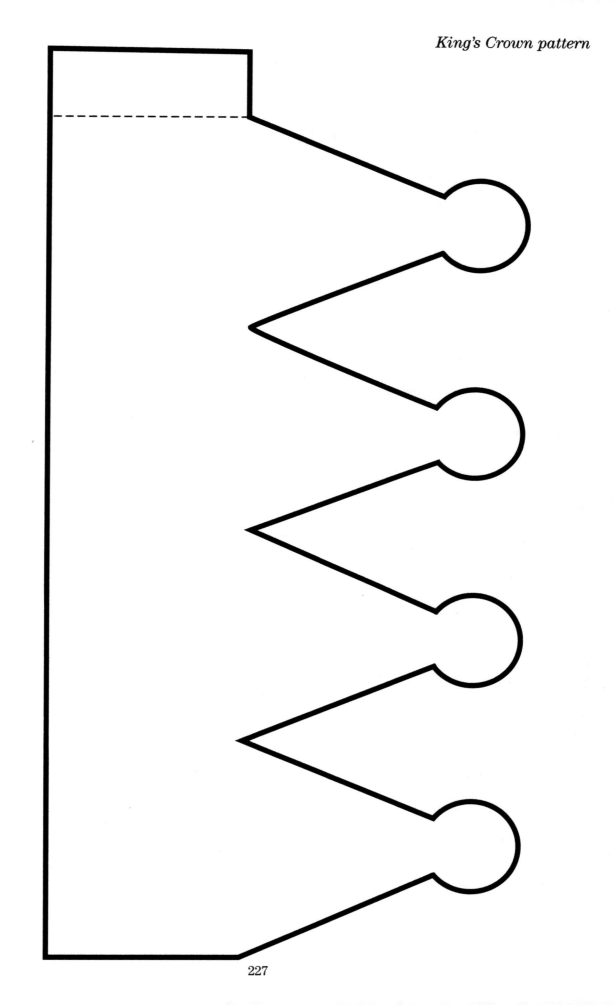

*King's Crown pattern*

*miniature poinsettia leaves*

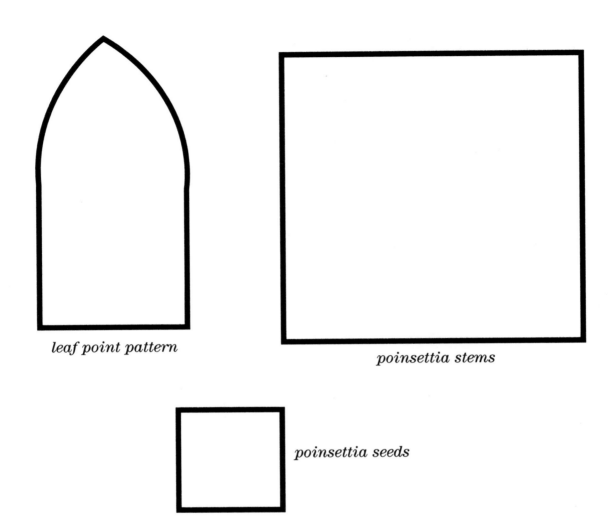

*leaf point pattern*

*poinsettia stems*

*poinsettia seeds*

# Diagrams for making Miniature Poinsettias

### Diagram 1

### Diagram 2

### Diagram 3

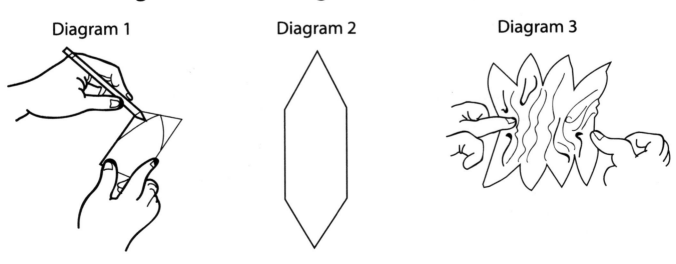

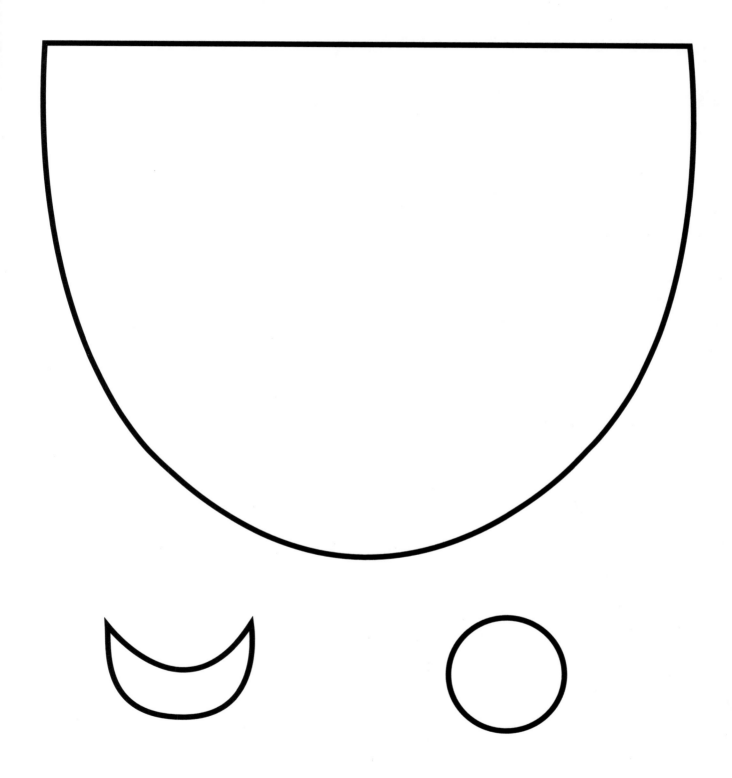

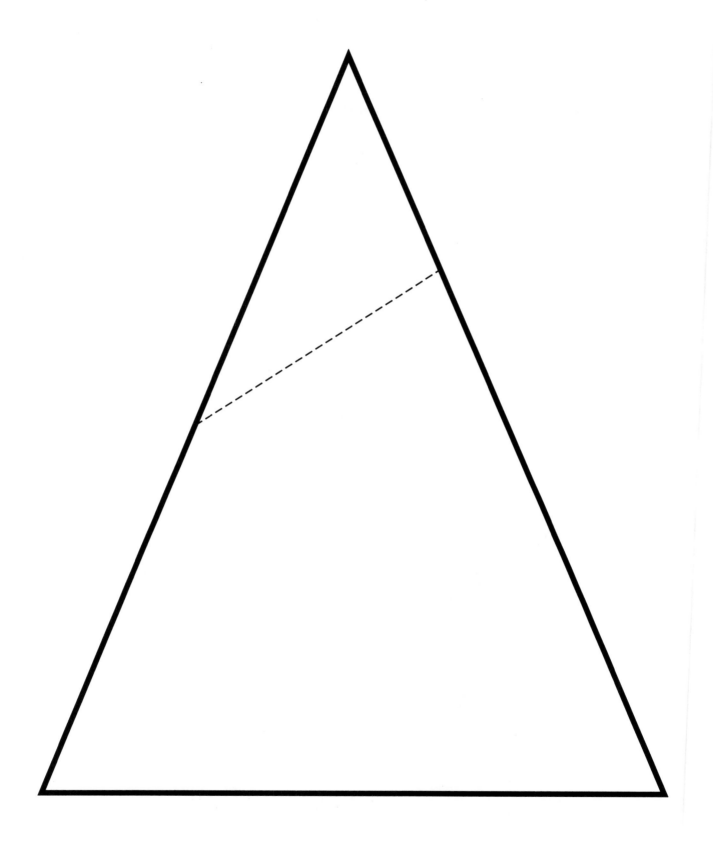

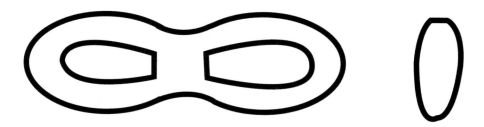

*Star of Bethlehem Pencil Topper pattern*

*Walnut Mouse patterns*

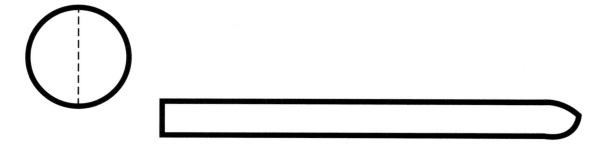

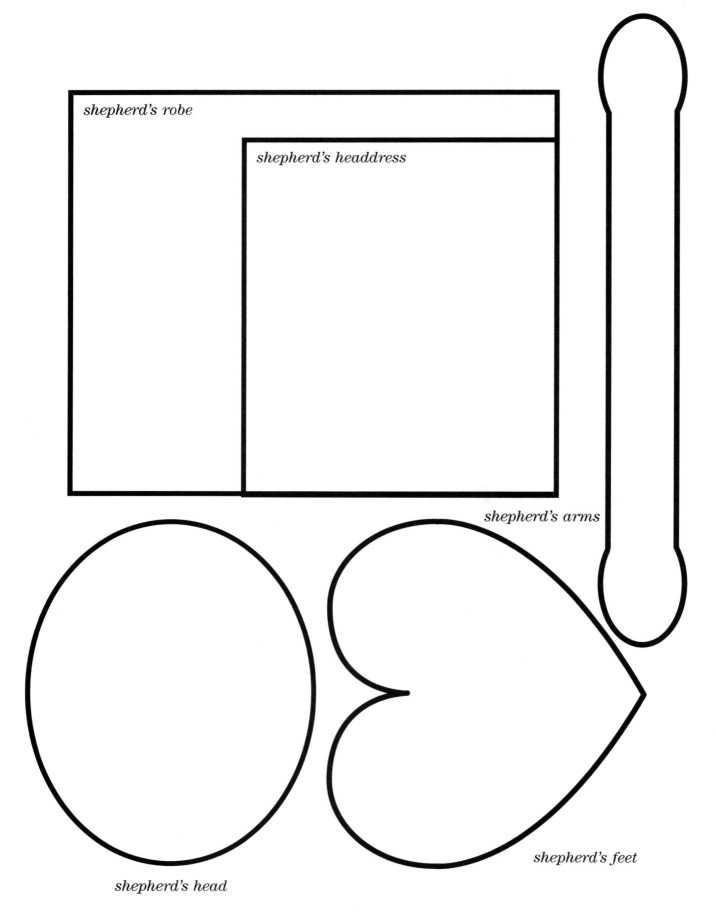

shepherd's robe

shepherd's headdress

shepherd's arms

shepherd's head

shepherd's feet

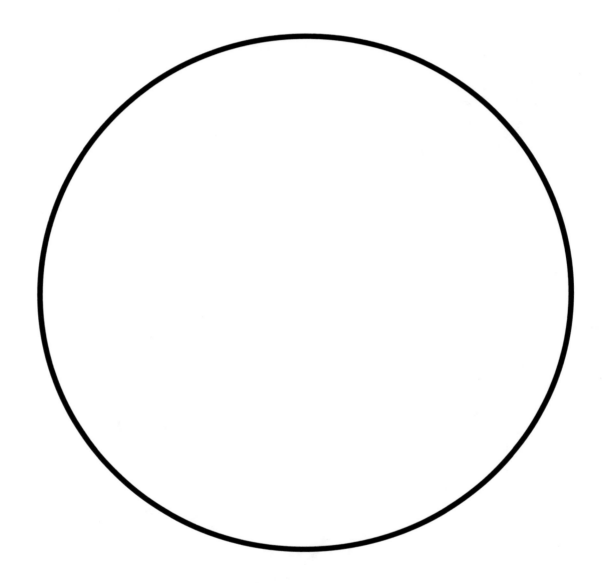

*Snowflake Fleece Scarf patterns*

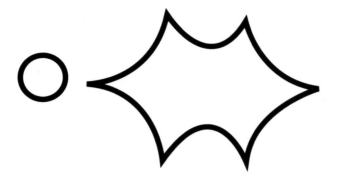

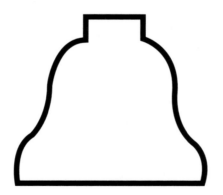

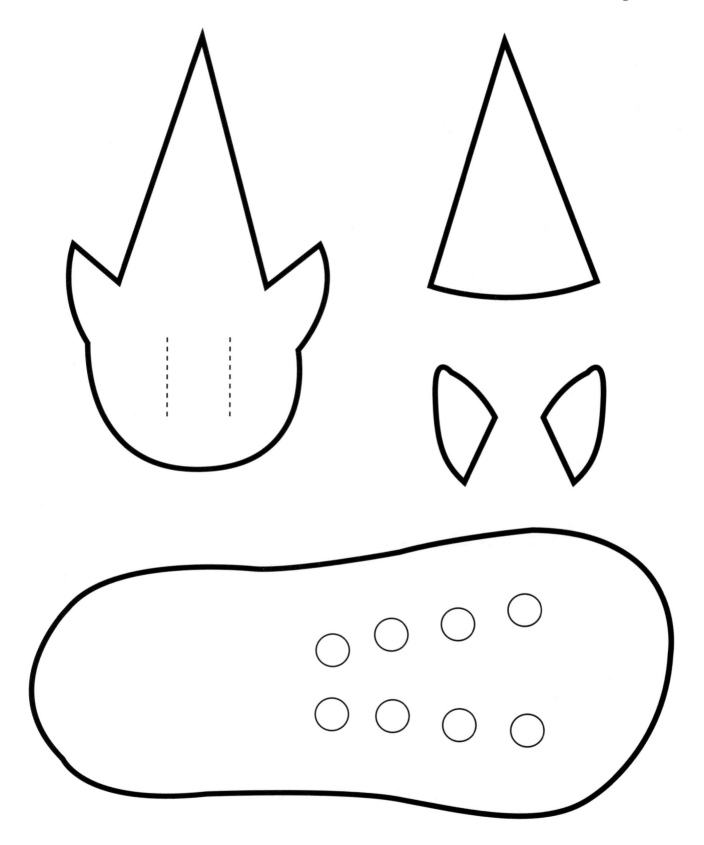

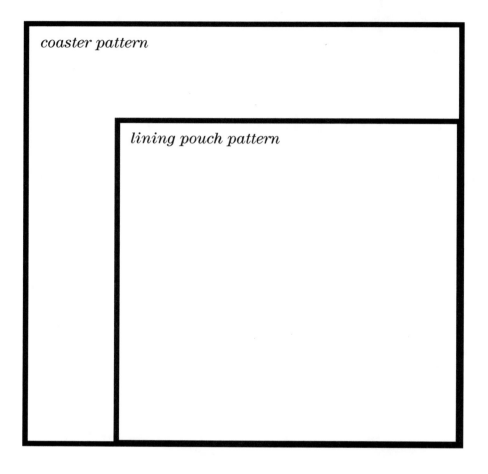

*coaster pattern*

*lining pouch pattern*

# 1,2,3...

| | |
|---|---|
| **Right Foot Jerusalem (Yellow)** | **Left Foot Jerusalem (Yellow)** |
| **Right Hand Jerusalem (Yellow)** | **Left Hand Jerusalem (Yellow)** |
| **Right Foot Egypt (Green)** | **Left Foot Egypt (Green)** |
| **Right Hand Egypt (Green)** | **Left Hand Egypt (Green)** |

| | |
|---|---|
| **Right Foot Nazareth (Red)** | **Left Foot Nazareth (Red)** |
| **Right Hand Nazareth (Red)** | **Left Hand Nazareth (Red)** |
| **Right Foot Bethlehem (Blue)** | **Left Foot Bethlehem (Blue)** |
| **Right Hand Bethlehem (Blue)** | **Left Hand Bethlehem (Blue)** |

# *Christmas Caroling Songbook*

# Angels We Have Heard on High

Angels we have heard on high,
Sweetly singing o'er the plains,
And the mountains in reply,
Echoing their joyous strains.
Gloria in excelsis Deo!
Gloria in excelsis Deo!

Shepherds, why this jubilee?
Why your joyous strains prolong?
What the gladsome tidings be
Which inspire your heav'nly song?
Gloria in excelsis Deo!
Gloria in excelsis Deo!

Come to Bethlehem and see
Him whose birth the angels sing;
Come, adore on bended knee
Christ the Lord, the newborn King.
Gloria in excelsis Deo!
Gloria in excelsis Deo!

1

# Away in a Manger

Away in a manger, no crib for a bed,
The little Lord Jesus laid down His sweet head.
The stars in the sky looked down where He lay,
The little Lord Jesus asleep on the hay.

The cattle are lowing; the Baby awakes,
But little Lord Jesus–no crying He makes.
I love Thee, Lord Jesus; look down from the sky.
And stay by my cradle 'til morning is nigh.

Be near me, Lord Jesus; I ask Thee to stay
Close by me forever, and love me, I pray.
Bless all the dear children in Thy tender care,
And fit us for heaven, to live with Thee there.

2

# The First Noel

The first Noel the angel did say
Was to certain poor shepherds in fields as they lay–
In fields where they lay keeping their sheep
On a cold winter's night that was so deep.
Noel, Noel, Noel, Noel!
Born is the King of Israel!

They looked up and saw a star
Bright in the east beyond them far;
And to the earth it gave great light,
And so it continued both day and night.
Noel, Noel, Noel, Noel!
Born is the King of Israel!

And by the light of that same star
Three wise men came from country far;
To seek for a King was their intent,
And to follow the star where-e'er it went.
Noel, Noel, Noel, Noel!
Born is the King of Israel!

3

# Hark! the Herald Angels Sing

Hark! the herald angels sing,
"Glory to the newborn King!
Peace on earth and mercy mild–
God and sinners reconciled."
Joyful, all ye nations rise;
Join the triumph of the skies.
With th'angelic host proclaim,
"Christ is born in Bethlehem."
Hark! the herald angels sing,
"Glory to the newborn King."

Christ, by highest heav'n adored!
Christ, the everlasting Lord!
Long desired, behold Him come–
Offspring of the Virgin's womb.
Veiled in flesh the Godhead see;
Hail th'incarnate Deity,
Pleased as man with men to dwell,
Jesus, our Immanuel!
Hark! the herald angels sing,
"Glory to the newborn King."

4

# Joy to the World

Joy to the world! the Lord is come;
Let earth receive her King.
Let ev'ry heart prepare Him room,
And heav'n and nature sing,
And heav'n and nature sing,
And heav'n, and heav'n and nature sing.

Joy to the world! the Savior reigns;
Let men their songs employ,
While fields and floods, rocks, hills and plains
Repeat the sounding joy,
Repeat the sounding joy,
Repeat, repeat the sounding joy.

No more let sin and sorrow grow,
Nor thorns infest the ground.
He comes to make His blessings flow
Far as the curse is found,
Far as the curse is found,
Far as, far as the curse is found.

5

# O Come, All Ye Faithful

O come, all ye faithful, joyful and triumphant.
O come ye, o come ye to Bethlehem.
Come and behold Him–born the King of angels!
O come, let us adore Him!
O come, let us adore Him!
O come, let us adore Him–Christ, the Lord!

Sing, choirs of angels; sing in exaltation.
O sing, all ye bright hosts of heav'n above.
Glory to God, all glory in the highest!
O come, let us adore Him!
O come, let us adore Him!
O come, let us adore Him–Christ, the Lord!

Yea, Lord we greet Thee, born this happy morning.
O Jesus, to Thee be all glory giv'n.
Word of the Father, now in flesh appearing!
O come, let is adore Him!
O come, let us adore Him!
O come, let us adore Him–Christ, the Lord!

6

# O Little Town of Bethlehem

O little town of Bethlehem,
How still we see thee lie!
Above thy deep and dreamless sleep
The silent stars go by.
Yet in thy dark streets shineth
The everlasting Light;
The hopes and fears of all the years
Are met in thee tonight.

How silently, how silently
The wondrous Gift is giv'n!
So God imparts to human hearts
The blessings of His heav'n.
No ear may hear His coming;
But in this world of sin,
Where meek souls will receive Him still,
The dear Christ enters in.

7

# Silent Night

Silent night! holy night!
All is calm, all is bright
Round yon virgin mother and Child.
Holy Infant, so tender and mild,
Sleep in heavenly peace;
Sleep in heavenly peace.

Silent night! holy night!
Shepherds quake at the sight;
Glories stream from heaven afar.
Heav'nly hosts sing, "Alleluia!
Christ the Savior is born!
Christ the Savior is born!"

Silent night! holy night!
Son of God, love's pure light
Radiant beams from Thy holy face,
With the dawn of redeeming grace,
Jesus, Lord, at Thy birth,
Jesus, Lord, at Thy birth.

8

# BEST NEWS NEWSPAPER

**Bethlehem, Judea**                                    **4 A.D.**

# Savior Born!

# Christmas Symbols and Their Meanings

**Mary and Joseph:** Jesus' earthly parents

**Baby Jesus:** God came to earth to live among us; Christmas is His birthday

**Donkeys:** Mary rode to Bethlehem on a donkey

**Stable:** Where Jesus was born

**Sheep and shepherds:** Came to worship Jesus the night He was born

**Angels:** Announced Jesus' birth to the shepherds

**Wise men:** Traveled from the East to worship Jesus and bring Him gifts

**Camels:** The wise men traveled on them

**Star:** Led the wise men to Jesus

**Candles:** Remind us that Jesus is the Light of the world

**Wreaths:** Remind us that Jesus' love is evergreen and eternal

**Crowns:** Remind us that Jesus is the King of Kings

**Shepherd's staff:** Remind us that Jesus is the Good Shepherd

**Trees:** Remind us that Jesus hung on a tree – the cross

**Holly:** Thorns and berries remind us of Jesus' sacrifice on the cross for us

**Mistletoe:** White berries remind us of Jesus' purity

**Gifts:** Remind us that Jesus is the best gift of all

# ❄ Scripture Reference Index ❄

Genesis 1:27 — Snowman Sticks ................. 140

Numbers 6:1-8 — Grow a Beard ...................... 117

Job 37:5-6 — Plastic Basket Snowflake .... 58

Psalm 1:1-3 — Candy Tree ......................... 50

Psalm 18:32-33 — Reindeer Candy Cane .......... 75

Psalm 23 — Crunchy Shepherd's Staffs .. 134

Psalm 32:10 — Tree Garland of Trust .......... 62

Psalm 47:1-2 — Jingle Bell Gloves ................. 96

Psalm 47:6 — Caroling Fun ...................... 148

Psalm 51:1-2 — Celebration Soap Bar ......... 85

Psalm 95:6 — Worship the King ............... 183

Psalm 104:24 — Walnut Mouse ...................... 82

Psalm 119:72 — Silver and Gold Sachet ...... 104

Psalm 119:103 — Cozy Christmas Cocoa ...... 133

Psalm 139:7-10 — Race Down the Chimney .... 120

Psalm 149:2 — The King's Cupcakes .......... 137

Isaiah 1:18 — Frosty Icicle Wreath ............ 54

Isaiah 9:6 — Holiday Heart Gift Tag ........ 93

Isaiah 9:6-7 — Why A Baby? ...................... 181

Isaiah 35:1-2 — Miniature Poinsettia ............ 72

Isaiah 40:3-5 — Getting Ready for Christmas ........................... 169

Isaiah 53:3-5 — Holly Door Stopper ............. 94

Isaiah 60:13 — Hanging the Greens ........... 158

Micah 2:12-13 — Grocery Sack Reindeer ........ 55

Micah 5:2 — Don't Miss the Party! .......... 167

Matthew 1:20-21 — Sugarplums ........................... 144

Matthew 1:23 — Immanuel ......................... 171

Matthew 2:1-2 — Camels and Donkeys .......... 112

Matthew 2:1-2 — Gingerbread Magi Men ........ 68

Matthew 2:1-2 — Jesus Came for Everybody 174

Matthew 2:1-12 — Christmas Card Magnets ......... 66

Matthew 2:1-12 — Christmas Story Match-up .... 114

Matthew 2:1-12 — Pocket Crèche Puppets ........... 73

Matthew 2:1-12 — Tabletop Crèche ...................... 61

Matthew 2:1-12 — The Christmas Story ............. 152

Matthew 2:1-12 — Which King Will You Follow? ......................... 179

Matthew 2:2 — Star of Bethlehem Pencil Topper ............................ 81

Matthew 2:7-8 — The Call from King Herod ...... 111

Matthew 2:9 — Bethlehem Sky Star Caper ...... 65

Matthew 2:9-11 — Worship the King ................... 183

Matthew 2:11 — Magi Gift Bag ........................ 71

Matthew 2:13-15 — Escape to Egypt ..................... 115

Matthew 2:13-15 — God's Messengers ................... 170

Matthew 2:13-15 — The Land Where Jesus Was Born ...................... 118

Matthew 3:1-6 — John the Baptist's Snack Mix ................................ 136

Matthew 4:18-22 — Shoelace Elves ...................... 102

Matthew 5:14-16 — Shining Light Votive Holder .. 101

Matthew 5:14-16 — The Light of the World .......... 175

Matthew 7:9-11 — Ask for Good Gifts .................. 166

Matthew 7:24-27 — Rock Trivet ............................ 99

Matthew 25:13 — Don't Miss the Party! ............. 167

Matthew 25:31-40 — The Mitten Tree ..................... 163

Matthew 27:28-29 — Cranberry Grapevine Wreath .. 91

Mark 1:1-3 — Advent Treat Calendar .......... 64

Mark 10:13-16 — No Room At the Inn ............... 177

Mark 12:30-31 — J.O.Y. ...................................... 172

Mark 13:26-27 — Angel Clouds .......................... 128

Luke 1:8-13 — Cinnamon Ornament .............. 53

*continued on next page...*

| | | |
|---|---|---|
| Luke 1:13-16 | Grow a Beard | 117 |
| Luke 1:15 | Stocking Stuffers | 124 |
| Luke 1:26-35 | God's Messengers | 170 |
| Luke 1:26-38 | Gabriel Macaroni Pin | 67 |
| Luke 1:37 | Im-pastable Canister | 95 |
| Luke 1:39-44 | Bouncy Balls | 84 |
| Luke 1:41 | Stocking Stuffers | 124 |
| Luke 1:46-55 | Cookie Mix in a Jar | 89 |
| Luke 1:67 | Stocking Stuffers | 124 |
| Luke 2:1-5 | The Census in Bethlehem | 113 |
| Luke 2:1-20 | Pocket Crèche Puppets | 73 |
| Luke 2:1-20 | Tabletop Crèche | 61 |
| Luke 2:1-20 | The Christmas Story | 152 |
| Luke 2:1-35 | Christmas Story Match-up | 114 |
| Luke 2:4 | The Land Where Jesus Was Born | 118 |
| Luke 2:4-5 | Camels and Donkeys | 112 |
| Luke 2:4-5 | Donkey Biscuits | 135 |
| Luke 2:4-20 | Christmas Card Magnets | 66 |
| Luke 2:7 | Animals in the Stable | 129 |
| Luke 2:7 | Build a Stable Relay | 110 |
| Luke 2:7 | Hand Towel for a King | 92 |
| Luke 2:7 | No Room At the Inn | 177 |
| Luke 2:8 | Sheep on the Hillside | 122 |
| Luke 2:8 | Shepherd's Dip | 139 |
| Luke 2:8-14 | Night of Wonder Headband | 97 |
| Luke 2:8-15 | God's Messengers | 170 |
| Luke 2:8-18 | Spread the News | 178 |
| Luke 2:10 | Jesus Came for Everybody | 174 |
| Luke 2:11 | Happy Birthday Pin | 69 |
| Luke 2:12 | Swaddled Dates | 145 |
| Luke 2:13-14 | Paper Clip Heavenly Host | 57 |
| Luke 2:16 | Mangers With Straw | 138 |
| Luke 2:17-18 | Cardboard Tube Caroler | 51 |
| Luke 2:19 | Confetti Treat Tin | 87 |
| Luke 2:19 | Live Nativity | 161 |
| Luke 2:20 | Noel Coffee Mug | 98 |
| Luke 2:22 | The Land Where Jesus Was Born | 118 |
| Luke 2:22-28 | Stained Glass Candies | 143 |
| Luke 2:25-32 | Luminaries for the Light of the World | 56 |
| Luke 6:1 | Cheesy Popcorn | 131 |
| John 1:9-11 | Don't Miss the Party! | 167 |
| John 1:14 | Why a Baby? | 181 |
| John 4:34-35 | Fields of Snow | 116 |
| John 7:37 | Spicy Hot Cider | 141 |
| John 8:12 | The Light of the World | 175 |
| John 10:11 | Shepherd Treat Holder | 79 |
| John 10:14-16 | Sheep Lollipop | 78 |
| John 12:35-36 | Snow Shoveling in the Dark | 123 |
| John 14:2-3 | Santa Take-Home Sack | 76 |
| Romans 6:23 | Wrapping Gifts With Jesus | 184 |
| 2 Corinthians 2:15 | Spicy Scented Coasters | 106 |
| Ephesians 1:13 | Santa Stamps | 100 |
| Philippians 2:9-11 | Chrismons | 52 |
| Colossians 3:12-14 | Snowflake Fleece Scarf | 105 |
| 1 Thess. 3:12 | Santa's Belly | 121 |
| 1 Tim. 6:14-16 | King's Crown | 70 |
| Hebrews 3:4 | Gingerbread Houses | 156 |
| Hebrews 13:8 | Cornflake Wreaths | 132 |
| 2 Peter 1:5-8 | Sprinkle Spoons | 142 |
| 1 John 4:10 | Cozy Cocoa Kit | 90 |
| 3 John 1:14 | Christmas Card Roundabout | 86 |
| Revelation 3:20 | Silver Bells Door Hanger | 60 |
| Revelation 21:3-4 | Ribbon Teardrop Swag | 59 |
| Revelation 22:16 | Bright Morning Stars | 130 |